A CHIEF IS A CHIEF BY THE PEOPLE

A Chief is a Chief by the people

THE AUTOBIOGRAPHY OF
STIMELA JASON JINGOES

———————————————

RECORDED AND COMPILED BY

John and Cassandra Perry

LONDON
OXFORD UNIVERSITY PRESS
NEW YORK   CAPE TOWN

1975

Oxford University Press, Ely House, London W.1

GLASGOW NEW YORK TORONTO MELBOURNE WELLINGTON
CAPE TOWN IBADAN NAIROBI DAR ES SALAAM LUSAKA ADDIS ABABA
DELHI BOMBAY CALCUTTA MADRAS KARACHI LAHORE DACCA
KUALA LUMPUR SINGAPORE HONG KONG TOKYO

ISBN 0 19 211727 0

Printed in Great Britain
by Ebenezer Baylis and Son Limited
The Trinity Press, Worcester, and London

This book is dedicated to

The Chiefs
and the people of Lesotho

CONTENTS

ILLUSTRATIONS

MAPS

Maps 3, 4, and 6 are based on sketch-maps drawn by Mr. Jingoes, in which locations have been identified by him to correspond with more detailed aerial survey maps.

GENEALOGIES

The genealogies in this book are constructed from information supplied by Mr. Jingoes. They are not to be regarded as complete or definitive, but are intended to assist the reader to trace his way through tangles of family relationships and descent referred to in the text.

INTRODUCTION

THE idea of this book was generated during sixteen months' field research in Lesotho, when Mr. Jingoes, employed by us as interpreter, became our constant adviser and companion. He is a gifted raconteur, and most of the incidents and anecdotes that comprise this book were already familiar to us before, three years after we first met Mr. Jingoes, we were able to record his life. What gave his recollections particular force and interest, was the way in which they expressed a man's involvement with his times and his awareness of the events that shaped his world. It was this, we concluded, that would constitute a loss if allowed to go unremarked.

The book was recorded in English, from the direct dictation of Mr. Jingoes, whose wife took part in many of the recording sessions and was invaluable in helping him recall details from the past. We ourselves prompted with questions when we felt that more information was needed to clarify certain points. As the work progressed, Mr. Jingoes became more and more involved with his narrative, and it became a question of keeping up with, rather than prompting, him; we were often forced to use a tape-recorder to keep up with the flow. In such sessions, Mr. Jingoes paced up and down for hours at a stretch, impatient of the present, and quite immersed in the immediacy of his memories. We soon fell into a routine of starting work at seven in the morning and pushing through to six in the evening, with a break for lunch, every day of the week. Our mutual interest in the project mitigated the effect of the long hours.

Mr. Jingoes had very definite ideas on what he wanted included in the book. In the months preceding the recording, he had sent us rough notes covering certain aspects of his life, notably his childhood and the early history of his family, but when it came to dictating, he did not make use of any of these. We, however, used them as a basis for formulating questions to enlarge upon his narrative. Mr. Jingoes dictated entirely from memory; he had no recourse to diaries or documentary sources in the recording sessions. Of great assistance was the fact that Mr. Jingoes has an astounding memory, almost photographic in its total recall. He remembers visually and dramatically, and prefers to act out incidents and conversations, imitating mannerisms, movements, and tones of voice, rather than to give a descriptive summary. Mr. Jingoes has critical insight into the workings of his own society, but he does not express his conclusions abstractly. When asked to comment, he always explains by means of examples. Thus the reader will find little analytic comment in this book; rather, it is in his selection of material that Mr. Jingoes conveys his view of the events he was involved in.

Inevitably, we found it impossible to include every facet of Mr. Jingoes's life. His experiences as a race-horse owner, teacher, and journalist had regretfully to go unrecorded. This is true also of his passionate interest in the running and organizing of soccer clubs, and his involvement in church affairs.

Moreover, Mr. Jingoes's account takes us only into the early 1950s, since when the history of Lesotho has taken on a quickened tempo. The years culminating in Independence, and the changes that followed in its wake, have been fraught with incident. For a man of Mr. Jingoes's temperament, these have been exciting and concerned years, and the recording of his commitment to, and interpretation of, these times could properly provide the substance of another book.

In writing up our field recordings, we had to excise considerable portions of the material as the first draft of the manuscript was too unwieldy. Essentially, we cut sections that were repetitive, leaving, for example, one case to illustrate a point instead of three. A further reduction in length was requested by the publisher, on whose advice we have pared down the manuscript by about a third.

During the compilation of the manuscript, we were compelled to rework much of the narrative. Although Mr. Jingoes's English is fluent, he often uses phrases peculiarly his own, and does not hesitate to express himself in Sesotho when he feels he would lose a vital nuance in English. He also made use of Afrikaans to colour certain incidents. We had to paraphrase passages that we feared might baffle the English reader, but we trust that we have not strayed too far from the original. He did not dictate the book in chronological order, but roughly in the sections that comprise the present chapters, often digressing to another subject in the middle of his account. In addition, the recording emerged in anecdotal form and, in order to systematize the material, we had, on occasion, to impose our own time-sequence. We tried, as accurately as possible, to recapture the tone of the original.

As each chapter was completed, it was sent to Mr. Jingoes for his detailed examination, correction, criticism, and approval. He made only minor changes, usually of names we had misspelled.

We experienced great difficulty, as any student of an oral culture will appreciate, with the spelling of names. Mr. Jingoes grew up speaking a number of languages, and the names of his relatives are drawn from both the Sotho and Nguni language groupings. To complicate matters even further, it must be remembered that Mr. Jingoes might have been writing many of the names down for the first time when we called upon him to do so. Proper names are not readily available in any dictionary and, unhappily, even the spelling of historians and other official sources is subject to great variance. Unable, then, to check the accuracy of every name, we retained Mr. Jingoes's spelling, idiosyncratic though it might sometimes be, whenever doubt arose.

The reader will have noticed that we refer to ourselves as recorders and compilers, rather than editors, of this autobiography. That is because this is Mr. Jingoes's book. The opinions expressed in it are his own, and we have not attempted to comment on them in any way. The historical data were recorded from his memory, which can hardly be expected, however keen, to be completely accurate or omniscient.

We are not interested in viewing his account critically, in annotating the descriptions of customs and events anthropologically, or in giving a history of any area in Lesotho. Our concern has been to present, as untouched as possible, one man's picture of his life. The book is his, and we have tried to keep out of it as much as one can in a recording of this nature, except in so far as adding footnotes to concepts, words, events, and so on, that might have puzzled the reader had they been left without explanation. At the request of both publisher's reader and publisher, however, we have compiled an Appendix to provide a background on Lesotho for the interested reader.

The title Mr. Jingoes first chose for his autobiography was *I am surprised* because, in his own words, 'I am, every day. . . .' We hope that this book will stand as a tribute to his curiosity of mind, his courage, and his undimmed enthusiasm for whatever life may offer. We are indebted to him beyond recompense.

John and Cassandra Perry
Grahamstown, 1973

ACKNOWLEDGEMENTS

WE are grateful to Mrs. NoMaqhesha Jingoes, who gave freely of her time to assist us. Because of her close and warm relationship with Mr. Jingoes's father, her contribution to this narrative is considerable. Our thanks are due to Chief David Masupha for allowing us to live in his village, and for giving us the opportunity to meet a man of Mr. Jingoes's stature. Our warmest thanks go to Mr. and Dr. Jacot-Guillarmod, whose assistance was, and remains, immeasurable. All our friends in Lesotho will be remembered for their open-hearted and generous co-operation and support.

I received my training as an anthropologist under Professor David Hammond-Tooke. It is through him that I was given the impetus to go to Lesotho initially, and his thorough and painstaking theoretical grounding stood me in good stead throughout my fieldwork. My initial fieldwork was financed by a fellowship grant from the Institute for Social and Economic Research at Rhodes University. To them and to Professor Hobart Houghton I am grateful. Rhodes University also contributed financially to my research with two grants.

Among friends and colleagues at Rhodes University we are indebted to Professor Philip Mayer, whose interest and encouragement fortified us throughout this undertaking. Mr. Peter Temple and Mr. Gerald Sack have read through the manuscript and offered us invaluable criticism and comment. To Dr. Horst Ruthrof and Dr. Nick Visser and their wives we owe a special debt of thanks for they gave unstintingly of their time in discussion and reading. Mr. Mike Berning of the Cory Library with unfailing patience found references and facts. Thanks are due also to Mr. Gebeda and Mr. Lesoro of the African Languages Department, and to Professor André de Villiers.

Dr. Ian Hamnett, the reader for Oxford University Press, made invaluable suggestions, and his advice has helped us immeasurably.

We are indebted to our parents, who read parts of the manuscript critically, and who believed the book was possible before we did.

The people and institutions mentioned above are, of course, in no way responsible for the opinions expressed in this book. But they, and the many whose names we have not included, have encouraged us more than they know.

J. and C.P.

GLOSSARY

ao! interjection expressing surprise, displeasure, sympathy, or disbelief

auk! see *ao!*

ausi elder sister; affectionate or familiar form of address

Gaudeng Johannesburg; literally means 'the place of gold'

hao! see *ao!*

helang! interjection expressing surprise or admonishment

helele! interjection: 'right!'; salutation to a chief

induna Nguni term equivalent to *letona*; also more generally used to indicate a black 'foreman' in authority over other black workers

jo! interjection expressing sorrow or amazement

khele! (khelek!) interjection of astonishment

leboella reserved pasture where grazing is only allowed at certain times of the year, and where thatching grass is often grown

lekhotla court of justice; formerly village gathering-place for men

lelapa small courtyard in front of a house often enclosed by a reed screen; home; family

lenaka (pl. *manaka*) horn; container in which *litlhare* or medicine is kept; charm; source of power; powerful ruler

lesiba (pl. *masiba*) feather; a musical instrument made of a piece of quill and a string fixed on a stick. The tunes played on it are traditionally associated with cattle-herding.

lesokoana stirring-stick; game played by women which consists in stealing a stirring-stick from a *seotloana* to bring rain

lethuela type of diviner and healer who has been cured of a form of nervous or hysterical affliction known as *motheketheke*

letona counsellor of a chief; officer

letsema (pl. *matsema*) company of people working together, especially on the fields of a chief; work done in common

likhomo cattle; salutation to a chief

liretlo pieces of human flesh used for magic purposes; ritual or medicine murders

lithakhisa wooden pegs treated with *litlhare* and driven into the ground to ward off evil

litlhare trees, bushes; protective medicine and the substances from which it is made

moli generic name of plants of the *Hypoxis* genus, some of which are used for making ropes *molutsoane* hunt; ceremonial hunt undertaken in order to bring rain

morena chief (*borena*, chieftainship; see p. 17, n. 1)

ngaka (pl. *lingaka*) witch–doctor, herbalist, doctor, medical practitioner, diviner

ntate my father; respectful form of address for any man

oho! interjection of sorrow, dismay, or supplication

pitso assembly, gathering, public meeting (from *ho bitsa*, to call)

seotloana reed fence enclosing a *lelapa*

tickey a threepenny coin

thokolosi a witch's familiar

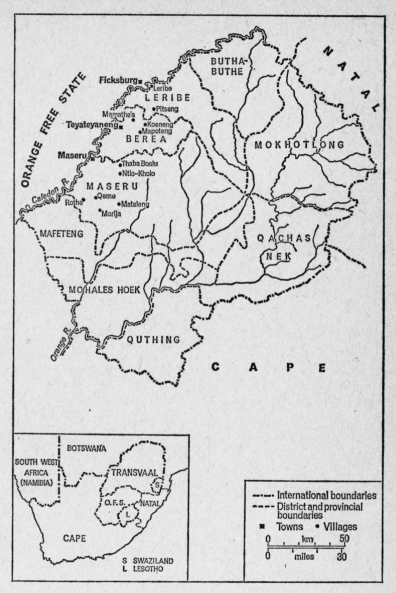

1. Lesotho

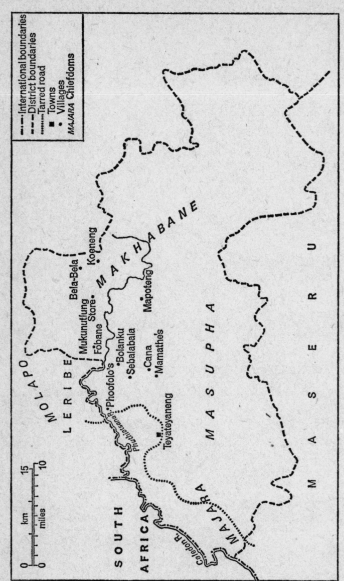

2. Berea District

Genealogy 1: Members of the Jingoes lineage who appear in this book

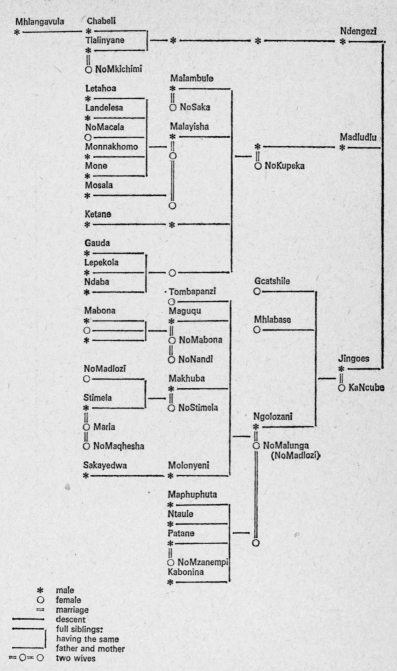

Genealogy 2: Members of the Makhabane lineage who appear in this book

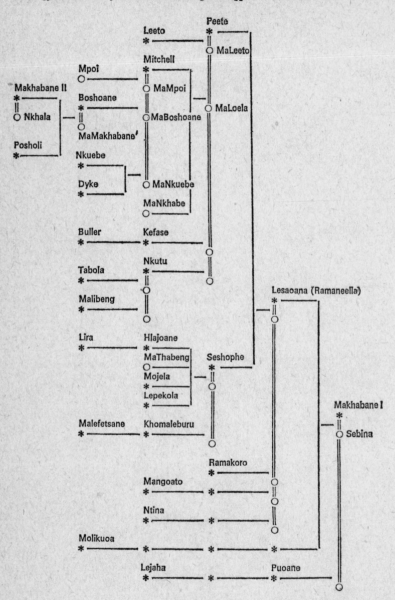

Genealogy 3: Members of the Chieftainship who appear in this book

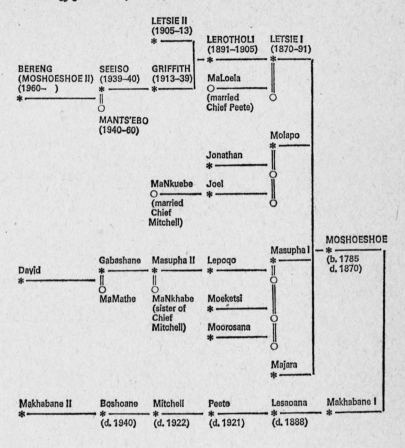

CHAPTER ONE

Ancestors

Litongwa of Mavuso, fall down
That the people may drink water.
You, Mtshengu of Tshabalala,
You, Mtshengu, talked
To the men at court and they trembled.
You, the sons of Sikova, the Owl,
Who has horns like a heifer,
You great liars:
You reported that the Chief was dead
When he was not dead.
You of dirty dresses,
Who can be buried at your mother's place;
You who pledge on the cobra snake
And say it is your clan;
You of loud applause,
What can you do to Mswati, the Swazi,
Who is a bull?

THESE are the praises of my ancestors, who are Swazi. When I
meet another Swazi, especially one of my clan, the clan of the
Cobra, we sing these praises together, and we cry. This is the
history of my forefathers as it has been told to me.

My ancestors used to live in Swaziland where the head of the
place was Sikova. When he died, his heir, Gatagata, was too young
to succeed him, so his *induna* or counsellor called Sitinga ruled as
regent for the boy. Gatagata came of age and demanded the position
due to him as head of the clan but Sitinga refused to surrender the
Chieftainship,[1] so Gatagata moved away from that place to another
called Mhlangavula, taking his followers with him. That is why the

praise-song refers to our 'mother's place': because we removed from our paternal home.

It happened while we were there that Madlangamphisi, the younger brother of Gatagata, passed away, and we sent word to Sitinga to report his death. In our report, we said simply that *Umntwana*, the Prince, had died, not saying his proper name out of respect for the dead. So when the report was received, people believed that it was Gatagata who had died.

Then one day a feast was held in Sitinga's village to which our people of Mhlangavula were invited. When we arrived, Sitinga's people discovered that Gatagata was still alive, and the whole village turned to us and asked us why we were such great liars, to have sent word that our Chief was dead. They accused us of having lied with a hidden motive: thinking our Prince dead, they might have invaded us, but we would have been ready for them under our Prince, hoping to kill them. That is how we came to be known as 'great liars'.

What became of Sitinga and his rule makes an interesting story. Sitinga also passed away, in time, and his *induna*, Dlamini or Sobhuza, became regent for Sitinga's son. When this son came of age he claimed his rights, only to be told by Dlamini, 'What are you, anyway? You claim the rights here, but you yourself are a usurper. Don't forget that you took Gatagata's place. Why should I let you rule here now? I have no time for you! Seek your own way before I lose my temper with you!'

It is said that at that time the nation liked Dlamini a great deal, so poor Sitinga's son also left the place. We are told that he passed by Mhlangavula on his way, but was too ashamed even to ask them for land there, and he came down to Lesotho.[2]

Recently, when King Bereng of Lesotho was installed, Dlamini's descendant, Makhosini, was here in Lesotho for the installation. He invited all the Swazi living in Lesotho to return to Swaziland, and to forget what mischiefs had made them leave the land of their forefathers. We learned from one of Sitinga's descendants that he had been to Swaziland where he had been promised lands if he could collect about two hundred Swazi to accompany him from Lesotho, but when he came to leave, most of the people he had gathered changed their minds.

When Makhosini visited Lesotho he was told that most of the Swazi living here are people of the clan of Mtshengu of Tshabalala. He heard that I was of that clan, and sent word to me to meet him.

But I did not go to meet him. I did not go because I thought of how my ancestors had left that place, and of how he rules the place that belongs to the descendants of Gatagata.

*   *   *

Genealogy 4: My forefathers

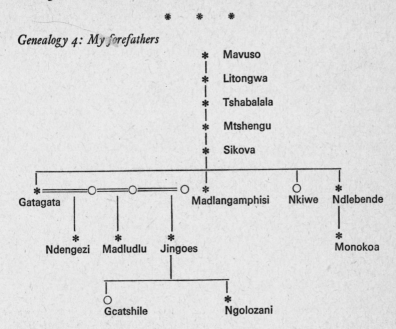

In the genealogy above, you will see that Gatagata's son in his third house is called Jingoes. He is my great-grandfather, and his descendants use the surname of Jingoes. I have been told the story of his life by my elders, and it was a life full of suffering. This is his story.

One day when Jingoes was herding cattle when he was a boy, some Europeans with hair like maize flowers came by and captured him. With other captives, they took him to a big river, so big that they could not see its farther shore.

I am telling this story now, you understand, as it was told to me.

When they arrived at the river, they found something like a house right on top of the water. They were taken inside that house, and those who refused to enter were whipped. Once they were inside the house on the water they felt the house begin to move. Jingoes did not say how many days they were on the big river, but he said that after a long time they saw land again, and they were surprised; they thought that perhaps they had been taken back to their own country, but when they arrived they were told that the place was known as America.

They found many white men waiting where they landed, and the people who had captured them simply sold them to those men. Jingoes did not know what their price was, for none of the captives could understand the language spoken there. They only saw one white man taking one of them away, another white man taking two or three away, and so on.

It is said that my great-grandfather was bought by a cruel man. His owner did not care whether his slaves were given food to eat before they were sent to work; he would simply say, 'Go there!' and his slaves had to obey him and go. I was told Jingoes remembered a time when he had nothing to eat for two days. Some of the slaves were useless to their master; they could not work because they were too weak from lack of food.

My great-grandfather could not stand the conditions under which he lived there. He was not alone. One day, five of the slaves disappeared from that farm, and Jingoes was one of them.

By that time they could speak a little English. It is said that they walked only at night, and hid during the day. They found their way by the following method.

If, during the day, they noticed anyone coming, and if it was a man of their colour, one of the five would go out and approach the stranger. When he reached the stranger he would say, 'I have been sent on an errand by my master. Would you kindly direct me which way to take to reach the sea?'

We are told the first man approached in that way replied, 'I don't understand what you mean, because America is surrounded by sea on all sides.'

Then the man who had been sent said, 'I mean where the things called ships are. I have been told to fetch a parcel from there.' So the stranger pointed out the direction in which the nearest port lay.

After a day or two days they reached the port, and found ships there. Jingoes said that there were *houses on the water* at that place, although later he learnt to call them ships.

You must understand that at first they did not know what their own country was called, but that on their way to America they had learned that their land was called *Africa*. Jingoes himself had thought that the place he came from was simply called *ESwazini*, or Swaziland, and he thought that all black people lived in *ESwazini*.

But now when they reached that port they knew what their country or continent was called.

Jingoes and one of his friends met a fine black man there, we are told, who was very kind to them. He told them that his ship was bound for Africa. Would he hide them on his ship, they asked him, until they reached Africa? He explained that there was no way to hide them, but that what he could do for them was to bring them to the notice of the captain of the ship, his master. He instructed them to help him while he was working on the docks and on the ship, just to help here and there, until his master noticed them.

They did as he told them and while they were there, it happened that the master of the ship asked their benefactor what those two men wanted. He replied that they were people looking for work on the ship and, he continued, 'They tell me that they were chased away by their master, who said he no longer wants them because they are lazy.' The captain of the ship asked Jingoes and his companion whether they were prepared to do the work of the ship, and they promised that they would.

So the master of the ship took them on as employees. Then one day the ship sailed from that port, and at last they came to Africa.

Jingoes, as I have been told, did not know the name of the place where their ship reached Africa, but it was not the same one from which they had sailed for America. The ship was there for some days, and its men were given leave to go into town. In town one day, Jingoes met a man who told him what route to take to reach Swaziland.

We are told that Jingoes then turned to his friend and said, 'Goodbye, my friend,' and then he disappeared from that ship. He took the direction that had been pointed out to him. It is said that he walked for many days before he reached Swaziland. At last, after suffering a great deal, for his feet were badly swollen, he arrived at his home again.

He was received, the story goes, like one who was thought lost.

*   *   *

I return now to Mhlangavula, where my people settled when Sitinga denied them their rights. I am told that the house there split up, perhaps because they were growing short of land. Some went to Natal; some drifted to other parts of what is now called the Republic of South Africa; some came down to Lesotho. I am descended from the ones who came to Lesotho, where we still live today.

Our branch of the family came to Lesotho in the following way. I understand that Nkiwe, a daughter of Sikova, was brought to Lesotho to marry the Chief of Rothe. She was accompanied by her brothers' sons, Madludlu and Monokoa, and by one of their bondservants, Kabinde. It might be that the Chief of Rothe had learned that these men were the sons of a ruler; I am not sure of the reason, but this group never returned to Swaziland. They all settled at Rothe.

*   *   *

This brings us to the story of how my great-grandfather, Jingoes, met his end, and of how his son, Ngolozani, was nearly lost to us.

It might have been that Jingoes was travelling with the marriage group to Lesotho, and that he was somehow cut off from them. Or he might have been travelling somewhere else, we do not know. The fact is that he was travelling with his wife, his son, and his daughter when they were attacked.

This was during the time of the *Lifaqane*, the terrible African wars of the early nineteenth century, when many people were homeless and starving, roaming the countryside. Some of the starving people formed bands and turned to cannibalism. Whether Jingoes and his family were attacked by cannibals or by a group of another kind, we shall never know.

Jingoes and his wife were both killed. Their son, Ngolozani, then about eighteen years old, managed to escape somehow, together with his sister, Gcatshile, but they lost each other in the confusion. Ngolozani became a wanderer, a *moshoti*, as so many people were during the *Lifaqane*.

It happened that one day Ngolozani came to a certain village late in the afternoon. We have never troubled ourselves to find out the name of that village, although I believe that Ngolozani must have told our fathers the name. What we do know is that the headman of that village gave the boy food and a place to sleep that night.

The following morning, when the boy wanted to leave, the headman asked him, 'Where to, my son? You have told me the tragic story of your parents. Now where do you want to go? If it happens that you too meet with bad people who kill you, what will Heaven and yourself say to me? You have told me that you still have relatives, who have come down here to Lesotho. If some of

those relatives are still alive, I will keep you with me in the hope
that, one day, they will come here and find you.'

So Ngolozani remained in that village.

Now one day Madludlu, Jingoes's older brother who had settled
at Rothe, went out to barter for food. It was still during the
Lifaqane, and it was impossible for most of the people to turn the
soil and plant crops, because of the wars. So people had to travel
about trying to buy grain from those who had managed to plant
and harvest a crop.

By good fortune, Madludlu happened to pass through the village
where Ngolozani had settled with the kind headman. He arrived
there, it is told, quite late in the afternoon, and was promised some
bags of grain. As it was growing dark, he decided to put up in that
village overnight, planning to continue his journey the following
day. It was the time of the afternoon when herdboys drive the cattle
back from the pastures to the kraal. The headman of the village
was calling to one of the herdboys, as they drove the cattle in. The
boy he called did not answer, so he turned to another of the boys
and shouted, 'Ngolozani! *Ngolozani!* NGOLOZANI!' Ngolozani
replied, and was given some orders by the headman.

Now when the headman shouted the boy's name, Madludlu was
torn between hope and fear.

He turned to the headman. 'I heard you calling my nephew's
name here. How does it happen that you name your children after
my relatives?'

The headman asked, 'What tribe are you?'

'I am Swazi.'

'The boy I called is also Swazi. Let me call him now, and see if
you know him.'

The man called my grandfather. As soon as Madludlu and
Ngolozani met, they recognized each other, and they both cried
for the joy of finding each other and for the sorrow of the death
of Jingoes and his wife.

When I think of this story now, and try to tell it, I also weep for
the joy and sorrow of my ancestors.

From Ngolozani, Madludlu also learned that Gcatshile, Ngolozani's sister, was not killed with her parents, but also managed to
flee from the killers, although Ngolozani had not been able to find
her afterwards, for she had run in a different direction.

Madludlu asked the kind headman whether he would let him take
his nephew back to his people, and he agreed, stipulating only that

he should be given a cow for having clothed and fed the boy during
his stay. Madludlu was satisfied with this, and said he would return
shortly with the cow.

When Madludlu arrived at his home he told his people that
Ngolozani had been found, and he also told them about the death of
Jingoes and his wife, and the loss of Gcatshile. He then returned
and gave a cow to the good headman, and Ngolozani was reunited
with his own people. Gcatshile was found later, and she married
someone at Matatiele.

My uncle, Maguqu, taught me the praise-song of Ngolozani; he
used to hear the old man praising himself when he was in a rage or
when he was about to go out to war. He said Ngolozani used to get
up with the morning star, and that was when one would hear him
singing his praises. His praise-song begins like this:

> Ngolozani, the brother of Gcatshile and Mhlabase,
> He grew up an orphan.
> Even at MaNcube's, where his mother's people lived,
> They knew that Ngolozani was an orphan.
> He was left by his parents, both father and mother,
> While they were on a journey;
> They were stabbed with spears
> By unknown people.
> Ngolozani became a stray,
> Like an animal.
> Madludlu! Hurry up! Jingoes's child has been left
> By his parents on their journey.
> He was left by Jingoes and KaNcube,
> As they were stabbed by spears.
> And you, the headman, who picked up our father Ngolozani,
> We are thankful to you.
> The Selibontshweni are praising you;
> The Selibontshweni, the sons of Ngolozani,
> Are thankful.
> Those thanking you are Maguqu, Makhuba, Molonyeni;
> You are praised by Maphuphutha, Ntaule, Patane, and Kabonina.

The rest of Ngolozani's story is a long one, and as it is bound up
closely with the history of a Chieftainship, it belongs, rightly, with
the stories about Chiefs.

*   *   *

I have related these tales about my ancestors not only because
they are the history of my family: I have told these tales mainly

Lesotho landscape showing contoured fields and erosion

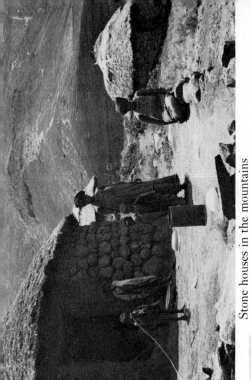

Stone houses in the mountains

Top left
Entrance of house

Houses and *seotloana*

because my ancestors are important in my life, even now; I cannot leave them out of any account of my own life.

When I was born, there were already missionaries and ministers of the Christian religion in Lesotho. Then, as now, they tried by every means in their power to make us do away with our custom of worshipping our ancestors; even in church, they preached against our ancestors. They would tell us not to pray to them, and they quoted from the Bible to support their view, especially from the Ten Commandments, where it says, 'Thou shalt have no other gods before Me.' They dwelt on that, and said that if we prayed to our ancestors we were breaking that law, by putting other gods before the Almighty God. So, many people tried to believe that it would be better to worship only the Christian Almighty God.

I was brought up as a Christian, and went to church from an early age. My grandfather, Ngolozani, was never converted to Christianity, and when he sacrificed a beast to the ancestors, as he must have done, I must have thought that he was simply slaughtering an animal.

My father became a Christian convert when missionaries came to Koeneng, where he was living. This was at the turn of the century. He was a devout Christian for most of his life, so although he sometimes mentioned them, he was one of those who had been persuaded by the ministers not to revere his ancestors. He was a lay preacher of such conviction that, even now, old people who knew him when he preached say of him, 'God hears that man when he talks.'

But he caused great pain to the ancestors, and just before he died he returned to their worship.

When I was young, the one who taught me a great deal about my ancestors was my mother. My father's older brothers Malayisha[3] and Maguqu also used to talk to me often about our ancestors and our customs. After my father became a Christian, he told me flatly not to keep listening to my uncles, because they were heathens, while he wanted me to be a good Christian. I obeyed him, but it was not easy: his brothers did not stop trying to influence me to follow our tradition, and I loved them both a great deal. At that time I did not like my father much because he was always rude or harsh to me, and I thought that he hated me. Today I believe that, instead of hating me, he loved me greatly.

Yet my father was a strange man. I realize now that he used to sacrifice to his ancestors, despite his Christian beliefs and zeal, but he used to pretend differently. I remember that when I returned

2

home from the Union of South Africa after an absence of fifteen years, he made a feast at which he slaughtered a ram. He called his relatives to the feast and told them, 'I am not making this feast for your ancestors, but I am sacrificing to thank my God, who has allowed my son to return to me after fifteen years.'

Ntate[4] Maguqu said to him, 'Don't come and tell us these things! You are thanking your ancestors because they have brought your child back.'

So I say that my father really did sacrifice to the ancestors even when he was a Christian, but he tried to hide this from people. What my father did then is what is done today by many Christians here.

Because their Churches forbid it, when people want to offer a sacrifice to their ancestors for some reason, you will hear them saying that they are making a table feast, a mokete oa tafole. This feast, although it is slightly different from a feast for the ancestors, is also an old custom. In this feast, one slaughters some animal for a relative who has died; in effect, for an ancestor. So if people do not believe in ancestors, why should they bother to slaughter for their people who have passed away? Therefore I say that most of the Christians of today have returned to their ancestors.

In former days, before the missionaries came here, we used to plait a thong of moli grass[5] and bind it around our heads as a sign of mourning. We did not wear black material then as we do now when we are in mourning. When the missionaries came, they stopped our parents from wearing the moli thong, saying it was a heathen custom. But although we wear black cloth instead of the moli thong today, we still believe that our ancestors are with us. Although we cannot see them often with our eyes, we believe that, in spirit, they are present, and that they see us.

* * *

When my uncles talked to me about the ancestors, they would say to me, 'We are sorry for you. We have noticed that your ancestors are with you, because we have seen many things. You are a lucky person, for you have often narrowly escaped being struck by lightning.' This was how they could tell that my ancestors were protecting me.

'But', they would continue, 'we are sorry for you because your father has forbidden you to worship and revere your ancestors. When you were small, you were once nearly hit by lightning, but you escaped. Again, while you were teaching in Vryheid, you wrote and told us how a bolt of lightning only just missed you. You yourself know how often this has happened. We are telling you now that the ones who protected you are your ancestors, and nobody else.

'When we warn you not to go about alone so much, you always say you keep out of trouble because you are so strong. But we tell you that you are alive because you are lucky, and not because you are strong. But how long can such luck be expected to last? Your ancestors have come to us; they have told us that something must be done about you, to give you protection against harm.'

This incident happened just before my first marriage, when an aunt of mine had been killed in a tragic accident. My uncles believed that the accident had happened because someone wished my death.

My cousin Chabeli was a *ngaka*,[6] what you would call a witch-doctor. Now he stood up and said to me, 'Come here. Put down your hat and your blanket and kneel down here.'

My father was present that day, and he tried to stop the others. 'What are you doing?' he expostulated.

'My uncle, please leave us here,' answered Chabeli. 'We need this our brother to live. When you were a youth, you were scarified to protect you against evil, and you were taught to honour your ancestors. Now you don't want this son of yours to be scarified. No!'

This scarifying is to ask for protection from all evil, and it is done with something like a razor blade. The small cuts are then anointed with a potion from the medicine horn or *lenaka*[7] of one's ancestors, and so it calls forth their blessing and protection.

At that point a problem arose about the *lenaka* they were to use.

My grandfather, Ngolozani, had given each of his sons a *lenaka* filled with special *litlhare*.[8] The secret of the mixture had been passed down right from our first ancestor, Mavuso. Chabeli and the rest, because they believed in the ancestors and the protection of their *lenaka*, had used up their *litlhare* in scarifying their children. They knew that my father had also been given a *lenaka*, and had hardly used it. So they asked him to bring that *lenaka* of his to anoint me.

At first my father denied even having a *lenaka*, but the rest persisted. They knew, they added, that Ngolozani had taught the recipe of the *litlhare* to my father alone, among all his sons. Ngolozani taught my father that mixture, I think, because he was his favourite, and was not as wild as some of Ngolozani's older sons. My father refused to teach the recipe to his children, fearing that we would misuse it. He taught it only to three people: Ketane, who is now dead; my brother's daughter, who will only tell others if they pay her; and Mhlangavula, who taught me that mixture only recently.

Even when my father admitted to having such a *lenaka*, he still refused to give it to them until the others had threatened to go to the Chief to ask him to force Makhuba to have me scarified. So he gave in, saying, 'Well then, do all these heathen things. . . . I don't care. . . .'

'Are you still denying what we keep telling you,' Ketane asked me, 'that your father is also a *ngaka*?'

Then I knelt down and Chabeli scarified me.

It is important that I keep a secret how he did it, and what he said, for if I tell it, people will learn how it was done and they will then be able to consult a *ngaka* to harm me. People have tried to witch[9] me in many ways, but they have not succeeded; if they were to know the manner in which I was scarified, they would be able to succeed.

Chabeli and those others taught me how to sacrifice to the ancestors as well.

'The ancestors will come to you', they explained, 'and ask you for something.' They may ask you for food, or for a blanket made from the skin of a slaughtered beast, or simply for a feast for their descendants. You cannot hold this feast alone: the children of your ancestors must be with you. When they have gathered, you say their praises, mentioning them by name, and you tell them, 'I, Jason, bring this animal to you, my ancestors, as a gift because you asked me for food.'

Now you cannot simply go and stab the animal.

If, while we are speaking to the ancestors, the animal urinates, we will all clap our hands, for that shows our ancestors have heard us. Or if, before we start praising, it urinates, we can stab it because our ancestors have heard us. We believe that if the animal does not urinate, our ancestors are not with us and do not agree to our slaughtering that animal. So someone is appointed to stand and watch the animal. If we finish our praises and it still has not urinated, we must wait until it does before we can stab it.

Here, you must understand, I am talking about the Swazi custom. I am not talking about other nations, for I do not know what their custom is about this; I speak only of my own tribe, and how I was taught.

Then once the animal has urinated, we stab it.

* * *

But I must make my beliefs clear here. Even though my uncles and others had talked to me about the ancestors when I was a youth, I did not believe them and I was not impressed by their tales, for the ancestors had never appeared to me; I had never seen them for myself.

When I was living in the Western Transvaal in the 1930s, my life was hard. That was a bad time for me.

One night in a dream, my grandmother, NoMalunga, appeared to me. She said she wanted food from me. I could not remember my grandmother, because she had died when I was very young, but in the dream she told me, 'I am your grandmother.' As I remember it, she was wearing a blanket, with a *thari* or cradle-skin under it, and she had beads on her head like they wore in the old days. She said, 'I am your grandmother, and I suffered a great deal for you when you were young. I ask you for food.' She went on to describe the type of cow she wanted.

I was worried and did not know what to do, so I wrote home to my father about it, and told him that an old woman with a light skin colour had appeared to me. I said in my letter that she resembled an aunt of mine, and that she wanted food. Then I described my dream in detail.

My father's reply was an angry one: why was I talking such nonsense, he asked. Why should his mother have appeared to *me*, when she had not appeared to him or to any of her other children? What did I think his mother was, a *ghost*?

I did not reply to that letter, but my father's words brought doubt to my mind. Because I believed him, I did not sacrifice the beast that my grandmother had asked for. Still, you must know, I was happy to meet my grandmother.

When I left the Union and went home, she appeared to me again. She asked me why I had not sacrificed the cow she had asked me for, and said again that she wanted food.

I was convinced, this time, that I should find her such a cow, but the difficulty was that my grandmother had chosen a difficult cow to find. She wanted a black and white cow, with a white face and a white tail. I combed my area for such a beast, but could not find one. Eventually I found in Ficksburg a cow that had just the right colours and markings; it was owned by a white man[10] called Mr.

Uys. I approached him, but he would not sell the cow as it was a favourite of his wife's. So I was beaten in my search.

With a sad heart I returned home and went to my grandmother's grave. I knelt there and prayed that she must not harm me. I said that I was not refusing to give her food, but that the kind of cow she had chosen was impossible for me to find. If she would only name me a cow of other colours and markings, I told her, I might manage.

About two or three weeks after I had been to my grandmother's grave, she appeared to me again. She refused to alter her decision: I had to sacrifice a cow with the markings she had specified, and she asked that I make a blanket of the skin, and not sell it.

I think my grandmother was troubling me because it is said that she bore the brunt of my childhood sicknesses. She had to nurse me, and even when I was not sick, I would insist that she, and not my mother, carry me. Even after I had suckled from my mother, I would run to her to be picked up. She worried a great deal, too, when once I became very sick. My throat swelled up. I was taken to a *ngaka* called Rasehlano; they say he gave me medicine and made a hole in my throat, of which I still have the scar. I think that is why, in my dream, my grandmother said she had suffered a great deal for me.

I still do not know why she chose those colours for the cow. She is of the tribe of Ndlovu's; perhaps the cow is of their colours. I do not know. I even went to ask my uncles, Maguqu and Molonyeni, and they were unable to tell me. Once, in desperation, I wanted to slaughter an ordinary cow for my grandmother, but they stopped me.

As I write this today, I have not slaughtered that cow yet. The ancestors trouble me about that still, and they are so many now.

*   *   *

There is a good and kind old man who always appears to me, not only in dreams, but even in broad daylight, when I am walking outside or sitting in a house. That man is my great-grandfather, Jingoes, whose story I have already told.

He is of a light-coloured skin. When I saw him the first time, he was holding a knobkierie and spear, a shield and a stick. I asked him who he was and he told me his name. I have seen him three times.

The last time I saw him was this year, 1971, when I was sitting in this very house, at this very table, writing. He spoke softly to me in Swazi, and I remember he said to me, calling me by the name his son gave me, 'Ndlayedwa, how long do you mean to stay here?'

I did not look up at once, and answered roughly, 'I don't know!' Then I lifted my head, and noticed that I was before my great-grandfather. I changed my tone to one of respect when I said, 'You are the one who knows how long. . . .'

'Ah . . .,' he said. Then he disappeared.

I did not really know what he meant by his question, whether he was referring to this house, or the village, or even earth itself, but I think he must have meant MaMathe's village, because I know the ancestors want to see me return to their home at Koeneng. They have troubled me increasingly of late to leave MaMathe's, where I live now, and return to my home at Koeneng, where I must rebuild my father's house. Even if I do not go to live there, I must rebuild the house, and use it when I visit there, instead of staying with relatives. Right now I am trying to find someone who can get me stones for my father's house, which is in ruins.

* * *

If you ask me the very good question of how I manage to believe in both Christianity—for I am a Christian still—and the ancestors, I will tell you.

Chief Moshoeshoe, the founder of the Basotho nation, was a strange and wise man. I have been told that whenever he learned that people who were strangers had settled near his stronghold on Thaba Bosiu, he would commission some of his own people to visit those strangers. He would instruct his people to observe and learn the ways and customs of the strangers. He warned them not to do away with their own customs or traditions, however, but to bring him word about the new things they had learned. Then he himself, with his people, would decide which of the new customs were good, and should be adopted, and which should be rejected. *He warned his own people most strongly not to throw away their own customs in favour of the new ones.*

I have been told that Moshoeshoe, although he was converted to the Christian faith by the French missionaries who settled in Lesotho, and although he died a Christian, never stopped saying that he had ancestors. He used to say that he was afraid of Mohlomi, the one who chose him to be the Chief of the Basotho nation.

The story is that when Mohlomi was about to die, he called his children, and said that no one among them would rule the Basotho, but that someone of a much lower house, younger than they in status, but of their clan, would be the Chief. All of that clan, the Bakoena, gathered and agreed upon Mohlomi's decision. The man Mohlomi had chosen was Moshoeshoe, and that is why Moshoeshoe venerated his ancestors, and refused to forget them when the missionaries converted him to Christianity.

The ministers of religion came here and told us to turn away from the tradition of worshipping our ancestors, and that was wrong. Their only subject should have been to teach us about Jesus Christ, and the Christian God; their concern should not have been to make us discontinue our customs such as initiation schools and ancestors. They spread hatred instead of their message of love, by telling the children of Protestants they could not marry Roman Catholics, for instance, and making people feel foolish when they followed the customs that had served them well for so long.

I must be fair here and state that without them, we would not have been the nation we are today. They brought us education, so that today most of the people in Lesotho are literate; it was they who advised Moshoeshoe to seek protection from the British against the pressure of the Boers; they were the ones who recorded our history. Even today, many people in Lesotho call a white man *Morena* or Chief, in honour of those early men whom Moshoeshoe called his brothers.

I believe in Christianity because I believe in Jesus Christ, that he is my Saviour. But I also believe in my ancestors, because it is through them that I came to this earth. They are closer to my everyday life, and understand my weaknesses.

I believe that when I die, the day I appear before the Almighty God, the first court I will enter will be that of my ancestors, and through them only, I will find my way to Jesus Christ.

If I am a sinner, and am turned away from Heaven, those are the people who will plead for me not to be sent away, so that I may remain in Heaven, with them.

When I am in trouble, or when I pray for anything, I pray first to my ancestors, and ask them to take my prayer to the Lord Jesus. Many Basotho say that Roman Catholics are worshipping their ancestors in the saints; why, they ask, should one appeal to ancestors who never knew one, and who are not of one's lineage, when one's own ancestors are there? I have never felt guilty, just because ministers say it is a sin to worship the ancestors.

*   *   *

Those who do not venerate their ancestors today are fools, and do not know what they are doing. But out of every hundred, I am sure, there are only two who do not.

When the ministers first started preaching against our old ways, many people believed them and followed them. People used to say that one should emulate Whites and their ways, but slowly they started to realize that they were being foolish, trying to imitate white people when they were not white themselves. Gradually, they started to be proud once more of their old customs, and of being Bantu. Even among Whites, there are different nations; they are all white, but each has its own customs. So with us, each clan or tribe has its own customs, and there is no need to be ashamed of them.

So the Basotho began to see that the ministers of religion had led them astray. They started to say it is dangerous to forget one's traditional ways, and to let one's customs die out, because their children and their children's children would not know anything about all these things.

They said, 'Let us return to our customs because we do not want, after we are dead, that our children should point a finger at our graves and insult them, saying, "Here sleep bad people; today we suffer because of them because they threw away our customs and traditions." ' We do not want our children to insult our graves.

NOTES

1. We have used the word *Chieftainship* as a composite word throughout the book to convey the nuances contained in the Sesotho word *borena*. It has been used to convey two main meanings: the state or position of being a chief, and a chiefly dynasty.
2. Under colonial rule, the country was referred to as Basutoland. Since Independence, it has been called *Lesotho*. We have used the latter name throughout.
3. Mr. Jingoes refers here to Malayisha as his father's brother in a classificatory sense, as Malayisha and Makhuba are on the same genealogical level and their grandfathers were brothers. He calls Malayisha his uncle elsewhere for the same reasons.
4. *Ntate* is a form of address meaning literally 'my father'. It is used by the Basotho as a term of respect towards any man, preceding either his given name or his surname, or by itself.
5. *Moli* is the generic name of plants of the *Hypoxis* genus, some of which are used for making ropes.
6. We use the word *ngaka*, or its plural form *lingaka*, throughout instead of any English translation, which can only approximate the concept.

7. The word *lenaka* (plural, *manaka*) will be used throughout. It literally means 'a horn', for example that of a goat. Specifically in this context it refers to the container in which one keeps *litlhare* or medicine. Today the container need no longer be a horn; the most common ones are small tins or bottles.

8. *Litlhare* means 'trees' or 'bushes', as well as 'medicine'. The word will be used to refer to herbs, materials, objects, potions, medicine, etc. that have healing or protective properties, but that may also be used by the malevolent. The Sesotho term will be used throughout the book instead of *muthi* or 'medicine'; the latter is perhaps the closest translation, remembering that this is in the context of magic. For ease of reference, we have not made the distinction between *litlhare* and *mohlabelo*, which is specifically medicine burned to ashes and then mixed with fat. This is the type used for scarifying and for rubbing on pebbles, pegs, doors, and so on for protection against witchcraft or misfortune.

9. Mr. Jingoes does not use the English word 'bewitch'. We have retained his usage of the term *witch* (as a verb) throughout.

10. There is, in southern Africa, a wide range of terms to denote a man's racial grouping. For an overseas reader, the term *European* (which Mr. Jingoes usually uses) means someone from Europe, and not, as it does in southern Africa, a white man. Elsewhere in the book, the reader will come across words like *Native*, *Africans*, *Bantu*, and *Motho*, all of which refer to black men. To simplify matters, we have tried wherever possible to keep consistently to the terms *Black* and *White*, when to do so would not distort the tone of the original.

CHAPTER TWO

The battles of my youth

By the time I was born, on 9 January 1895, my grandfather Ngolozani had settled at Koeneng, which was then in Leribe District, and I was born there, at Tsokung or Dark Brown Hills.

My father was Makhuba, the second son of Ngolozani Jingoes in the house of NoMalunga, his first wife, whose other name was NoMadlozi, which means 'mother of the ancestors'. My mother was of the Bahuruts'e tribe, followers of Langalibalele. She was brought up among the Zulu in Natal. Her mother was of the Zulu tribe of Mthimkulu.

According to our tribal custom, the parents of a new-born child cannot give him a name if his grandfather is still alive; my grandfather Ngolozani was therefore the one to name me, and he called me Stimela Ndlayedwa.

These two names have a meaning. It is said that when I was born, people were starting to talk about trains for the first time as there was a railway line established between Cape Town and Johannesburg. So my first name, meaning 'train', was given to commemorate the events of the time.

I am told that my grandfather then said, 'The second name I give this boy is Ndlayedwa, because his uncle Maguqu does not share meat with me and his mother when he slaughters anything; he eats all the meat with his wife, NoNandi, or he shares it with NoNandi's parents. Besides, two days ago Ndlayedwa's mother brought some sweet cane up from the lands, and she shared it with nobody, not even her sister's child. That is why I will call this boy Ndlayedwa . . .' which means 'he eats alone'.

As I was the first son of Makhuba, my father had to make a special report of my birth to his parents-in-law who, as is the custom, also had the right to name me. The name they gave me was Ntshanyana which means 'little dog'. This is a name given to boys who are born after older children in that house have died. This was what had happened in Ngolozani's house.

Ngolozani's first son, Maguqu, had a son called Mabona who died when he was about three or four years old. The girl who was born after him also died. This caused their mother, NoMabona, to return to her own people, saying that she was not prepared to live in a village full of witches. But when she left she was pregnant for the third time, and that child also died.

Maguqu went to consult some *lingaka* to discover why his children kept dying. They divined by means of bones, which we call *litaola*, and told him that NoMabona had been witched to ensure that she would have no children. The bones said that the village hated her husband and indeed all of NoMalunga's descendants and wanted to make sure that all their children died.

I was born six months after NoMabona's third child died.

In my father's house there had also been tragedy: my older sister, NoMadlozi (named after her grandmother), had also been killed by witchcraft. It happened then that I was the first son born, in all of NoMalunga's house, who survived.

It is the custom, when a child is born, to place reeds in the thatch of a house to warn people that that place is a *motsoetseng*, where a woman has just been confined; nobody can just go into such a place.

Four days after my birth, an old lady called NoKholomeni simply rushed into my mother's hut, paying no attention to the reeds. I had been placed outside in the *lelapa*[1] or courtyard because, as was the custom, people were smearing the hut freshly. My grandmother cried out, 'What are you doing? Why have you come in? Can't you see this is a *motsoetseng*?'

But the old lady simply snapped, 'I am already inside!'

She scooped me up from where I lay on the ground and kissed me. Then she took out her honed razor. By now my grandmother was screaming, trying to get me out of her arms, because NoKholomeni was known in our village as a witch. But the old lady scarified me, first on my chest, and then under my left arm; she anointed the cuts with *litlhare* from her *lenaka*, and then put me back on my blanket.

Then NoKholomeni turned to my grandmother and said, 'This child will live.' She went on to tease, in the way women do about

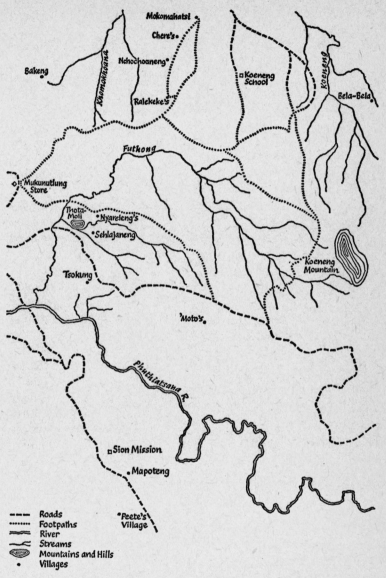

3. The places of my childhood

babies, saying, 'He is my husband.' She bent down to look at me closely and said, 'Oh no, he won't marry me, but he will marry my granddaughter Ndabazana, and become my son-in-law.'

My grandmother was still terrified, so the old lady known for her *litlhare* turned to her again and said, 'I am tired of things here. Every time a child is born to your house we learn after a few months that that child has died. This one here will live. They won't manage to do anything to him now.'

*   *   *

The reader must remember that all these people I have written of so far never went to school. My uncle Maguqu was the exception, and he went to school with children when he was already a married man.

I understand that a merchant arrived in Ngolozani's village, a man called Charles Stevens. His Sesotho name was Seanamarena, or The-one-who-takes-his-oath-by-Chiefs; he was called that because he was proud of our Chiefs when he came to live in Lesotho. Stevens said he wanted to open a trading store in Ngolozani's village, but he could not do so unless he found literate people to help him. Among Ngolozani's sons and grandsons he picked Maguqu, and sent him to the Roman Catholic school, Our Lady of Sion, at Mapoteng. With Maguqu was another man, Semema Solomon Marabe. Both children and adults laughed at the two men going to school with children, but they did not mind, for at last they could write and read and do arithmetic.

Then Mr. Stevens approached Ngolozani for a hut which he could use as a store. He was lent NoMalunga's hut, and he employed Maguqu and Semema. In return for the use of the hut, he would give Ngolozani luxuries like sugar and tea.

I was born some days after that shop was opened, and Maguqu and Semema recorded the date of my birth. That is how I know when I was born.

*   *   *

When I was between two and three years old, I was taken to live with my mother's parents. It is said that my maternal grandparents feared I might die, as Mabona had when he was of my age. My mother's people and their whole village could speak only Zulu, and that was the language I learnt.

At last, after about three or four years, my father fetched me back because he wanted me to go to school.

A boy in Lesotho spends most of his time herding. Even if he attends school, he is expected to herd during weekends and holidays. When I came to herding, there were no cattle in Lesotho because of the Rinderpest,[2] so my task was to herd horses belonging to our family along with Moloi Phahlane and Mafuroane Mthengi Sotshangani.

I still remember that while I was with my mother's parents, the last two cattle in their village died. They were skinned and the people wanted to eat their meat. I can barely remember all this, but I do recall clearly how my grandfather scolded the people and forbade them to eat the meat. The meat was buried and the hides were kept.

Instead of using oxen, people harnessed horses to their ploughs. I do not know how difficult it is to plough with a horse, but I saw people using them.

Ploughing was not the only difficulty the Basotho had to face during the Rinderpest. Our whole system of marriage is founded on cattle. What were we to do without cattle? Marriages could not stop. Instead of paying for brides with cattle, people used horses, and when the horses were finished, they used stones.

If a family had no stock, they would go to the parents of the girl and sit down and explain their difficulties: that they had no cattle in that time of hardship. I understand that stones would be taken and placed before the people who were arranging the marriage, and these stones represented cattle. The number, age, and type of cattle were agreed upon, and the stones were set aside to be redeemed later when times were better.

Once the Rinderpest was over, men went to the mines to earn money to buy cattle again. On their return they came back driving cattle. When I first saw cattle again after the hard years I would always hear people saying that they were taking the cattle to exchange them for the stones of a marriage debt.

Using stones to represent cattle was not an entirely new concept among the Basotho, for there was an old arrangement called *ho bala majoe*, or counting stones, among our marriage customs. If a man did not have enough cattle to pay the bridewealth demanded, he paid what he could, the balance being counted with stones which he redeemed with cattle whenever he could. The whole transaction would be witnessed by people of both families, and by a representative of the Chief or headman, so that there would not be disagreement later about the number paid and the balance.

Remember also that, according to our tradition, a debt does not die with the man who contracted it. One family may owe another cattle even for several generations, but the debt will eventually be paid.

* * *

There is a type of grass known as *moli* which is valuable for making ropes and enclosing courtyards. Wherever this grass grows, you will find people disputing about it, and especially Chiefs and headmen, who will always try to claim the area where *moli* can be found.

On the banks of the Futhong stream, near Tsokung, there was a beautiful stretch of veld where *moli* grew abundantly when I was a child. The Futhong was a boundary: the area to the south of it was directly under the Principal Chief,[3] Chief Peete; to the north lay the area under the jurisdiction of Peete's younger brother, Chief Seshophe. Our village was in Peete's area.

Although the *moli* grew on Peete's side of the Futhong, Seshophe was always claiming that it was his and, being a warrior, he was not averse to resorting to force of arms to prove this.

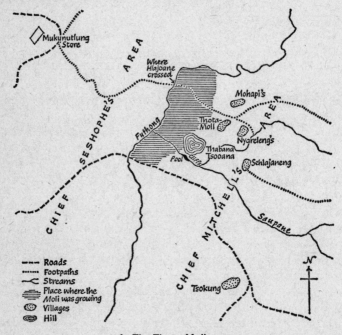

4. The Thota-Moli area

Seshophe had a son, Hlajoane, who was even wilder and fiercer than his father. One night Seshophe sent Hlajoane across the Futhong with many men, and they gathered as much *moli* as they could carry.

Chief Peete could not take any steps against his brother, but he looked around for men he could trust as headmen as well as fighters to guard the grass for him. He sent for Ngolozani and Sotshangani, the headman of Tsokung, and asked them to send their sons to live near the *moli*, to act as a buffer against Chief Hlajoane's incursions. Sotshangani sent his son Mthengi, the father of the Mafuroane with whom I used to herd; Ngolozani sent his son Makhuba, who was brave, but not as wild as some of his brothers. With them went men called Tente and Ramarathane and all their families. They founded the village called Thota-Moli.

There was a man living at Mapoteng near Chief Peete called Potjo Phenethi Masekoane whose grandfather was headman of Sehlajaneng village. Potjo was impatient for power, and he used to nag Chief Peete to let him have a village to rule as headman. Chief Peete always told him that he could found his own village near the *moli* veld, to act as its caretaker, but Potjo was a born coward, and Seshophe and Hlajoane were renowned warriors, so Potjo always refused to go there.

When Potjo saw that a village was being built at Thota-Moli by brave men, however, he approached Peete's first son, Mitchell, to whom he was related by marriage, and asked to be placed over that village as headman. Chief Mitchell readily agreed to Potjo's request, but he did warn him.

'Hlajoane is Hlajoane,' he told him. 'He does not play when he is after something.'

Potjo had no intention of actually living at Thota-Moli while there was the chance of having to do battle with Chief Hlajoane, so he sent one of his men, Phahlane, to act as headman for him there. With Phahlane came two other men, Mongali and Sekhamo.

So I spent my early childhood at Thota-Moli, a small and newly founded village, guarded by my father and a handful of men.

They did not wait long for their first battle with Chief Hlajoane. At the outset things were very quiet; perhaps Hlajoane was waiting until the village had settled down and the men's vigilance relaxed. Potjo, from the safety of Mapoteng, must have thought that Hlajoane would not raid us after all, for he moved into Thota-Moli with his two wives.

Two days after Potjo's arrival all hell broke loose.

My father and Mthengi often went to the Mukunutlung store, in Seshophe's territory, to listen to the gossip there. If there was to be a raid on the *moli*, they would be sure to pick up murmurs about it at the store where all the women of the area did their shopping. It was there it came to their ears, one afternoon, that Hlajoane planned to cross the Futhong during the coming night.

It was a bright moonlight night. I remember that our mothers were still awake long after night fell, and we could hear my father and Mthengi riding their horses along the banks of the stream, watching for Chief Hlajoane and his men. I had gone to sleep outside in the *lelapa* instead of in the hut, but I was just old enough to feel how tense everyone was, and I was sleeping lightly.

DAAA! It was a shot!

I leapt up, but my mother pushed me flat, hissing, 'Keep down!'

I could hear the drumming of my father's and Mthengi's horses as they raced back to the village, shouting, '*Ooeoeooo! Hlajoane is here! Up, men! Hlajoane has arrived!*'

My father strode past me into his hut and came out carrying his gun, his barbed spear, and his ordinary spear, and also his battle-axe. He ran out of the *lelapa*, still shouting to his men.

There were only nine horses in the village at that time, so some of the men would be on foot. The others were saddling their horses and shouting, '*Get up! Get up! Hlajoane is here!*' All the men gathered around their horses, waving guns and spears, except for two. When the alarm was raised, Potjo was sitting in the hut of his second wife, MaMpoi, and he made no move to go outside. With him was Mongali, waiting for an order to saddle up Potjo's two horses.

Like an owl, I watched the men getting ready to confront Hlajoane.

'*Hlajoane is Hlajoane!*' they were shouting. '*This is the night we meet Hlajoane!*' they cried. I remember Ramarathane lifting his face and bellowing, '*A man dies on a spear; a woman is killed by childbirth.*'

Our mothers did not need to be told what to do. Women were running about, packing their possessions and gathering their children, crying, 'Let's go! Let's go!' Some children were tied to their mothers' backs; others to their sisters'. I was old enough to walk. We were only some yards from the village, heading for a valley that would lead us towards Tsokung, when the first bullets came thudding into the village. We could hear them over our heads: *TCHEUUU! KA-TCHEEEU!*

Potjo was still sitting in MaMpoi's hut when one bullet went through the wall, passing between them, and going out through the other wall. MaMpoi had been making a fire in the hearth—where could she run when her husband was sitting there like a stone?—and she snatched up a stirring-stick.

'You damn coward!' she shrieked at Potjo, and struck him with all her might behind the neck. 'Get up! *Get up, you dog!* You dog of a man! People are dying on enemy spears while you crouch here!'

Half blinded by the terrific blow, Potjo staggered to his feet and stumbled towards his saddle, but he could not find the bridle. While he was fumbling around, his first wife, Polo, appeared in the doorway.

'Come on, MaMpoi!' she shouted fiercely. 'Give me that saddle and bridle at once. I'm going to war now. I'm sick of this coward of a dog! We'll die right here, but he stands there shivering and won't fight! Who will lead the men?'

'I'm also sick to death of this dog!' shrilled MaMpoi, as she hit Potjo in the small of the back with her stirring-stick.

'This dog is not fit to be a husband!' added Polo. 'He's a damned coward!' and she snatched up the saddle, found the bridle, and ran outside to saddle up.

That lady could ride!

Polo was already on her horse among the men when Mongali came running up, saying, '*Ooe! Ooee! Mofumahali, ooehle!* Please, Chieftainess, wait. . . . You disappoint us. . . . You put us to shame. . . . Wait! . . .'

We only heard Potjo's story after the battle. The last I remember as we left the village was my father, on his horse in the moonlight, singing the praise-song of Chief Hlajoane.

> Hlajoane, whose praise-name is Mokoara,
> Defended the land of his father.
> Mokoara, cross the river,
> Let the children of senior houses remain;
> Those who should remain are Seeiso, son of Maama,
> Masupha, son of Lepoqo, and Mitchell, son of Peete.
> Seeiso and Masupha remained on the banks
> Of the Mejametalana in Maseru,
> Mitchell remained on the banks of the Caledon;
> 'Go, young brother!' he said. 'If we both go,
> 'Who will stay with Peete and Seshophe?'
> Brother of MaThabeng, cross the river!

Bulwark of your brothers, Mojela and Lepekola.
Under orders, Mokoara left his home.
He went to war.[4]

My father Makhuba was shouting Hlajoane's praises to make
Potjo know how brave the men of Thota-Moli were; Potjo, who had
come to spoil their village as headman only because he was related
to Chief Mitchell through Mitchell's wife.

You might well ask whether singing your enemy's praises does
not make your own men afraid. The answer is that if you face a man
in war, knowing nothing about him, you might start to tremble
simply because he is unknown. You ought to be told what kind of
man you are facing, then you can face him with full knowledge and
courage. That is how my father put heart into the men that night,
by telling them that Hlajoane was a brave and violent warrior, who
had defended the country of his fathers against the Boers.

The rest of the battle I was told about later, for I was running
by then with my mother and other women and children for the safety
of Tsokung. Some women ran to Nyareleng; others fled to Sehlajaneng; each was heading for the village she had lived in before
moving to Thota-Moli. As we fled, we heard the guns over to our
right and bullets cutting air above our heads.

While the women fled and the men galloped to meet Hlajoane,
Potjo was on his blue gelding, riding distractedly back and forth
behind the village; first he went towards Mohapi's, then back
towards his grandfather's village, Sehlajaneng; from there he
turned back and headed for Nyareleng. He never came to blows
with anyone that night.

Thota-Moli's men split up into groups to meet Hlajoane. A man
called Lerata was with some men near the hill, Thabana-Ts'ooana.
When Lerata saw Chief Hlajoane and his men crossing the Futhong,
he started shooting at them. It is said that Lerata was an arrogant
man, insolent to Chiefs and savage in a fight. When Hlajoane heard
the shots, he recognized the sound of Lerata's gun, and headed
straight for him, determined to make an end of him right there.

Lerata was on foot, and when the Chief bore down upon him on
horseback, he fled around the back of the hill, with Hlajoane in
pursuit. Fred, a companion of Lerata, climbed frantically up the
hill, and hid at the top until the battle was over. Lerata kept going,
as fast as he could, all the way around the hill, keeping to the rocks
where Hlajoane's horse could not find a way. At last Lerata could
run no more. He threw himself off the cliffs at the south of the hill

and plunged down, straight into a deep pool in the stream below.

On the cliffs above, Chief Hlajoane reined in his horse, and looked down. *PHAAAAM!* he heard Lerata strike the water. Hlajoane threw up his gun and fired wildly into the pool, afire to get Lerata, but Lerata had already crawled out of the water and was pressed to the ground in deep shadow. Finally the Chief yelled, 'You haven't escaped me! I'll meet you one day!' and turned back to rejoin his men.

By this time men were arriving from Tsokung and the other villages to help Thota-Moli fight off Hlajoane. We met *Ntate* Molonyeni leading the young men of our family.

'My brother . . . ?' he asked my mother, and I was surprised to see tears glimmering in his eyes.

'When I left him,' my mother replied, 'he was alive.'

Heavily outnumbered, Chief Hlajoane was forced to retreat, and he was driven back across the Futhong into his father's area. But he left wounded enemies behind him: Mohapi lost a toe from his right foot, and Likotsi was wounded in the right thigh and could never walk without sticks again. Only one of Hlajoane's men was wounded. While the battle was on, Chief Hlajoane's men had split up, leaving a group to gather *moli* while the rest fought. They were forced to leave what they had gathered behind them, and the next day our people collected it and took it to Chief Mitchell.

The British Government did not fine anyone for taking part in that battle, but they reprimanded Hlajoane.

After the battle, Chief Mitchell made Potjo return to Mapoteng and stripped him of his rights as headman, because he was not even among the men of Thota-Moli during the battle, much less leading them, as he should have been. I heard that Chief Mitchell ordered Potjo not to be seen anywhere near the Chief's houses, because he was a born coward.

I have never heard of *litlhare* to make a coward brave. The Basotho have a saying, *Ha bolekoala ha ho lluoe*, which means that a coward's people never mourn. I have only heard of *litlhare* to make a man an accurate marksman. Apart from that, there was a ceremony for men about to do battle, at which they were *lekisoa* or fortified for their coming ordeal.

Those were exciting times for a young boy.

* * *

I will describe the *lekisoa* ceremony I saw once.

When I was a boy of about twelve, I was sent on an errand to a man called Ratumo who lived in Chief Peete's village. Along the way, I saw my father in a group of about ten men, all armed, riding towards Mapoteng, where the Chief's village was. When I think back on it now, I realize that an order must have arrived in our village from the Chief, telling all men to arm themselves and gather at the Chief's place; at the time, of course, I did not know what was going on.

When I arrived at Mapoteng I went to Ratumo's house to give my message, but his brother said to me, 'Wait a bit, my child; we'll talk later,' and he walked to the *lekhotla*.[5] It was clear that there was to be a *pitso*,[6] a gathering called by the Chief, that day, for men were streaming into the village, all carrying arms, and they were singing a war song. I cannot remember the words of that song, except these: 'A man of war does not die at home.' All these men—there must have been more than one thousand of them—dismounted and tethered their horses near the *lekhotla*, in front of which they gathered. We were about fifty yards from them, a group of boys, playing. No woman was in sight; they had all withdrawn to their *malapa*.

One of the Chief's advisers stepped forward and said, '*Tsielala*', which is how silence is called for at a *pitso*. The men fell silent. Then Chief Mitchell stood up and said, 'People of Mats'ekheng,[7] my father, Chief Peete, would like to talk to you; I know you will all pay attention to his words.'

Chief Peete was sitting on a straight-backed chair outside the *lekhotla*. Beside him was his brother, Chief Seshophe; close to them sat Chief Hlajoane, and next to him Chief Kefase, son of Peete. The last chair was Chief Mitchell's. This was the time that chairs were first making their appearance in this country and we boys were very intrigued by them.

Then Chief Peete stood up to address his people. He was wearing what the Boers called an *onderbaadjie*, a long waistcoat of red flannel —a colour he loved—with short sleeves. He wore a conical grass hat, of the same type as Basotho men wear today. He was holding his stick, the one called *Mohlakola*. This word means 'to sweep clean'; it is also a name given to a certain position of the divining bones which indicates a total loss or a very bad omen. I think the name of the stick signified that Chief Peete was so powerful he could sweep away any opposition he met. The men of Mats'ekheng were ranged in front of the Chief.

'Sons of Makhabane,' Chief Peete was speaking. 'We were brought up as orphans because our grandfather, Makhabane, was killed in battle with the Xhosa. Yet we have never been anxious about our fate; we have never cared or worried because we are only a small group. I don't care how strong a man might be; I don't care how brave a warrior a man might be; I only know that however brave, however strong our enemies, and however small our band, we have never been defeated by a group strong in numbers. I am not simply praising us; I am saying what we all know to be true, and I am saying what has always been so.

'Now I must tell you that I am getting tired of Chief Masupha, our neighbour to the west. The area known as Khokhoba was allocated to me by Chief Moshoeshoe—you know this. I cannot understand why Chief Masupha is now claiming that Khokhoba is his, that it *belongs* to him, only because my father allowed him to run a cattle-post there. Yet Masupha is now starting to settle his own subjects at Khokhoba. The dispute between us has gone before the Paramount Chief, and I am awaiting his decision. If that decision is not final, if that decision does not come soon, I am going to take the law into my own hands and face Masupha.'

When the Chief had spoken, he turned and looked at his *ngaka* who was sitting about a yard to his right, on a stone. I did not know this man, for I had not seen him before; he was not one of the Chief's regular *lingaka*. To this day I do not know his name. He was wearing on his head the old headdress of men, a feather cockade or tuft, black in colour. In his hand was his iron digging-stick, used for digging out the herbs of his profession, and also a spear. His assistant sat near him, dressed in an ordinary blanket and grass hat.

'Will you do it?' the Chief asked this *ngaka*.

That man got to his feet and said, 'My Chief, I am only a *ngaka*, but I believe I will do it, if your *lingaka* will help me. I should like them to approach me now.'

At this, four men moved forward. They were Nqhoboi, Mabefolane, Ramaile, and Chabeli, all *lingaka* of Chief Peete. The *lingaka* of Mats'ekheng did not dress up particularly because of their work; anyone who did not know them would have taken them for ordinary men, because they dressed like ordinary men.

These four walked up to the strange *ngaka*; with them were their acolytes or assistants. The *ngaka* pointed to a place apart from the crowd, and they went to hold their private council there, inviting Chief Mitchell, Chief Hlajoane, and Chief Kefase to join them.

Chief Peete and Chief Seshophe remained on their chairs. After they had talked for a while, they returned and Chief Mitchell reported in a whisper to his father.

By this time, we boys had realized that this was no ordinary *pitso*, but something we had never witnessed before. We crept forward, watching everything raptly, and joined the group of men.

The Chief's kraal was about twenty yards from the *lekhotla;* it was a very big kraal, built of stone. In it, there was a fierce brown bull. *Ntate* Nqhoboi led the *ngaka* we did not know towards this kraal, with the other three *lingaka* and their assistants following.

The five men entered the kraal and surrounded the bull. They were all holding spears which looked like any other spears, but which must have been treated with special *litlhare*.

There was no singing now: everyone was watching the group in the kraal, standing in a circle around the bull.

As one man, the five *lingaka* lifted their spears and pointed them at the bull. Then they leaned forward together and touched the bull with the tips of their spears. They drew back, their spears still pointing at the bull, and felt in their pockets or their leather bags for their *litlhare*. Behind them, the assistants were scurrying around, each pulling forth *litlhare* from bag or pocket and putting it into his master's hand. The *lingaka* smeared their spearheads with this *litlhare*. When they had done, the five turned and pointed their spears towards Chief Masupha's area.

There was still no sound to be heard anywhere.

As one man, the five *lingaka* turned back to point their spears at the bull again. Once more, they touched it with their weapons, and then drew back. Once more, they smeared the spearheads, and once more, their assistants bustled around frantically to hand them their *litlhare*. This time they turned to point their spears towards Chief Molapo's area, to the north of Mats'ekheng.

For the last time, the five *lingaka* swung back to face the bull. They touched it with their spears. . . . They withdrew their spears. Then, still moving at the same instant, like one man, each took his spear by the haft and lifted it high above his head.

The five spears came down together, and stabbed the bull through its ribs.

'*Ho eona, Mats'ekha*!' Chief Peete's order cut through the silence, telling the men of Mats'ekheng to fall upon the bull. A deep sigh arose from the men, '*Helele*, Chief . . . .'

Within twenty minutes, nothing was left of the bull except its bones and some intestines.

The men fell upon the bull, hacking off chunks of flesh with hide still on them. They cut with their knives and their spears. They ate that bull, and they ate it raw and hot. I have seen that. They hacked up the bull with their knives and they ate it raw.

When they had chewed off the meat, they threw away the tatters of hide. As boys are, we also wanted to taste that raw meat, and be warriors like our fathers. We fell upon the bits of hide thrown aside by the men and gnawed at them. They tasted like dust-caked bits of hide, but we felt we were warriors too.

That is how warriors are given strength and protection before going into battle, and I have seen it.

* * *

In my youth our Chiefs at Mats'ekheng and throughout Lesotho observed the customs of our fathers, and people did not want. If we had no rain for a month or even three weeks, you would hear people saying we were having a drought. I never saw a drought that lasted over six months, like the bad one we are having now.

When there was a drought in those days, the Principal Chief would be approached by his advisers and sub-chiefs, who would tell him that the people needed rain. The Principal Chief would then send out word that all men should gather on a certain day to go on a communal hunt, a *molutsoane*, to bring rain.

I was told when I was young that there were still leopards and cheetahs in the mountains, but I never saw these animals. We did see many buck, like the vaal rhebuck, the springbok, and the klipspringer. We were also told that there used to be black wildebeest and eland; we children did not see these, though. I remember being told, even then, that hunters were driving all these animals away from our country. My father once killed a buck, but in our custom, if a man shoots a buck, he cannot take it to his own home but must give it to the Chief, who may give him a portion of it, but who is not obliged to do so.

When the Principal Chief gave orders to gather for a *molutsoane*, it often happened that rain would fall even before they left on their hunt, and then the Chief would hold a *pitso* of thanksgiving to thank his ancestors for the rain.

If the rain did not come at once, the Chief led his men out to hunt, especially for buck, which are great animals in our customs.

I saw one hunt like that at Koeneng when I was about ten. I was herding near Koeneng, where many buck were to be found in those days, when I saw men from all over the Chief's ward coming together for the hunt very early in the morning. When they found the buck—it was particularly the klipspringer they were after—it would be chased by men on horseback, with sticks. The man whose stick struck the buck first would be the one to take it to the Chief, who would carry it to a stream. As soon as possible the buck would be skinned there by the Chief's men, and then the Chief himself would hasten to take the partly digested grass from its intestines. This he would mix with water from the stream, and with *litlhare* from a *lenaka* which is used only for rainmaking. With this mixture, the Chief would wash himself and his son, and then he would sprinkle all his men with it. If the people wanted to eat the buck after this, they could, but it should not be cooked properly; it had to be partially roasted over an open fire and eaten half raw.

The Chief needed no *ngaka* to perform this ceremony; he himself had the power to pray for rain. You must know that in this prayer the Chief would address the ancient God of the Basotho, whom we call *Molimo*, but who has many other names. This God created man out of clay, working without cease for so long that he developed holes in his hands. He is sometimes called The-God-whose-nose-gives-water. When we have to give him a form, we think of him as a cow.

The hunt would end after the first buck was killed. If, by accident, the men killed a second buck, both could be skinned and used together, but only one was needed. By that time all the men would have gathered round in a large group, singing a war song.

I do not know of any *molutsoane* when the men did not return wet with rain from the hunt.

I have been told that even Chief Lerotholi, the Paramount Chief, came to Koeneng once to make a *molutsoane* for the whole country. If, right now, the King called a *molutsoane* for the country, you would see a wonderful thing: it would rain—for certain—*it would rain*. It is because our ancestors see us using the wrong prayers today that we suffer these droughts and hardships.

In the old days when there was rain and game, and when we gave reverence to our ancestors, people were not seen hungry as they are today. You would never see beggars going about asking for food as you see them in numbers today. During that time, if a person was hungry or poor, he would not be ashamed to ask for food, and no one would turn aside from him. A man would come to your door and say his children went to bed hungry the night before; you would turn to your wife at once, and she would see how many baskets or bags of grain she could spare him. If someone was sick, he would never be left alone to die alone in his house as people do today. These days, when a person is dying and in need of nursing, people ask, 'Where are his relatives? Why don't they come and see to him?' In former days sick people were attended by villagers: some would bring water, some would take the dirty clothes and wash them, and some would cook and grind grain.

In the last two years I have turned increasingly to my ancestors and to our old customs. Our ancestors need us back, for things are growing bad. There are painful things here in Lesotho, and not only here, but in Africa as a whole. We have lost our ways, yet we expect miracles. We have made a mistake, a great mistake, and unless we return, nothing can be done for us. If we do return to our old ways, surely we will meet our ancestors easily and peacefully.

* * *

Ao, children! Those days! *Those days!*

It was not only our men who could bring us rain: our mothers had their own way of praying for rain.

I remember vividly how, in my boyhood, our women once went to steal a *lesokoana* or stirring-stick from another village to bring rain to us.

The Chieftainess of our village, Thota-Moli, gave the order, and very early one morning, before dawn, our women arose and went to Chere's village in Chief Seshophe's area. You cannot just arrive at a village and announce that you have come for a *lesokoana*; no, you have to plan your campaign as carefully as you would a battle.

At strategic points, all along their route, groups of women are positioned to wait until their turn comes to fight for the *lesokoana*. As the main group gets close to the village they are to invade, they place women around the village and inside the village, all being very quiet and hiding carefully. The woman chosen to steal the *lesokoana* goes to the headman's or the Chief's house, where she finds the women of the household up and doing their early chores, for by then the sky is growing lighter with the coming dawn.

She knocks and goes inside, looking carefully to see whether the *lesokoana* is in its customary place, tucked into the reed enclosure

of the *lelapa*, or whether someone is still stirring porridge with it.
To allay suspicion, she sits down next to the fire, quietly chatting.
As soon as she sees that the people of the house are relaxed, she
leaps up and snatches the *lesokoana*. Now she must *run*.

She races out of the house, ululating loudly to call her companions: *Helelelelele!*

At once, behind her, there is an outcry: '*Oooooooo*! Women!
The *lesokoana*'s gone!' Even the men who are up and about shout in
angry voices, 'What are you standing there for, crying? It's gone
already! Go and get it back!'

This is when the real battle starts. The men and boys stand
on the sidelines, encouraging and scolding their women, while the
village women and girls turn out to recover their *lesokoana*.

This game is not unlike rugby. The stick is thrown from hand to
hand, and if anyone manages to touch it, it is hers and she throws it
to her companions. All the while, the invaders try to make for their
line of retreat, where fresh runners await them, while the defenders
do their very best to stop them. Once the invaders manage to cross
the boundary of their area, the chase usually stops, for the losers
ought to give up.

After this the winners cannot simply go home. Having succeeded
in stealing a *lesokoana*, they stop at the stream near their home and
smear themselves with clay. There they sing their rain-prayer songs
for the rest of the day. Late in the afternoon, singing and clapping
their hands, they return to the village, and take the *lesokoana* to
their Chieftainess's house, where it is placed in the *seotloana* or reed
fence enclosing the *lelapa*. By the time they come into the village,
singing, it is raining.

This time, as I have said, the *lesokoana* was taken from Chere's
village. This Chere was a headman living at Nyareleng's village
when we first moved to Thota-Moli. He did not want to fall under
the command of Matebele, as we were called, so he moved across
the Futhong into Seshophe's area. There had been friction between him and Tsokung's people because he wanted to rule us all,
but when he was offered the headmanship of Thota-Moli by the
Chief, he refused to go there, being afraid of Chief Hlajoane and of
having to defend the *moli* from him. He was the uncle of Potjo, the
younger brother of Potjo's father. So there was a history of friction
between us and Chere, and perhaps that was why our mothers chose
his village when they went to steal a *lesokoana*.

Chieftainess MaMpoi, wife of Chief Mitchell, was very angry

when she heard of the *lesokoana* of Thota-Moli's women. It had brought rain, but not very much. She sent out word to say that she was both angry and sorry, and added, 'If you want to pray for rain, don't go and take a *lesokoana* from a village of Mats'ekheng, for you are all subjects of the late Chief Makhabane. You ought to go to Masupha's, Molapo's, or even to Matsieng, the place of the Paramount Chief, and get one there.'

This, you understand, was before *lesokoana* became the game for children it is now, when girls go to their neighbours' villages and ask for a *lesokoana*. In those days it was a serious affair, because it was a prayer for rain.

After two or three weeks, Chieftainess MaMpoi announced that she was going to invade Fobane's, a village then in Leribe, under Chief Molapo, for *lesokoana*. The best runners were chosen from all over Mats'ekheng, and the Chieftainess herself was to lead her women.

Those days were so pleasant . . . .

I do not know what time the women left home, for I did not see them go, but we were told that when the dawn broke they were already at Fobane. All along their route groups of women were stationed, waiting to run.

A famous runner, a woman called MaMoliehi, was chosen to enter the hut of MaMohato, Chieftainess of Fobane, to steal her *lesokoana*. That was a good, fierce battle, for all along the way, more and more women came to defend their Chieftainess's *lesokoana*; if you had seen the numbers of people, you would have thought there was a feast there. From her house, MaMohato was encouraging her women, and they gained courage and managed to snatch back the *lesokoana*.

Then two men arrived with Chieftainess MaMpoi's horse, and she leapt on its back and raced to the centre of the mob, crying to her women not to give up, but to fight. 'Come, Mats'ekha! Come and help!'

She was not playing a game that day; she was riding in earnest, to guide and put heart into her people. When she appeared among them on her horse their courage grew, and they would not let the *lesokoana* return to Fobane.

'Now! Now!' yelled the girls.

'We've got it! We've caught the *lesokoana*!' their Chieftainess shouted.

Some of the women wanted Chieftainess MaMpoi to catch the *lesokoana* and gallop home with it, but the Chieftainess herself and women who understood what it was they were trying to do objected that that would be unfair.

Slowly the Mats'ekha won ground; from Fobane's donga they moved to Outspan; from there to Mabunyaneng's veld, where they found reinforcements; from there they raced to Rakoto's village, right near the Mukunutlung store. Just as they were about to enter that village, a girl from Fobane managed to snatch their prize from them. She raised it high above her head and ululated: *HELELE-LELE*! Everyone knew what a runner that girl was, and Fobane's people were gloating, 'Now we've got you!'

The girl was at Mabunyaneng's donga before one of our women, UnoMocinelo, could make a grab for her. She missed. Moliehi, a lanky girl also of Thota-Moli, reached for her, but she escaped. NoStimela, my own mother, grabbed at her; again the girl slipped away, and she tossed the *lesokoana* to her companions.

Then a champion appeared. MaKhokolotso from Mokomahatsi, Chief Seshophe's village, intercepted the *lesokoana*. By now it was noon. Our women started to win back the ground they had lost. Again, they entered Rakoto's village, and this time they managed to pass through it. By now the sky was clouding over.

They could not afford to relax yet; Chieftainess MaMohato, accompanied by some men from Fobane, was on horseback among her women, trying to lead them back to victory.

By the time the cattle were coming back from the pastures it was clear that the Mats'ekha had won, and they went to the Futhong stream to bathe and sing their songs. I am not sure of all the things women do at such a time, for men do not go near them. When they left the stream, singing and clapping, it was raining hard.

We had good rain for a week that time.

Fobane's women came to try to steal back their *lesokoana* from Chieftainess MaMpoi's *lelapa*, but they failed to get it outside, so well was it guarded.

A *lesokoana* is one of a woman's most important household utensils. It is not made of any special wood, but it still has some significance. With it, if her husband annoys her, a woman strikes him, as Potjo's wife did during the battle at Thota-Moli. She uses it to stir the food she cooks. If there is no rain, a woman cannot cook, for there will be no grain, and there will be no water. Without water, we all die. It is the *lesokoana* that blends water with grain to make food.

*   *   *

By the 1910s there were cattle to be herded again, but by that time I was attending school at Koeneng and could only herd during the weekends and holidays. The cowardly headman, Potjo, had made his peace with Chief Mitchell and had come back to Thota-Moli as head of the village, and this caused my father to return in disgust to Ngolozani's village at Tsokung. We had suffered to protect the *moli* and the village of Thota-Moli from Chief Hlajoane while Potjo ran around like a whipped dog, and we would have been fools to live under a coward just because he had made his peace with the Chief. That was why we moved back to Tsokung.

The Tsokung area as a whole was under the headmanship of the Rachakane family, descendants of Ngolozani's friend Sotshangani, but Ngolozani's village itself was under one of Ngolozani's sons. At the time I speak of now, my uncle Malayisha was our headman and he was strict with child and adult alike.

Whenever we boys went out to the fields with the village cattle, Malayisha would say to us, 'My cattle must not return hungry. If they do, you must not come back with them! Let my cattle graze wherever they like; if they graze people's grain, I will pay for any damage caused by them.' He was like that. If anything happened to the cattle of his village, he would not sleep, but would spend the whole night cursing.

We knew that he really meant what he said.

'Do you understand what I'm saying, you, Ndlayedwa?' he would growl at me. When he talked to me that way, my heart contracted and my eyes prickled with tears I could not stop. I might have been a fool to cry at that, but he hurt me, and I felt that he thought me a bad herdboy who did not know how to keep the cattle fat.

Our village had over thirty beasts. When we went out to seek pasture for them, we would allow them to graze anywhere at all, even on the reserved *leboella*[8] and the crops in people's lands; any good stuff we found, we would drive our cattle to graze, for my uncle had said he would pay damages.

Uncle Malayisha's instructions, and the way he backed us up when people complained, made me a difficult, stubborn child, because I gave no thought to the consequences of my actions. My father saw this and tried to counter it, but I paid no heed to him. He would go up on a hill and shout to me to stop the cattle from grazing on reserved places but I ignored him, knowing that if I kept the cattle away from the best grazing, my uncle would thrash me.

At last my father saw that he could not control me from afar, and he began to keep his stallion in the stable instead of sending it out to pasture. That stallion was used only to chase me whenever I drove the cattle into forbidden places. My father used to ride down to the lands where I was, clutching a sjambok to thrash me. When I saw him coming, I trotted over to broken ground, never to a level place where his horse could outdistance me easily. As he came up behind me, I did not run flat out: I loped along to save my breath until he caught up with me. As soon as he dismounted to thrash me, I raced away as fast as I could, and this used to infuriate him. He used to tell my second wife, NoMaqhesha, who was his favourite, that I was an unspeakably stubborn child who used to take perverse delight in making him angry and that he had never known such a child before or since.

Sometimes, of course, he caught me and beat me with his sjambok, forcing me to drive the cattle where he wanted. On those evenings when I returned to the village I knew we were in for a scene.

'Why are these cattle hungry?' uncle Malayisha would start ominously.

'*Ntate*,' I always replied, 'your brother went to the fields and stopped me from letting the cattle graze their fill.'

'He was there?'

By that time I could no longer speak. I bawled with rage and terror, knowing I was caught between two hard-necked men. Ndaba, son of Malayisha's sister, who made up in grit what he lacked in years, used to reply for me, 'Yes, my uncle was there, chasing us.'

That was enough for us all: we boys turned and ran while *Ntate* Malayisha grabbed a stick or a stone or anything else that came to hand and hurled it at my father, yelling, 'I told you long ago to keep away from the herdboys!'

'Why should I?' my father always shouted, ducking the missiles. 'They drive their cattle to graze the *leboella* and people's wheat.'

'That's none of your business! I am responsible for the cattle of this village. I have never asked *you* to drive them into anyone's land.'

*   *   *

It was when we had to enter the territory of another village with our cattle that our real battles started, for herdboys defend their grazing rights jealously, and our own band contained some notable

A young woman

An old lady.
The reeds in the thatch
behind her show that
it is a *motsoetseng*,
where a mother and a
new-born infant are

Boys with clay cattle in
kraal

Looking from the lowlands to the mountains

Mountain trail

cowards, so that we were often beaten up. The strongest band at that time was made up of boys from Raletsae's village, led by Mokete and Kubatse, fearless fighters who were respected by most herdboys in the area. Their territory lay just across the Futhong from ours, in Chief Seshophe's area, and as it had a fine *leboella*, it was a constant temptation to us. Our feud with them was long and bitter, fanned by the covert rivalry between our fathers and our Chiefs.

The last chapter in our feud started one day at about midday when we drove our cattle from Tsokung's *leboella* where they had grazed all morning down across the stream to the fresh green grass of Raletsae's *leboella*. We were herding about forty cattle that day. I was with Sefako, my friend, Monnakhomo, Malayisha's son, Molisana, Lepekola and young Ndaba, sons of Malayisha's sister, and Sakayedwa, Molonyeni's son. As we went slowly down towards the stream we could see no one anywhere near the area we wanted our cattle to graze, so we crossed the stream without a qualm and moved on to the *leboella* relaxed and confident.

They took us by surprise. I think their elders must have seen us from their village and sent the youngsters out after us. There was a hollow like a small valley to our right, and they appeared from there without warning, armed with sticks and stones. Without a word, they started to drive our cattle before them.

We made no attempt to resist them for we were afraid that their older brothers might suddenly appear to help them if a fight started, and so they drove our cattle along, with us following them silently. Then we realized that they were not heading for the stream, to escort us back into our territory; they were driving our cattle towards their village. We asked them where they were taking the cattle, and they replied that they were capturing them and were going to impound them at their village.

'Your parents can come and pay for damages to the *leboella*,' they continued, 'and after they have paid the pound fee as well, we will let them have their cattle back.'

We feared *Ntate* Malayisha more than we feared a thrashing from those boys, so we started arguing at once.

'We only came down to the stream to let our cattle drink,' we pleaded.

'If that's so, why didn't you stop them from crossing the Futhong?'

That was unanswerable. To add to our misery, they started beating

3

our cattle with their sticks as they drove them, to show their contempt for us.

Brave young Ndaba turned to us and hissed furiously, 'You're such cowards!'

'Yes,' Sakayedwa chimed in, 'why should people drive our cattle away from their grazing? We'll tell *Ntate* Malayisha when we get home!'

'We will say,' Ndaba warmed to his task, 'that you are useless. We will say he must not let you herd his cattle again.'

I was about fourteen then. The others clearly expected me to take the initiative. I felt the hot flush of shame creeping into my neck.

'Please,' I called out to Mokete, 'stop driving our cattle! If you don't want them to graze your *leboella* you can come and tell us to leave, but don't drive them yourselves, and don't beat them with sticks.'

'What can you do about it?' Mokete taunted us, and gave our cow called Ts'oanyane a hard whack.

'Mokete! That's enough now!' shouted Sefako, for Ts'oanyane was his favourite cow, and he rushed forward, lifting his fighting-sticks.

Our fear fell away from us at once, and all of us threw ourselves upon Mokete's company, fighting with sticks. We might have stood a chance, for although Mokete was a big fellow, we out-numbered his band, but at that moment a horde of younger boys appeared, all armed with stones. Under the barrage they hurled at us we saw we were beaten, and we started falling back to the stream, taking our cattle with us. Once we were in the stream-bed Mokete's group stopped attacking us and turned back to their village, but Mokete stayed long enough to yell, 'If you come back here again, I'll show you!'

Ashamed and trembling we decided there and then to get our own back on Mokete. That day, we said, we were unprepared; we did not know if their older brothers were hiding in the long grass to help them fight; we had been taken by surprise. We went home and stayed up late that night, making plans. Our final decision was to split our herd into two groups when we went to graze Mokete's area the following day; one large herd of cattle can be noticed too easily from afar while two smaller ones might well pass undetected long enough to give us time to prepare for the battle.

The following day the herd of oxen and heifers went out along the usual path down to the stream while Monnakhomo, Ndaba, and myself led the milk cows down the path that leads to Qoboloto's village. On the way we met *Ntate* Mahamane, the headman of Tsokung as a whole.

'Where are you going?' he asked us. 'That is the way to our *leboella*, so turn back.'

'We are just passing Qoboloto's on our way to the stream, *Ntate*,' we assured him.

'If you graze my *leboella*, watch out!'

We moved on past Qoboloto's and down towards the Phuthia-tsana, crossing the Mataheng stream three times, allowing our cattle to graze on the banks of the Phuthiatsana, but heading always towards the Futhong. At last we reached the stream and crossed over, and still we had not been spotted. When we met up with Sefako and the rest with their herd of oxen and heifers, we learned that they had crossed without incident as well, and we settled down quietly together, letting our herd spread out across the *leboella*. So far, our plan had worked well. For an hour or more we were disturbed only by a few birds and a cool breeze.

Then there was a hoarse shout, 'Malayisha's boys are grazing our *leboella*!'

This time the men of that place did not send youngsters like Mokete; they sent young men. There was Likoto, Nyatso, Mosiuoa, and some others whose names I forget.

When they appeared they said at once, 'We know that you have come to fight. This matter is no accident.'

As soon as they started to drive our cattle away Sefako cried at once, 'What are you trying to do, you people?'

'We are capturing your cattle to go and impound them. This is a *leboella* here, you boys. That means no grazing.'

I started pleading with Nyatso, the older brother of Mokete. Our fathers were close friends, so I thought he would be the most likely one to listen to reason, but his reply was simply, 'Why did you do this when you know this is a *leboella*?'

'I did not know you would be sent to stop us. I thought they might send someone else.'

'Then', he said, 'drive your cattle away from here.'

We complied with alacrity; we had managed to graze our cattle on their *leboella* for some time, and we were getting off lightly. But just then Mokete appeared, followed by his company. They were racing to catch up with us, their blankets flapping. Without further word, they started beating our cattle with sticks.

'Cattle don't herd themselves!' shrieked little Ndaba. 'Don't take out your anger on dumb animals. *We* are the herdboys of those cattle!'

At once Mokete turned back to Ndaba and Sefako. I was still trying to plead with Nyatso, but Ndaba and Sefako started playing a war song on their *masiba*,[9] the instruments herdboys play, and the rest of us started a dance to their tune, showing we were ready for battle. The two groups of youngsters faced each other lifting their sticks, but Nyatso separated us before we came to blows.

'They're too full of themselves,' Mokete pleaded with Nyatso; 'yesterday they came here and we warned them and today they've come looking for trouble on purpose.'

'Why didn't you stop us earlier?' I flung back at him. 'You saw us coming. Why did you wait until Nyatso and the bigger boys were sent after us?'

The insult went home, as I had meant it to. Mokete whirled on Sefako with his sticks up. Nyatso stepped between them quickly saying, 'Mokete, you must remember that they are our brothers,' referring to our fathers' friendship. Then he said to us, 'Please drive these cattle away from our *leboella*. I would not like to have to capture *Ntate* Malayisha's cattle.'

'Don't let them get away!' Mokete wailed, nearly dancing with fury. 'Don't be soft! They came here on purpose!'

I was exulting in our victory now and could not help goading Mokete further: 'You're a coward! You did not come. You waited for your older brothers and yet you *knew* we would be here today. We told you yesterday. You only came to stop us when you had these men to back you up. You want to fight in their presence, forgetting that they are our older brothers and we cannot, according to custom, fight in their presence. We cannot fight today, but one day we will meet!'

Mokete still wanted to fight, but he was powerless; if you try to fight in the presence of your elders when they do not want you to, they will simply whip you for disrespect.

Mokete was like that. He never backed down from a fight, and he was always ready for one. He was a renowned fighter until his early twenties, when he was killed in a gun-fight.

'One day . . . *Yes*! One day we will meet!' Mokete echoed.

That day came that summer during hoeing time, which was earlier in those days than now. It was about November or December. During that time Lesotho was rich in grass, and Lesotho was rich in marshes. Water was plentiful in the streams and rivers, but our cattle did not drink much from running water, however thirsty they were; they would head straight for a marsh, where the water was sweet. It was an important thing to herdboys to have their cattle drink in a marsh every day, for they soon grew fat and sleek. Naturally, there was fierce competition among companies of herdboys at every marsh, and only the leading boys, the ones who dominated everyone else, could have their pick of the marshes. Their herds drank before any others, and if you were not a leader like that, your cattle had to wait, and often did not get a chance at all. If you arrived home without your cattle having drunk their fill at a marsh, your elders would always scold you.

How could they tell that the cattle had drunk at the marsh? If you know anything about herding, you will realize that while the cattle are drinking from a marsh, they have to wade through mud, reeds, and water, sometimes up to their bellies. When they swat at flies with their tails, they splash muddy water on their flanks, and when this dries it leaves distinctive marks.

It so happened that our nearest marsh was in Chief Seshophe's area, right where Mokete and his company ruled as leaders in matters of grazing, and they defended their marsh from other herdboys, especially us, with all their might.

I arrived home from school one Friday night that summer to be greeted with the news that our cattle had not drunk at the marsh that day. *Ntate* Malayisha was scolding the boys.

'Why have my cattle not drunk from the marsh?'

Sefako and Ndaba tried to explain to him that they had failed because two alone could not take on Mokete's gang, and Mokete was trying to exclude us from that marsh altogether.

'But where were Lepekola, Monnakhomo, and Molisana?'

'They were there. . . .'

'Why didn't the cattle drink then?'

'Mokete's lot came upon us . . . we couldn't do anything . . . they drove us away. . . .'

'I'm sick and tired of feeding cowards!' uncle Malayisha burst out. 'I'm sick and tired of clothing cowards!'

When he was angry, *Ntate* Malayisha would scold and swear the whole night. He started then, swearing and pacing up and down. Of the three cowardly boys who had not wanted to face up to Mokete, only Lepekola and Monnakhomo were of his house, for Molisana was only an inhabitant of the village and not related to us.

He could not be punished, but *Ntate* Malayisha gave orders that Lepekola and Monnakhomo were not to be given food that night, '. . . just as my cattle were not fed today!' Then he had an even better idea: none of us herdboys related to him was to be fed that night. He wanted to be sure we knew how it felt to be denied nourishment.

He sent for me and told me, 'Tomorrow you are not to go anywhere. You must herd my cattle tomorrow. You must go with Sefako, Ndaba, and the rest. My cattle must not drink from the Futhong as they did today!'

I helped the boys drive the cattle to the place where they are milked in the middle of the village before being closed up in the kraal for the night.

While we were milking, Molisana whispered, 'Why don't you give Nkai,' for that was my nickname then, 'why don't you give Nkai Mokete's message?' There were murmurs of agreement, and I saw their heads nodding, so Molisana resumed, 'Mokete said we must tell you this: "Tell Nkai that all the cattle of Tsokung's village did not drink from the marsh today; it was we who stopped them. Even tomorrow we will stop them, because tomorrow our second leader, Chabana, will be here."'

It was a challenge.

This Chabana, of whom Mokete was so proud, was attending the same school as I was, but he was a year older than the rest of us.

I was in a fever of disappointment and anticipation, so full of emotion that I could not stop tears from my eyes. The old man, my uncle, saw my humiliation, but he said only, 'I'm telling you, Ndlayedwa, that my cattle must drink at the marsh tomorrow.'

We herdboys were not allowed to go to our homes that night, for our mothers were sure to take pity on us and give us food; instead, we all had to go straight to our separate sleeping-huts.

The following morning we were up very early indeed, knowing that we would have a very difficult day to face. *Ntate* Malayisha had given instructions to all the women of the village, mothers and sisters, that no food was to be taken out to us at midday as a punishment because his cattle had not drunk at the marsh. Yet he expected us to fight hard anyway, even without food.

As soon as we had milked the cows, we set out for the fields. Sefako and Ndaba were playing strange melodies on their *masiba* that morning; so full of feeling was their music that people passing by, who did not know anything of our shame and our resolute hearts, said in wonder, 'How these boys are playing! When the cattle return this afternoon we will hear news, for sure!'

They were playing like men going to war who did not expect to see the next sunrise; their tune was the age-old one played by the leading herdboy to tell his companions to prepare to face their enemies. This tune always has a strange effect on cattle: they seem to catch the subdued excitement and graze right around the player's feet. I used to play a *lesiba* too, in my youth, but Sefako and Ndaba were artists on that instrument. Now I cannot play at all, having few teeth left.

When we passed headman Mahamane he said, 'Go, you damn cowards! If the cattle do not drink at the marsh today you needn't come back!'

We felt very alone, and very hungry.

Our sisters and the friendly girls of the village had gone to the fountain when we were leaving the village, but they slipped secretly down along the donga from the fountain and met us along the way, bringing food to us. They found us weeping with hunger, overwrought with feeling that our elders had abandoned us, and lifted our hearts with their gifts of food and their warm encouragement and sympathy.

After the girls had left us our cattle started driving us on, grazing as they walked, but never stopping anywhere. I think our elders must have done something to them with *litlhare*, for they gave us no rest, as if they knew they had to get to the marsh quickly. They drove us on and on, along the banks of the Mataheng stream. By now the cattle of the surrounding villages had joined ours, but they were moving slower; our herds still moved with a purpose. We were about to cross the Mataheng for the third time when Mokete and Chabana spotted us from their *leboella*.

'Yes!' their voices came across the valley. 'That cocky Nkai is here today! This is the day we meet!'

Their company started shouting, '*Heeeeee*! Stop your cattle! *Hanela*! Stop your cattle!'

My favourite cow was called Khomo-ea-lona-maoma, which means 'your cow, you heroes of the mines'.[10] My father had bought this cow with money he had earned on the Jagersfontein diggings. This one and Sefako's favourite, Ts'oanyane, would not graze any longer, but started out for the marsh. We tried to stop them, telling them it was still early—for herdboys talk to their cattle all the time—but they were wild. 'What are the cattle doing?' we wondered. We had never seen them like that before.

We did our best to slow them down, not really wanting to face Mokete and Chabana just yet, but Gauda, Lepekola's older brother, was passing on his way from the shop and he shouted to us, 'Let the cattle go and drink, you boys! If you don't, I'll go for you!' Then he added the final insult, 'You are just like your mothers and sisters!'

It seemed that some of our cattle understood his words, for they broke into a trot, heading straight for the marsh. They were the three cows, Ts'oanyane, Khomo-ea-lona, and Tsielala, and the two oxen, Free State and Goldberg. I do not know how this last ox got its name, for it was named by our parents; it was only after I grew up that I learned that Goldberg is a Jewish name, and I never asked whom it was named after.

When these five started running, all Tsokung's cattle started after them. We had no choice but to follow.

After we had crossed the Mataheng, Mokete and his boys started running towards us. Mokete himself was running like a fat calf, bouncing along, tail up. They were brandishing their sticks, yelling at us to turn our cattle back.

The same Gauda who had shouted at us owned a cow called Lea benya, which means 'there is lightning'; she was a most strange animal. She was lifting her head as she ran, bellowing a high-pitched protest, as if she were saying, 'Again I won't get to drink, just like yesterday!' She had a fine voice that cow.

Just opposite the marsh, where the stream runs into the river, there was a land on which Tsokung's people were hoeing together in a sort of work company, and we were conscious of their eyes on us.

Still moving at a good pace, we crossed the Futhong. I noticed, as we passed, a small land of peas near the marsh; another land to our right had mealies about six inches high on it. I remember thinking that we must keep the cattle out of those lands.

While Mokete was yelling at us to stop, the men hoeing across the stream were shouting abuse at us: 'Let the cattle drink! You'll have us to reckon with if you don't, you boys!' We ran on, Mokete's voice ringing in our ears. What a man he was, even then. 'Stop! I tell you, stop! I told you yesterday to warn Nkai not to bring his cattle here to drink today. *Jooo Ooeeee!* We'll show him today!'

I was usually a great talker, but that day I had not a word to say, for I was thinking so hard—what could I do about what was going to happen?

Now when we had crossed the Mataheng stream for the last time, Molisana and Monnakhomo had remained there, making the excuse that they should stay to watch the cattle coming along behind us, to see that they did not go into people's lands. Lepekola had gone with us as far as the Futhong, where he too made this excuse to be left behind. When we crossed the Futhong then, there was only myself, Sefako, and Ndaba. Those other three, along with the cattle and herdboys following us, never crossed the Futhong at all. We were on our own.

Those lands I had noticed were close to the marsh, so we asked Ndaba to stay back to see that none of our cattle entered them. When Mokete arrived, he found those five magnificent beasts of ours up to their bellies in the marsh, while Sefako and I watched them from the bank, leaning on our sticks, silent.

'What did we tell you yesterday?' demanded Mokete. 'Didn't we tell you not to bring the cattle here? Didn't you get my message, Nkai? Drive those cattle out of the marsh *at once*!'

Sefako said quietly, 'You'll have to make us.'

'Why did you bring this arrogant Nkai here?'

'I gave him no instructions. He looks after his own cattle.'

'Drive those cattle OUT!'

'No.'

At this time I was thinking of our God, the *Molimo* whom we think of as a cow. And of my ancestors. I was neither talking nor laughing, but weeping without a sound. That habit of mine, of crying whenever I was angry, used to make my father beat me often. He said he hated to see me like that, because I was despising people; my face looked, he would say, as if I wanted to take someone and break him in two. I never felt like that, though. It was just my face. I would rather cry than smash someone because I am big; if I smash someone, he will not get up until he has water poured over his head. But my father could not understand how one can cry without having been hit.

Mokete's company that day was Chabana, Kubatse, Liphaphang, Kompi, and Mofuama. Their names ring in my head even now like a praise-song. Mokete was not very big, but he was wild; he was unbeaten in a stick-fight up to that day. Chabana and Kompi were also devils with sticks. If I close my eyes, I can feel the grass under my feet, see every reed in that marsh, hear the cattle as they moved through the water.

Then Mokete grunted, '*Ho bona*! At them! But leave Sefako for the moment—let's get Nkai first!'

'We daren't!' Chabana held him back. 'If we all go for Nkai, Sefako will beat in our heads from behind!'

There was a girl from Tsokung called NoMadlozi passing by on her way from the shop. When she saw our sticks go up, and how Mokete's band of little boys started throwing stones at us, she lifted up her head and ululated to give us heart: *Helelelele*! From behind us, the men hoeing the land shouted, 'Fight to your death, you boys! We learned yesterday that our cattle did not drink. Today *they must drink*!'

It was a wonderful battle. Sticks were thumping: *QAQA* ... *QA* ... *QA* ... *QAQAQA* ... *QA* .... Stones were whistling around us. There were some women hoeing with the men, and their strong voices joined NoMadlozi's shrill *HELELELELE*! How hard we fought!

The cowards who had stayed behind did not move to come to our aid, even though it was only Sefako and myself fighting. But at this point stout little Ndaba left the cattle to help us. He was about eleven then. He came running, and he was screaming as he ran. ...

'Why do you stand there doing nothing when you see our men outnumbered?' he shrieked at the cowards, and all the while he scooped up stones and threw them at our opponents. Those cowards across the valley stood watching us with their jaws hanging, as if they were watching girls from the initiation school dancing.

With Ndaba's help, we could start an orderly retreat, back towards the Futhong, with our cattle. We had to run backwards, glancing over our shoulders to see where we were going, because we had a hail of stones to duck and sticks to ward off. The Futhong was very deep because it had rained the night before, and we came up short on its bank, unable to cross without picking our way. But Ndaba could throw a good stone. He hit Kubatse in the short ribs, winding him, and that stone gave us the necessary break to get across the swollen stream with our cattle.

This time Mokete did not stop at the Futhong, which was the boundary between us, but followed us and drove us back across the Mataheng as well. Unlike Chiefs, boys chase each other right across boundaries in a fight like this one, and Mokete wanted to whip us into our own village, even into our homes. We picked up stones to defend ourselves and kept falling back.

Across the Mataheng, we met up with the other Tsokung herdboys who were only just arriving with their cattle, so fast had our own cattle driven us down to the marsh. With them to back us up, we settled down to hurl stones at Mokete on the far bank of the stream. Chabana made it across the stream to our side, and was creeping up behind me to hit me on the back of the head with his stick when Ndaba threw a stone that knocked his stick aside. That youngster could throw stones. We fought with both stones and sticks, and our boys refused to let Seshophe's boys cross the stream easily.

We saw that day how Mokete had come by the power to be so fierce: it was not his courage alone. His father was a *ngaka*, and we realized that he had given his son *litlhare* to be so strong. Across the stream from us, Mokete dropped to his knees, his blanket draped down low in front of him and filled with stones. He was making downright fearful faces, and screaming like a madman. This was done to scare us, but although it did indeed terrify us, we still fought on. It was there, at the Mataheng, that Mokete proved to be a champion in evading stones. On his knees, his face contorted, he ducked and weaved about and we failed to hit him. Even Ndaba and Moeti, our best stone throwers, were defeated.

Kneeling down, Mokete sang his song of war:

> Mokete, older brother of Sekoboloana,
> He left his home as he was ordered
> By his father, Letsae,
> And his older brother, Motseki.
> They pointed their *lenaka* at him,
> They said, 'Mokete,
> 'When you come to war,
> 'Become a whirligig beetle,
> 'That none may strike you.'

At last, despite our efforts, Mokete and Chabana broke across the stream with their company and chased us back towards our home, saying that they wanted people to laugh at us there, to see their sons being such cowards. We were about two miles from our village, when two older youths, Likotsi and Tlalinyane, arrived with Gauda. They rushed at those boys who were nearest the village and running hard, among them Lepekola, Molisana, and Monnakhomo, and went for those cowards with their sticks, abusing them, 'Where are you going, you youngsters? Where are the cattle? You leave the cattle to graze people's lands, and run away, eh? Back! *Back to your cattle!*' We could hear the *lephu-phu-phu-phu* sound of their sticks landing on backs.

There was no use in going anywhere after that; there were sticks ahead of us and sticks behind us. So we turned to face Mokete and Chabana once more.

Sefako called out, 'Mokete, man! I'm not a coward . . . people who fight with stones are cowards!' and he threw away his stones and went to meet them with his sticks. That fight must have been a beauty to watch. We had taken our stand near a grove of wattles, and above us, on the mountain slopes, people had gathered to watch. '*Jo! Jo! Jo!*' we could hear them saying in amazement, 'Please separate those children—they'll kill each other!'

I had stopped crying. I was laughing now. Chabana, Kompi, and Mofuoama went for Sefako; Mokete, Kubatse, and Liphaphang came for me. Within a minute, those fighting Sefako numbered five, for little ones had joined in to throw stones; my group also grew like that. Ndaba and Moeti both came running, screaming; Moeti threw stones to help his cousin, Sefako, while Ndaba helped me. The people on the mountain were still shouting for someone to stop the fight, and all around I heard stones and sticks thumping and clashing. Lepekola, Molisana, and another one called Mzimukulu had black eyes when they fled from the sticks of their elders; they were running blind, not knowing where to turn in their desperation.

Then at once Sefako and Chabana stopped playing: their fight became serious, what we call *khahla*. In a normal stick-fight, the fighters stand about the length of two sticks apart, dancing in to land a blow and then leaping back; it is little more than a game, in which one delights in skill, even though people do get hurt. *Khahla* means the fighters close in, only two of them, and they do not lower their sticks until one has found its mark. No quarter is asked or given. It is single combat, not just feinting and getting in the odd blow, and it is serious. This is when stick-fighting changes from an exercise to a battle.

Sefako brought his stick through Chabana's guard to land a blow on his head, cutting a wide gash from which blood poured. At that moment, Moeti managed to hit Chabana on the calf with a well-aimed stone, and his leg gave way.

Meanwhile, Mokete was discovering how bitter my sticks could be, although we were not fighting *khahla*, but just sparring. Then a stone from Ndaba hit Mokete's thigh.

Our followers took courage from that moment. NoMadlozi had followed us all the way, and her high-pitched '*Helelelele!*' took on a triumphant note. Slowly Mokete's boys started retreating. They broke into a backward, shuffling trot. They turned. They ran.

We followed them, all the way to the Futhong.

Then we fetched our cattle and drove them to the marsh to drink, while Mokete's band watched us from close by, whipped and silent. When the cattle had drunk their fill, at about three or four in the afternoon, we told Mokete at great length to keep his cattle from drinking at the marsh at midday, for that was when our cattle would come to drink. From that day on, our cattle drank there every noon, under their eyes.

After that we turned and headed home.

Some of us, like Sefako and Ndaba, were limping; others felt bruised around the ribs and shoulders, like me. Our cattle started driving us at a good pace again, as they had in the morning, and we did not try to slow them down. Sefako was playing the happiest song on his *lesiba*, a melody in which the sound of the humming of wings is imitated. Only Lepekola, Monnakhomo, and Molisana were downcast, shuffling their feet in the dust.

From afar, we could see smoke rising in the still air from the *lekhotla* of our village: something was being cooked there. When we entered the village, the old man, *Ntate* Malayisha, was at the *lekhotla*, clutching his stick and pacing up and down. No one, not even my father, would he allow near us, and he was totally caught up in a fury of pride and exultation. Striding up and down, he chanted a praise-song in our honour, one he had composed himself that day.

> They are the children of Ngolozani,
> Whose name is Let-the-bulls-kill-each-other,
> In the house of KaKupeka,
> In the house of KaMalunga.
> Warriors are borne in those houses.
> They are just like Ngolozani,
> They are like Malayisha
> And his young brother, Maguqu.
> They went out to take on the warrior's mantle
> Of Makhuba and Molonyeni.
> At midday they threw away their stones
> In the veld of Tsokung;
> They said they wanted a war of sticks.
> Ndaba is a sister's son here at Swazini;
> He is just like his mother's brother, Malayisha;
> He is like his father, the son of Hosha,

Who was left on the battlefield at Tsikoane,
While men decorated themselves with weapons and guns,
Spears and guns, the blankets of men.
The son of the daughter of Ngolozani,
The warrior of KaKupeka's house,
He refused to part with his cousins' lives
When the Basotho wanted to take them;
When they wanted to kill Sefako and Ndlayedwa.
The child who took into his mouth food
That bravery had spat upon to bless
And imbue him with valour.

'Landelesa!' *Ntate* Malayisha started shouting for his son.
'*Landelesa*! . . . LANDELESA! Are the *liholane* not cooked yet?'
Liholane are parts of lungs and intestines that can be cooked only
at the *lekhotla* and not in a woman's *lelapa*, to be eaten only by men.

'Give the meat to the three herdboys, and get porridge for them
from your mother's house.'

Landelesa's younger sister, NoMacala, soon prepared the
porridge, and we sat down among the men to eat. Although *Ntate*
Malayisha was still praising, talking to the three of us as his own
sons, he was praising with tears running down his cheeks.

* * *

Everybody remembers his childhood as a golden time. I am
particularly fortunate in that I have memories peopled with great
warriors, strong relatives, and good friends, and that I grew up at a
time when herdboys were not regarded as simple peasant folk, and
when people still had a love for cattle, and when fathers of households could stay home for most of their lives. I drew on these
memories of an ordered existence, governed by tradition, when in
later years I met the dust of the mines in South Africa and travelled
across the ocean to work as a labourer on the battlefields of France.

NOTES

1. The *lelapa* (plural, *malapa*) is the small courtyard in front of a house,
   enclosed by a *seotloana* or reed screen. It also means 'family' in the sense
   that a reference to, for example, 'MaLoela's *lelapa*' means the children
   born to MaLoela. The Sesotho word will be used throughout.
2. *Rinderpest* is a specific malignant and highly contagious fever characterized
   by acute inflammation of the mucous surfaces, affecting cattle, game, and,
   in a minor form, sheep. It made its appearance in Southern Rhodesia in

1896 and within twenty-five days it had spread southwards almost to the borders of the Cape Colony. The epidemic of Rinderpest in Lesotho in 1896 took the lives of more than 100,000 animals.

3. At the head of the traditional hierarchy of chiefs in Lesotho there is the Paramount Chief or King. Below him are twenty-two principal and ward Chiefs, each having jurisdiction over a ward with an administrative network of chiefs, sub-chiefs, and headmen. See also Appendix.

4. The praise-song refers to Chief Hlajoane going out to do battle with the Boers.

5. The *lekhotla* is the place in the village where men meet to transact business, discuss village affairs, and settle disputes. The word is also used to denote a court of justice. The Sesotho word will be used throughout because the English word 'court' does not have the same connotations.

6. A *pitso* (from *ho bitsa*, to call) is a gathering, assembly, or public meeting, usually called by a chief. Again, the Sesotho word will be used throughout the book.

7. Chief Lesaoana's regiment and age-mates were known by the name *Mats'ekha*. The area where he settled with his followers took the name of *Mats'ekheng*, meaning 'The place of the Mats'ekha'. People from that area are still known as Mats'ekha.

8. A *leboella* is a reserved pasture where grazing is only allowed at certain times of the year, and where thatching grass is often grown. The Sesotho term will be used throughout.

9. The *lesiba* (plural, *masiba*) is a musical instrument made of a piece of quill and a string fixed on a stick. The tunes played on it are often associated with cattle herding.

10. *Maoma* means literally, 'men coming back from the Goldfields'.

CHAPTER THREE

Gaudeng—the place of gold

I WAS still at school when, for the first time, I crossed the Caledon River during my holidays to work for the white man.

Through a contact of my father, I found work as a groom at the police stables in Ficksburg. I knew horses, and at first the work was not unlike working with horses at home, but I soon found that more was expected of me than I had reckoned.

I was sent to the railway station one day with some money that had been marked by the police to buy home-made beer from two women who used to come from Lesotho to sell their beer in Ficksburg. In those days there was a kind of Prohibition in South Africa for Bantu, for we were not allowed to make, sell, or buy liquor. I went to the railway station with mixed feelings.

Luckily, just as the two women were about to sell me a mug of beer, a Mosotho working on the railway station called out to them, 'Beware! This chap is a spy. He's been sent to trap you. Do you know him?'

'No,' said the ladies, they did not know me.

'I know he works for the police, and I also know he does not drink beer himself. Who are you buying this beer for, boy?'

'I'm buying it for myself,' I told him.

'Then drink it right here,' he said. 'You cannot leave the station with it. This beer I am giving you is not for sale. It is the food these women have prepared for their lunch, but they'll share it with you. So drink!'

He was right. I did not drink beer then, and could not manage to down the mug, so I explained sheepishly that I had been sent to buy some beer for my cousin. Of course, they would not sell me any after that. As a trap for beer merchants, I was a failure.

The next time I was sent to trap a woman selling beer I was instructed to get hold of the beer before the woman reached the station, because the men working there would expose me. I found the two women who were suspected by the police, and although the same man from the station yelled at them to look out, he was too late: I took the beer and handed over my marked note. Just then a white police sergeant and a Mosotho, a constable, came up and demanded, 'What are you doing here? Are you selling beer? Have you any right to do so? Produce your licence!' .

Naturally, the women had no papers licensing their beer-dealing. I was asked roughly whether I had any right to buy beer in a municipal area, and I replied, 'No, *Baas*, I was just buying it for my friend.'

I was relieved to be in on this deal, and not really guilty. We were all taken to the charge office where the women were charged.

'You!' the police were addressing me, 'tell the truth! Have you bought this beer or were you given it?'

'I bought it.'

The women pleaded not to be sent before the Magistrate, and each paid a ten-shilling admission-of-guilt fine.

I was ashamed of this work, but I needed the job.

The railway workers told the women selling beer to look out for me after that, and I thought my troubles over, but there was a man working as a waiter at a hotel in Ficksburg who was suspected of selling brandy to Bantu in the hotel bottle store. I was sent to trap him.

The police got onto his trail because of a man called Sehoapa, a rich fellow from Lesotho, who always used to be found drunk in Ficksburg. He was getting drunk on hard liquor. No one ever saw him buying the stuff, and no one ever saw him drinking the stuff, but he was getting it illegally somewhere, and the police were very keen to have the supplier apprehended. Sometimes Sehoapa was so drunk he could not move his legs, but he never fell down. A policeman asked me whether I had ever seen Sehoapa drinking, and I told him I had, often.

'Next time he's in town,' he said to me, 'just tell me when he arrives.'

Then he gave me two half-crowns and sent me to buy brandy from the hotel.

Charles, the waiter, was highly suspicious of me when I asked him for brandy; he might well have started hearing rumours about me. I assured him that I needed the brandy for my sick brother. At last he was satisfied with my assurances; he took my five shillings and handed me a bottle.

Just then the policeman came rushing in.

'Hand me that bottle! Come-come-come-*come*! Hand over that brandy! Have you people got a licence to drink brandy, eh?'

I handed him the bottle.

'Where's the money for this?'

Charles said he was giving me the brandy, and that he had not taken any money for it, truly. As Koos, the policeman, was about to search Charles, the money clattered to the floor. Charles and I both went to the charge office, and so did Charles's master, who paid a £2.10.0. admission-of-guilt fine for Charles.

The town began to suspect me, and people said I had left my work as a groom to become a detective. Some promised to beat me up if they ever caught me alone. I saw then that what I had was not a job—it was a bad job. I left at the end of the month to return to school.

The next job I had in Ficksburg was as a houseboy. I loathed this work as well. When you work as a house servant for a White, you have to be up early every morning. Some ask you to make early morning tea. You are told to sweep and scrub the house, if you work as a houseboy. That was the work I hated most, cooking, scrubbing, sweeping, making tea and making tea and making more tea.

My term as a houseboy was a difficult one because the woman of the house was hard on servants. She could not manage to keep one: if you stayed a week with her, people around town congratulated you for your perseverance; two days was usually enough.

I lasted a month, because I wanted the money and because when she scolded me I paid no attention whatever to her. At last she saw that I would stay long enough to draw my wages, so she said I had stolen some of her sifted flour. She told her husband, who did not believe her. 'What would he want with flour?' he asked her. She said I might have handed it to some of my relatives when they were in town. Her husband asked what proof she had and she showed him how the level of the flour in the tin had dropped. He searched around on her shelves and finally found the packet of missing flour hidden under some other tins, but when he asked her how it came to be there, she said she had no idea—perhaps one of the children had put it there.

I wanted to leave at once, seeing that she wanted to have me sent to gaol as a thief, but her husband asked me to work out the month so that he could find someone to replace me. At the end of the month I was given a wage of one pound sterling, a high wage for a houseboy then, and I left.

In those two school holidays I learned enough to know that there must be an easier way to earn a living. I never went back to work in Ficksburg again.

* * *

Every boy in Lesotho grows up with stories about working on the mines, because just about every man in the country, at some stage of his life, goes to earn money in the South African labour market.

My father once told me how he had spent three years working on the mines without going home once, until his family became worried that he might never return, and Ngolozani sent *Ntate* Maguqu to go and fetch him back.

When my father told the story, he said he was working at Klerksdorp, getting sick and tired of the way his white masters used to insult him, saying he was lazy and bad and things like that. Then one day my father went underground with a white man who always used to beat and scold the Bantu, and that man kicked my father, as he had often done before.

My father was not an easy man.

'I'm tired of you!' he snapped. 'You keep kicking people and yet you have never done the work that we are forced to do. You seem to be a lazy bugger!'

Those words incensed the master, who threw a lamp at my father's head. When my father ducked, the man kicked out at him, but my father caught hold of his leg, jerked him off balance, and started in on him with his fists.

'I feared my master was not feeling my fists properly,' he would say to me, 'so I started looking around for my hammer.'

As he was going for him with the hammer, the chief *Baas*, as my father called him, appeared, shouting, 'Stop it! Stop that!' Both of them started talking at once, trying to explain their provocation to the chief *Baas* and at last, not getting much sense out of either, he ordered them to the surface where their case could be heard properly. After they had knocked off work, they went up.

I am told that while they were still speaking, the mine captain arrived from the compound to say that Makhuba was wanted there.

'Who wants him?'

'The compound manager.'

My father was escorted to the compound where he found his older brother, Maguqu, complaining that Makhuba had not been home for three years; that he had never written home in that time; that he was needed at home. Maguqu was painting an unfavourable picture of my father, not knowing what trouble he was in. But indirectly this helped my father.

The compound manager said my father might have got into that fight because he was tired, having been in the compound so long without a break. He reminded everyone that my father had not caused any trouble at all for the three years he had worked there, and he pleaded that the men involved pardon my father for this one incident. They agreed and my father went home.

He taught me at home that some white people are troublesome to Bantu, but whenever he told me this story, he would also remind me that people are not alike; he himself had met many fine, gentle white men who never tried to make a black man's life unpleasant.

*   *   *

I did not really think that tales about the hardships Bantu suffer on the mines would ever have any relevance to my life, for my intention was to become a teacher in Lesotho. I was good at school and studying was easy for me; there seemed to be no reason for my having to earn money in any other way.

So after I left school at Koeneng, I enrolled at the Morija training school for teachers. The first months there were hard ones, because the older boys used to torment us newcomers, but after I got used to it, and told myself it was more important to become a teacher than to give up and run home, I enjoyed the work.

But during my nineteenth year my eyes developed a disease: there was some kind of growth forming in my right eye. I consulted a doctor in Morija, who kept me out of school for two weeks. After the second week I returned to him and when he examined me he told me that if I returned to school, the strain would be too much for me. He advised my teachers not to let me write my final examinations in November. That was in October.

I returned home bitterly disappointed, but I still thought that this was merely a trivial setback. I would return the next year to complete my studies.

While I was home my cousin Chabeli, the one who was a *ngaka*, came to visit me one day. He threw his divining-bones and said my eye was diseased because someone had witched me; he was sure he could cure me. My father simply muttered that he did not believe in such things, and refused to let Chabeli try to cure my eyes.

In those days, I did not believe much of what anyone told me, so I simply sat back and waited for the new term.

When the schools reopened in February I returned to Morija. My teacher advised me to see the doctor again before I started lessons. I tried to get out of it, knowing that the doctor would not pass me as fit because my eye had, if anything, deteriorated during the past three months, but he forced me to go. The doctor said my attending school was out of the question for that whole year; he also advised me to see a *ngaka* because he himself could do nothing to help my eyes.

Chabeli was the one who finally cured them.

Well, I could not stay home doing nothing, so my thoughts turned to the mines, where many of my companions and relatives were earning money. My father tried to find me work as a teacher at home, and went to see our minister about it, but there was no hope, he was told. There were vacancies in mission schools, but I was still a youngster, the minister explained. There were pupils at school older than me; I would not be able to keep discipline; even if I did keep order at school, my older pupils might wait for me after school and beat me up.

'Would you be satisfied with that?' the minister asked my father.

My father had no choice but to say he would not. But he did not give up the idea of educating me further.

By this time I was thoroughly fed up. I did not raise the subject of the mines at home. One day I simply walked to Leribe, without telling anyone where I was going, and I was recruited as a mine labourer by one Sitwell Nkoko, a clerk at the Native Recruiting Corporation office, who had been a former teacher of mine. That was in 1915.

I went without asking my father's permission, and to this day I do not know whether he would have allowed me to go, although I doubt it.

* * *

The train journey to Johannesburg fascinated me: it was the first time I had been on a train.

The N.R.C. sent me to Block B compound at Langlaagte Mine on the Reef. I was to stay there for four months. The compound

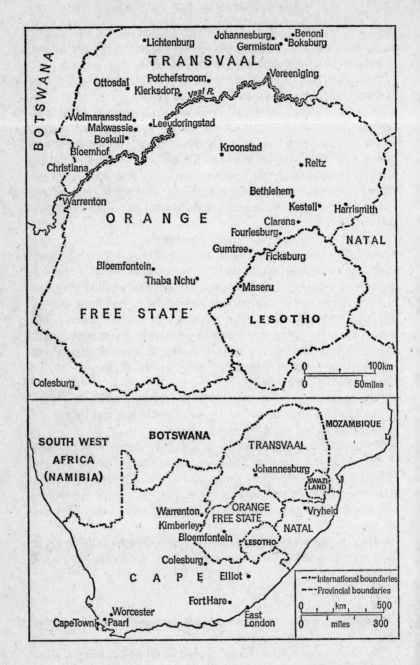

5. Western Transvaal, Orange Free State, and Lesotho

manager was a Mr. Miller, known as Rabasotho or Father-of-the-Basotho because of his command of Sesotho and his fondness for the Basotho. He was a fine, very tall man.

Because I was still a youngster, Mr. Miller did not want me to go underground; he said I should be given a desk job on the surface in view of my age and my education. His assistant or compound *induna* was a man called Ben, a Mosotho who had worked with Mr. Miller for many years. They had started together at Premier Mines and when Mr. Miller was transferred to De Beer's in Kimberley, Ben went along with him. They were like father and son, except that Ben wielded most of the power.

For some reason I have never been able to fathom, Ben took a dislike to me from the first instant, or at least that was how it seemed to me. Perhaps he resented Mr. Miller's wanting to favour me with a desk job. Whatever the reason, Ben insisted that I should be sent underground. They argued about it for a while, until Ben gave me a pen and some paper.

'Write the name "Pietermaritzburg",' he said.

I had never had occasion to write such a word before, and I still remember clearly the hash I made of it, something like 'Peitermartzburg'.

'What kind of a clerk is he going to be?' Ben asked, showing Mr. Miller my effort. 'He ought to go underground. When he has gained some experience we can let him work on the surface.'

'Why did you leave school?' Ben asked me.

I explained that I had not left of my own choice, and told him about my eyes.

'Have you a doctor's certificate to prove that?'

I produced the certificate, but of course my eyes would not affect work underground, so I was put down as an underground worker. I was not the only one to run up against Ben in that compound. He was just a rude fellow by nature. He seemed to have his knife in for anyone who could read or write or who tried to better himself.

I was given free choice about what work to do underground. I had heard that hammer-boys earn a lot of money, so I picked that job. There were some hammer-boys on that compound knocking out twenty pounds cash a month, a very high wage indeed—even now it would be considered a reasonable wage on the mines—and I knew about them through a cousin of mine who was earning about eleven pounds a month at that job. I saw that that was where the money was. I had never been underground before, nor had I worked

with hammer and chisel on rock before, but I had watched my
father breaking stone and I was confident that I could do it.

I had been told by another cousin, Mokoena, 'You take care when
you first go underground. There will be old-timers in the cage with
you, the cage that takes you down to the level where you will work,
and they are sure to try to frighten you. They will say a lot of things.
Try not to scare easily.'

I felt prepared for whatever underground held in store.

The next morning a whole batch of us newcomers waited at the
top of the shaft. At first we saw only a rope turning, and then
suddenly the cage appeared from out of the mine. It opened.

'Go on! Get in! Get in, you new ones!'

Mokoena was right. There were old-timers waiting for us in the
cage. The door closed, and a bell signalled that we were ready to
lower away. That signal must have been rung in a certain way to
inform the controller that there were new ones in the cage, for at
once the cage shot straight up. It stopped dead. Then it fell like a
stone. We gaped at each other, with eyes like pebbles, our stomachs
heaving.

'Speak, boy! Who's your love?'

'If you don't tell, the rope will split . . . .'

'We'll all die . . . .'

'I'll tell you . . . . Stop . . . .'

'Talk up!'

'Who's your mother's lover?'

'How many sheep did you steal at home?'

'We don't want to die . . . .'

'Did you eat the fowls you stole?'

'Oh God . . . !'

'Who's your lover?'

'Yes! Yes! I stole them . . . . Yes . . . . Please . . . . Please . . . .
Stop . . . .'

The questions came so fast, from all sides, that none of us could
think straight. I clutched at the thought of Mokoena.

'. . . Try not to scare easily . . . .'

I need not start talking, I told myself. *If I close my mouth firmly . . . .*
How those others babbled . . . . They were confessing to the most
dreadful deeds. The truth must be spoken: I was terrified.

'You! You quiet youngster! You're cocky, eh?'

'You think we're playing a game here? If we're not all killed here
when the rope snaps, you'll be taught manners!'

'*Molimo* .... We're all dying ....'

As the cage plunged down, it grew dark as night. At last it stopped. We were all panting, but we were alive, and from there we went to our various stations to work.

I had watched my father breaking stone, it is true, but I had not expected that the stone underground would be any different from that at home. I was soon to learn otherwise. No stone of my experience had ever fought back before.

On the surface I had been supplied with a hammer and three chisels; we were now given candles. The white miners and their boss-boys had lamps. If your candle went out or burnt out before you got back, it was your problem; if no one came to lead you out, it looked as though you could stay in those tunnels for ever. As we went down them, the tunnels were wide and high at first, but as you went on down, they grew shallower, and you had to stoop or crouch to move forward.

I was given a funny Afrikaans gentleman to work under; he was short and stout, and I call him funny because he was so kind and friendly to us Blacks, and would defend us if anything went wrong. He went ahead of me, tapping the sides of the tunnel with his hammer, and when he heard a different note, he told me to start breaking the rock there.

I had a four-pound hammer and three strong chisels; I attacked the rock face with energy, sure that I would have made five feet before the end of the day.

The first five inches were easy. Then my chisel stuck fast. I fiddled with that chisel for two hours. There was a hammer-boy working near me who, I am certain, used some *litlhare* on my chisel to make it stick, perhaps because he resented my being given the job so easily. I suspect him because after two hours of wiggling the chisel about to make it move, he came by and said to me, 'Just pull it out,' and it came out just like that. He went on by to call our boss to come and measure his work for the day: it was five feet. Remember, I had only made five inches. This man reminded me that I had a long way to go, so I started on the rock again.

When I had made a further four inches, it was time to go home.

Cruel people! I had been down the mine the whole day, from seven in the morning to two in the afternoon; when the boss came to measure my work, he asked me to bring my ticket. On it he wrote: *Nine inches. No pay.* Hammer-boys were paid two shillings a foot then.

Well, the next day I tried again, and broke through eleven inches. The third day I made one foot. The next, one foot two inches. They said I was wasting their time, and I was not inclined to disagree; I felt I was wasting my own time as well, trying to master that job.

I then became a trammer-boy, shoving the carts that carry ore underground along rails. One day one of these things fell over and while we were picking it up, it crushed my finger and I nearly had to have it amputated. In those days there was no compensation for this kind of injury. I was promoted after this to boss-boy over a group of trammers because of my finger, and my salary jumped from fifty to sixty shillings a month. It is nonsense to promote someone instead of paying him compensation, and just a cheap way of covering over mistakes. I was not satisfied with my pay or with compound life under Ben, and after my four-month contract expired, I left Block B.

*   *   *

I never mixed much with men of other tribes while I was in the compounds, simply because I was afraid of them, not knowing their languages. Each group usually kept pretty much to itself; for example, the Basotho would sleep in one dormitory and mess together if they could.

But it was seldom, in the compounds, that one found the Basotho on good terms with one another. One would find, in a room housing thirty to fifty Basotho, men from several chiefdoms, and they brought their quarrels with them from their homes, quarrels that usually started because of disagreements between their Chiefs.

There were several distinct factions. The group from Mats'ekheng and part of Masupha's called themselves the Liakhela, which means 'habitual thieves'. Another group was the Russians, who were from Matsieng and a part of Masupha's. The third group was from Molapo's area in Leribe, led by one Sankatana. These factions seemed to be a constant challenge to one another, fighting at the drop of a hat, and fighting hard, so that people got killed.

Their hatred began at home. For example, the Matsieng Russians would say, 'We know you Molapo's don't like us because our Chief was disliked by your Chief!' and then they would fight.

The cause of their wanting to fight goes far back, to the time of Chief Molapo and Chief Letsie, both sons of Moshoeshoe. It is said that when Letsie was installed at Morija, before he became Paramount Chief, Chief Moshoeshoe instructed people to build a hut for Chief Letsie and his *lekhotla*. He also had a hut constructed for Matela, son of Chief Lethole of the Makhoakhoa tribe, and another hut there at Morija for the son of Moletsane, Chief of the Bataung tribe. Then Molapo asked his father to build him a hut at Morija as well, but his father said to him, 'Bear in mind that you are not a Chief. I have helped Letsie because he is the future King of the Basotho. His two counsellors, Matela and the son of Moletsane, also have their huts. I cannot build your hut or your *lekhotla* here at Morija because you will one day be Letsie's subject.'

It is said that from then on Molapo did not like to be reminded that he was junior to Letsie, and anything he or his people did would be frowned upon by Matsieng's people who said, 'You do this because you have learnt it from your Chief Molapo, and you do it because you despise us.'

Molapo's would say in reply, 'You hate us without cause just as your Chief hated ours. Your Chief did not want ours to rule: he recognized the Makhoakhoa and Bataung better than his own full brother.'

Then sticks would be raised at these words, and they would fight. These quarrels started first in the compounds, where men live under pressure, but at last they spread outside until everyone, even Whites, knew about them.

I remember we once read in the newspapers that the Matsieng group and the Masupha's group had challenged each other and that they would meet in a certain field between Boksburg and Benoni, where there is a good valley for that sort of battle. The date was mentioned, a Saturday. When this announcement appeared in the papers the Union Government tried to stop the fight, but they failed because the men said they were going to fight about things connected with their homes, and did not want to fight any of the Union's subjects. The Union men were free, they said, to go and watch if they chose.

On another occasion two groups met at a place called Molapo's Location. People were killed in both fights, on both sides.

There is nothing that creates bad feeling as quickly as the praisesongs of Chiefs, for they often contain stinging words against some Chief or other. So if in the compound a man started singing the praises of his Chief, it could be enough to spark off a fight, for someone would want to retaliate to make his Chief's name respected.

I was once walking with a Chief descended from Moshoeshoe's grandfather, who was captured and eaten by cannibals shortly before Moshoeshoe entrenched himself on the mountain Thaba

Bosiu.[1] We were visiting the cave in which those cannibals used to live. Along our way, we met a man descended from those same cannibals and stopped to pass the time of day with him. The Chief I was with was named after that unfortunate old man who had died at the cannibals' hands. He turned to the cannibals' descendant and asked him laughingly, 'Do you think you could manage to eat me today?'

That is what I mean. If those two men lived in close daily contact in a compound, and kept up their banter for too long, factions would form and there would have to be a fight. We are not divorced from our past: we are descended from our ancestors. As Moshoeshoe said, when his people wanted to slay the cannibals who had eaten his grandfather, 'They are the grave of my grandfather. Give them cattle and grain and let them stop eating people.'

When I was still in the compounds, these fights were not as numerous as they later were, perhaps because the Paramount Chief would commission Chiefs to visit the mines and see how the Basotho were treated, and they must have acted as a restraining force on us. But, as with not wanting to mess together, there was still not good feeling among us and we were always conscious of our home associations.

*   *   *

When I left Block B I went to Simmer East compound in Germiston. The compound manager there, whom I shall call Smith, was known among us as the Wild Ox. He really was wild. Some mornings he would get up early and take his sjambok in his hand when he went into the compound, and those days no one would willingly go near him. The compound watchman, when ringing the bell to wake us on those mornings, would shout, 'Wake up! The Wild Ox is here!' and everybody would *move*. He would go from room to room; anyone still in bed tasted his sjambok.

I remember one day he took up his usual post beside the compound gate, waiting to whip anyone who left late. We had had enough. Nobody moved from his room. The compound police were sent to fetch us, but people refused to leave unless the Wild Ox left the gate.

'We're tired of being sjambokked for nothing. He still expects us to work after he's always thrashing us. No! We refuse!'

At last the mine captain arrived to find out why no one had come to work on the six-thirty shift. He found Smith at the gate, and made him move away, asking him how he expected men to work for

him if he beat them. Once the mine captain arrived, we came out
of our rooms. The last people, I remember, went underground at
eight o'clock. I think this incident might have been the one that
caused Smith to be dismissed from that compound.

When I first arrived at this compound I walked in to the main
office and met a man called Ben Dube, a Hlubi from Herschel,
working as head clerk. We liked each other at first sight. He wanted
to find me a place in his office, but I preferred to go underground
where the pay was better.

Underground workers are the heroes of the mines. They are the
ones who keep the mines operating. Without them, no mining
could be done. They despise the surface workers, who usually
work on top because they cannot manage heavier duties for reasons
of health or because they are lazy. So I did not want to work
anywhere but underground, not wanting to be called a weakling.
Besides, my uncle Maphuphuta was in that compound, and he
would have thrashed me had I taken a surface job.

Even as I talk now, there has been a news broadcast that 28
Bantu have been killed in mine disasters: two in a gas explosion and
26 in the collapse of a coal mine. Some of these men are Basotho;
two of them are from this village, and I will attend their funeral on
Saturday. Underground workers are truly heroes.

I had more or less dropped out of sight of my family by this
time, and had changed my name. Now my uncle notified my
family of my whereabouts. One consolation was that my pay had
increased: as a boss-boy over trammers I was now getting £4.10.0. a
month. I began to send money home to buy cattle and goats.

I had no sooner settled down when, late one Saturday evening,
my father entered my room. He told me he had had some difficulty
in finding me, because he did not know I had changed my name.
He wanted me to go home because he had applied for me to attend
the Leloaleng Industrial School at Quthing. So I went home in
December 1916 only to find that my application to the school had
been turned down. They then applied to the Lerotholi Technical
School in Maseru, which also replied that there was no vacancy.
I had to recognize that I should never be able to continue my
education, and prepared to go back to the Union to look for work.

*   *   *

I was back in Germiston in January, no longer interested in
working on the mines. Some of my home people were working in

town in Germiston, and they had always urged me to work in town with them, saying I looked like a town fellow and not a miner. I also thought there was bound to be more money in town. It is always easy to be convinced by a friend, and my friends painted gay pictures of life in town—anything would be lively compared to compound life—so I started going around the shops, asking for work. It was not as easy as I had thought. A friend from Mapoteng promised he would find me a job with the chemist he worked for, but when I went there the owner told me he already had seven boys working for him, and could not find work for another.

That's another thing to get used to—being called a boy when you are already a man.

I went to a store where a black salesman was wanted, thinking that sort of job would suit me well, for it is true that if there is anything I can do, it is talk, but the vacancy had just been filled when I arrived.

Then I remembered two chaps I had met in the compound, Solomon Masitenyane and Henry Malebu. They were salesmen, going about the compounds selling trousers and suits for a Jewish tailor, and we often used to chat when they came to Simmer East. I looked Solomon up, and he promised to introduce me to his employer, Mr. Sacks. I was soon employed as a travelling salesman, and it was a great job. Mr. Joseph Sacks was a fine gentleman in every respect.

Our wages were thirty per cent on orders for trousers; £1.5.0. on suit orders. On ready-made clothes we got a five-shilling commission on every pair of trousers sold. Mr. Sacks supplied our accommodation, but we had to find our own food. It was an excellent arrangement.

I was a success as a salesman. It suited me far better than fighting rock with a chisel or supervising the transport of ore underground. I found the work absorbing. I loved talking people into a sale, telling them the material was from overseas and not low-quality local merchandise. I would lift the article of clothing, letting the light play on the coloured threads woven into it, and talk without cease until I had sold it. For the half-month I worked in January, I earned £4.15.0. I can speak Sesotho, Sechuana, Zulu, and Xhosa, so I could get across to most people.

As travellers, we found out the days on which each compound was paid, and we would visit the compounds only on pay-days, knowing that it is easy to buy when the money is in one's pocket.

Some compounds did not like our going there to sell to the men, and would not allow us in if we were carrying any kind of parcel. So if we wanted to get something into such a compound, we would stand at the gate and ask for someone by name, usually picking a Mosotho we knew, because Basotho wear blankets. When the man came out to us, we would slip our parcel under his blanket and go in with him. Once in, the rest was easy.

One day I went to Simmer East compound. Someone came out to fetch my parcel and I got in without trouble to make my sale. That day I was lucky: I had six pairs of trousers and some shoes, and I sold everything. When I was selling the last pair of trousers, the compound policeman came in. He had been looking for me in every room, for he knew me, and he knew what work I did, and he knew I would not go in there just to visit, especially as it was pay-day. As he came through the door he said, 'Yes! Oh Yes! I said I'd catch you one day! You didn't like working with us here, when we wanted to work with you; no, you wanted to go to town, to be a town fellow. Why come and do your business here? Why don't you go and sell your things to the other townies? I've got you now!'

The men tried to plead for me, but Matela the policeman paid no attention to them. I also started pleading with him, but he interrupted me.

'If you come back to the mine to work, I'll let you off. If not, I've got you!'

He wanted me back so badly because we both sang in the same choir in the compound when I lived there, and it was a good choir.

So Matela locked me up in the compound. The next morning he took me to the Germiston Magistrate's Court. I still tried to convince him that he should let me go, but he was quite immovable, that fellow. On our way, we had to pass Mr. Sacks's shop, and I asked Matela to let me go in and tell Mr. Sacks, but he refused. Luckily, Malebu saw us passing and he ran to tell Mr. Sacks, who followed us to the court. I was called before a clerk and asked whether I pleaded guilty or not guilty. I pleaded guilty and my employer paid a one-pound admission-of-guilt fine, releasing me.

NOTE

1. Thaba Bosiu is a flat-topped mountain where Chief Moshoeshoe established his stronghold. Its name means 'mountain at night' or 'mountain of night'. There is a legend that the mountain fortress was never captured by enemies because the mountain itself grows at night, making it impregnable.

CHAPTER FOUR

France—1917

WHEN the First World War broke out, I, as a member of the British Commonwealth, felt deeply involved. The picture that the newspapers drew of men doing battle in trenches in the mud and the cold of France, fascinated and horrified me. I followed closely the progress of the war, as our papers wrote it up, and I felt growing in me the conviction that I should go and help in some way.

There had been many appeals in our Bantu newspapers for black people to volunteer. One such appeal was along these lines:

'The present war is a world war. Every nation must take part in it. Even we Bantu ought to play our part in this war. Some of you have done a great deal in German East Africa and South West Africa already. You are still expected, even across the seas, to go and help.

'Without you, your white comrades cannot do anything, because they cannot fight and provide labour at the same time. So you must go and do the labour while your white fellows are doing the fighting.

'Please, everyone who loves his country and respects the British Government, join this war without hesitation. Forward! Forward!'

The newspaper *Leselinyana* printed word songs, like this one, exhorting us to join up:

> Europe is our work
> Of our head the King.
> Who are going?—Boys!
> Who are going?—Girls!
> Europe is our work.

When I read words like these, my blood rushed in my veins and I felt, *Why should I hesitate? I must go and die for my country and my King!* I had not talked to men returning from the war then, and I had not heard of any of my home people volunteering. Some people in the Germiston location had recently returned from German East Africa; I had not talked with them, but I had seen them in their khaki uniforms.

Then again I argued: *Why should I go? I'm getting a good salary here; Mr. Sacks is a fine employer. I'm having an admirable time right here. Over there, people are dying!*

One evening, in the midst of one of these arguments with myself, I jumped up and went to the table. Before I could change my mind again, I wrote to my father asking him and my mother to give me their permission and blessing to go to war.

The next week passed slowly.

At last I realized I was simply trying to put off having to take this plunge into the unknown. I said to myself, *I'm a pure coward! What am I waiting here for? My father fought against the Boers; his older brother was also there and, more to the point, so was his younger brother. Why am I putting these things off then? I must have been born a coward.*

Then a novel and splendidly silly thought struck me: *How nice to die without having a wife!*

That decided me. I rushed to the table again and wrote to my father, telling him that I had already gone to join up; by the time he received my letter, I wrote, I would probably be on my way to France.

About five o'clock the next morning I was knocking on Mr. Sacks's door.

'I'm sorry to disturb you,' I said to him, 'but I must tell you that you have never done me any harm. You have always treated me well.'

'Whatever has become of you, Jingoes?'

'No, nothing. I just want to tell you. . . .'

'Have I ever said you've made mischief?'

'No.'

'Then why, man, are you talking this way? It's five o'clock in the morning!'

'I want to join the army.'

'The *army*?'

'Yes.'

I had not seen or heard Solomon walking up behind me, but now he exclaimed, 'You don't know what you're saying!'

'Yes I do. I want to go to France.'

4

'Think it over, man. Does Mr. Sacks treat you badly?'

'No, he treats me very well. But the time has come for me to go to war.'

I left them talking, shaking their heads, and ran to my room to fetch my order book. I thrust it into Solomon's hands saying, 'Go and collect this money for these orders.' I explained to him about a suit and a pair of trousers that were on order and told him where to deliver them.

'They're nearly ready now,' Mr. Sacks interposed. 'Why don't you wait a day or so and deliver them yourself?'

'I can't. I'm sorry.'

I was afraid that my father would come to stop me from going to France.

At 7.15 I was on Germiston Station and at 7.30 I boarded the train to Johannesburg. There I stopped people in the street and asked them where I should go to join up. Someone directed me to the Native Commissioner's offices, where, on 3 March 1917, I presented myself.

'Are you prepared, of your own free will, to join the army to die for your King and your country?'

Oh yes, I said, I was.

'Sign here.'

I signed.

I think about fifty of us joined up that day.

I took a train back to Germiston at four o'clock to collect my things and take my farewell of my friends. I left some of my belongings, like two paraffin stoves and three blankets, at Abnar Molupe's place. The rest of my blankets and trousers I left with Laban Moeti in Johannesburg. Both these chaps were from my home, but not from the same village.

I went to see these two fellows to try to persuade them to join up with me, telling them at length how it was their duty to go to war. Abnar said he was too young to die. Moeti said he wanted to live long enough to look after his children. Another friend from home, Paulus Marabe, said, 'You're crazy! You want to go to war before you're even married. I couldn't do that! Marry first, and then think about volunteering. If I were to die, I'd like to know I'd left a wife and children behind me.'

'By all means,' I told him, 'go and get married if that's what you want. As for me, I have decided *never* to marry.'

*　　*　　*

There was a girl at home, Jemina Mkuzangwe. We were in love, and we wanted to marry. It was all perfect; even my father was fond of Jemina. When I said I wanted to die rather than marry it was because of that girl, because I did love her a great deal. But some people persuaded her to drop me.

It was a stupid thing. I had visited her at her home at Cana, and people saw us together; rumours like that spread so fast. Some of her people went to her after I had gone, and asked her, 'Why are you so quick to admit that you love Jingoes?' They reminded her of their own Zulu customs.

'You disappoint us,' they said, 'for among our people we let the man walk several times before we confess our love. We don't accept a man in one day, as you have done.'

The next day I received a note from Jemina:

Please don't be surprised that I have turned back on our agreement. My relatives and some of my nation have blamed me for accepting you so quickly. I have had to listen to them. Please don't mention the matter of our marriage to your parents, as we agreed with each other, until later, when we can come to a good understanding with everyone.

When I had read the letter, I threw it down. My cousin Mone picked it up and asked, 'What is it? What's wrong?'

'The girl is mad!' I shouted. 'She thinks I'll keep going to her home for the sake of some old women!'

Mone tried to persuade me that Jemina meant well, and that I should do as she suggested, but I refused.

'There are many girls expecting me to court them!' I snapped.

I was present the day Jemina married, after I had come back from France. I was proud of myself that day, for I had come a long way, and seen many things; I was not sad at all. But it was because of Jemina that I wanted to die in France without a wife.

* * *

When I left my friends Abnar and Moeti I returned to the Native Commissioner's offices, where we volunteers were put up for two nights in a hall, with meals of bread, fish, beef, and other things provided.

We left for Cape Town by train on 5 March 1917.

We were a mixed bag of recruits. I could find no one from my home among us, but I soon made friends. Many youngsters in our position, having volunteered to die in a strange land fighting someone else's war, might have considered themselves superior, feeling that their fellow human beings owed them some kind of debt. And this was exactly how we did feel.

We behaved so badly on that train that at Colesburg our four coaches were uncoupled and the rest of the passenger train went on without us. We were young, scared, and excited, and we got up to some amazing high jinks. Whenever we stopped at a station, we simply poured out of the train, and took whatever we wanted from the railside stalls: food, fruit, magazines, anything that took our fancy. When people tried to get us to pay, we told them gleefully to ask the Government, for we were off to war. When the train was ready to pull out, and the last whistle blew, we would all leap off the train again, forcing it to wait for us. There were some white volunteers on the train with us, and they were in the same mood.

So the train simply left us behind at Colesburg. The people of Colesburg were sorry. The station-master was even sorrier. He rang someone to ask for an engine to be sent at once to get us off his station.

When that engine arrived, we tried to behave soberly, and we were a pleasure to be with until the 7th, when we pulled into Worcester Station. There we found a small store-room on the platform, packed to the ceiling with boxes of grapes. We made a real mess there. We pulled all those boxes aboard our train. Orders were given to the guard and the engine-driver that if they came to a station where there was anything edible, they were not to stop but were to pass straight by. Our next stop was at Paarl, where we were given a meal. From there we went straight to Cape Town, where we arrived the following day.

It was the first time most of us had seen the sea, and we all spent hours talking about it and repeating, 'So this is the sea!' The thing that amazed me about it was how the sun came up out of it every morning. We were not at all frightened of the sea then; the time was to come when it would strike fear into us.

We boarded another train which took us to Rosebank where the army camp was pitched on the Show Grounds. One novel experience I remember about Rosebank was that when we arrived there, some white and Coloured ladies met us at the station with tea and food. This was the first time it had occurred to any of us that a White or a Coloured would consider serving an African with food.

Officers met us at the station and marched us to camp in four lines. After we had eaten our midday meal it all started. Many of us did not understand half of what was going on; when someone shouted '*Attention*!' you could hear people all around you asking, 'What's he saying?'

We began to realize that being a soldier was not a pleasant matter. Our officers, we thought, were very rude to us, but it might have been worse, for it soon became clear that most of our people were dunderheads, and the officers were not so rude to those of us who could follow what it was they wanted. We slept about ten or fifteen to a tent and every day we were drilled. Within seven days, seven of our group had disappeared because they could not stand the life.

When we had been in Rosebank for about two days, another group of volunteers arrived from Johannesburg and among them were two friends of mine, from my home. Filemon Marabe, the brother of the Paulus I had left behind, was from Mats'ekheng; we were overjoyed to see each other again. Also among them was Nuoe Lechesa, related to me on my mother's side, from Cana. Nuoe's father and mine had been friends from their youth. I did not feel lonely any longer.

Filemon and Nuoe told me how they had joined up. They had met my friends Paulus and Moeti in Johannesburg, and had learned from them that I had volunteered.

'Why did you allow him to go by himself, without friend or relative?' Nuoe had asked them.

'We are afraid of dying,' those two had replied. 'It seems to me that you people are not following the newspapers. If you had been reading your papers you would not have asked such a question. Nowadays the Kaiser and Hindenburg are angry; they have been telling us through the newspapers that they don't want black men in this war. They say that this is a war among Whites; that we should keep out of it.'

So Nuoe and Filemon had left them and come to join me.

I soon realized that drilling was not a waste of time, because I was always conscious of the fact that we were going to war, and I found that we were being trained in how to behave on the battlefield as soldiers and how to react when we came under fire.

We were given uniforms and other kit. Our commissioned officers were all white; they addressed us through an interpreter, a Mochuana, who was not very popular because we Basotho could not follow him easily and the Zulu and Xhosa were completely in the dark. Later an assistant interpreter was appointed to solve this problem.

On 27 March we were called out early and told to be on parade at seven o'clock. We were informed that we would be leaving that day for Europe, and we mustered on the parade-ground again at ten o'clock with our kitbags. We were brought to attention, and then the Major, a Scot, came out to address us. He was a fine, grand man. When he walked, his back very straight, he would tilt his hat and swing his stick, showing by his every gesture that he was *alive*, you know, and a *Major* indeed.

'You are about to go to the place where, when you joined up,' he started, 'you knew you would be sent. While you were here, I may say, you behaved yourselves well. You were quite different from what I had been led to expect by the reports I had of you on your journey from Johannesburg.'

There was a long pause.

'I am sorry', he resumed, 'to have to inform you that your ship is the first to follow the *Mendi*, which has been sunk in the English Channel. The *Mendi* was carrying troops of the South African Labour Corps—men like yourselves.'

Our hearts fell.

'I do not mean to imply', continued the Major, 'that your ship, also, will be sunk, but you ought to know what has happened. You knew, when you volunteered, that you might have to fight; you knew what war is. Go in peace. Fight a good fight. Honour the name of South Africa. Let South Africa be honoured by all involved in this war. Make a name for your country. Make a name for your King, King George the Fifth. I shall look forward to hearing that you are doing good work in France, where I shall be following you.'

The Major's words were followed by a bugle call which put heart into those of us who were still trembling. Then we marched from Rosebank to the Cape Town docks, having been told that we should be prepared for conditions in France, where we would not travel about in trains much. When we arrived at the docks, a further seven men had disappeared from our 21st Company; nobody knew how, but they had gone.

We went aboard our troop-ship, the *Durham Castle*.

When my feet touched her decks, I thought of my ancestor Jingoes entering his 'house on the water', and I felt misgivings, but I reminded myself that I was not sailing as a slave, but as a proud volunteer, and I soon cheered up again. We had accomplished a great deal in three generations.

*   *   *

We took about 45 days from the Cape to Liverpool.

Along the way, one has to pass through the Bay of Biscay. Have you ever come across that sea? When I think of going overseas, now, my trouble comes when I think of that Bay. *It was a very wild sea.* The water of this Bay rises up into something like hills; it gathers itself up . . . up . . . up . . . into a mountain and with it the boat goes up. When the ship is right up there, suspended far above the rest of the water, the water suddenly spills down, and down comes the ship, spinning and sliding and *PUKHE!* hits the bottom.

We were in that Bay for three full days and nobody liked it one bit. All of us were told to put on our life-belts, and to keep them on, day or night. We asked why, and were told that should some accident happen, that life-belt would protect us in the water—unless, like Jonah, a whale found us first.

It was not being seasick that worried us here, because we had all spent our first two days at sea vomiting and with upset stomachs. After two days we were all right again and could say to the sea, 'We know you now, so let's move!'

As soon as we escaped the Bay of Biscay, a destroyer in our convoy was torpedoed by a submarine. Fortunately only the rudder was damaged, and another destroyer could take the damaged one in tow. Some torpedo boats arrived from England to meet us, and they chased the submarine but did not locate it. Those little boats were as fast as lightning.

It took us a long time to sail from the Cape to England, and this was because the Kaiser did his best to stop us. Off Sierra Leone we were driven back a long way by German submarines; at other places we had to steam ahead carefully because the water had been mined.

That was the Kaiser, or Mkiza, as we named him, after a legendary Zulu warrior who, we were told, feared no opposition at all, but crushed whatever came in his way.

Our papers reported that the Kaiser did not want us Africans in the war. He said, according to the reports, that he had been about to win the war when we entered to help the British Government. Before we came to provide labour, England and France were weak because their supplies of food and ammunition were not getting through to them. We had changed all that by working on the supply lines, leaving the other troops free to fight, and the Kaiser was being driven back. So the Kaiser tried to dissuade us from entering the war which, he said, was a European one and not our concern at all. By then he had already lost his possessions in East and West Africa.

I have had many arguments about the two world wars; Basotho fought in both. I maintain that the Kaiser and Hindenburg were men of far greater stature than was Hitler. They fought their war directly and bluntly, whereas Hitler was more devious. Some men in this village say that the Second World War was the more horrifying to have been involved in, but I disagree, and I have also read that the trench warfare of the First World War involved far more casualties among soldiers and civilians than did the Second. Trench warfare in mud was hell. While I was in France, it seemed that the Kaiser's presence was everywhere: on the land, in the air, and on the sea.

The more we learned about what the Kaiser had to say about us, the prouder we were to have caused so much discomfort to that strong man.

*　　*　　*

We disembarked at Liverpool at about ten in the morning, delighted to find an electric train waiting for us on the docks, under a large shelter, so that we did not have to go out in the rain. It was, for me, as though all my geography lessons at school were coming alive. I knew, for instance, that when the wind came from the Atlantic, we would get snow at home, and now I had sailed on the Atlantic. I had learned at school that England is a beautiful place, and I was pleased to find that my teachers had been right. Cape Town is a lovely city, but not as exciting as a place like Liverpool.

Thrilled by the speed of the train, I watched the lush countryside race by. English mountains are so different from ours, being covered with grass and rounded, with not a stone or rock in sight. Its trees are of a different green, and very beautiful.

When we boarded the train, before we left Liverpool, the girls of that place arrived with teapots, cups, and biscuits to serve us with tea. They were so friendly, and we warmed to their concern for us.

'Go and fight', they said, 'for your country and for your King, but we think that most of all you will go and fight for us, because you would not like us to die.'

Although white women had served us with tea in Cape Town, we knew they were only doing it because we were going to war. These girls were different.

One of our preachers had told us that we would find no colour bar in England, but we did not believe him: how could there be a country where black men were treated the same as white men? On our ship coming over there had been an Indian called Cassim who had told us the same thing. He seemed to be very well informed. He had come from German East Africa with his Captain, whose batman he was.

'I've been there,' he told us on the ship, 'and I assure you that there is no colour bar in England or France.'

'You tell a good story, my friend,' we mocked him.

'As you look at me, I am a French-speaker.'

We only laughed louder.

'You'll believe me when we get to France!'

The girls at Liverpool talked to us so easily that it seemed Cassim was right, but it was a little early to judge yet, so we kept open minds on the subject until we had had more experience of the place.

There was another thing that amazed us. When we disembarked we were told by our officers to put our watches forward by two hours, for we were then to go by European and not South African time. *Khelek!* We had been taught at school that places are not alike; that in some places it was night while we were having day, and we had found that hard to believe. We learned now that it was possible, for we had left home in autumn and in England it was spring.

It had been announced that a trainload of African soldiers would be stopping at certain stations along the route to London, and all along our way we were met by parties of women who brought us tea and whatever food they could spare. We behaved ourselves like people on that train, not wanting to disappoint our Major or the ladies who were being so pleasant and kind to us. At about six that evening we reached our destination at Folkestone.

* * *

On our first evening at Folkestone there was an announcement circulated—the British can be expert liars when they choose!—that our ship, the *Durham Castle*, had been lost at sea with all its African troops, and that there was no news to be had about its fate. We were astonished, and started questioning our officers about what was going on, but they told us to be quiet: they were playing a trick on the Germans. If they could spread the rumour that no one knew where we were, the Germans would not know when we were going to cross the Channel to France and we would then have a good chance of a safe crossing.

Two days later we went to Dover and embarked on a short, wide ship that would take us to France. That morning the whole Channel was full of torpedo boats—it seemed that every torpedo boat in England was there that day to escort us to France safely. These tiny, swift craft were darting about like bishop birds, moving in three rough lines, circling back, changing course, keeping the water safe.

We were told that had the morning not been misty, we should have been able to see France across the Channel, and that staggered me: I had always thought the Channel to be at least a hundred miles across, so well did it guard England from her enemies.

On board, we put on our life-belts, and Captain Hees gave us detailed orders.

'My people,' he said, 'wear your life-belts all the time. If anything were to happen, and we tell you to abandon ship, try to swim as far from the sinking vessel as possible, because when a ship goes down, she sucks the water around her down with her and you will drown if you are in it. Those who cannot swim must move their arms like windmills; this will move them forward and the life-belts will hold them up.

'I must warn you that the water is very cold, but these torpedo boats will be near by, and they will pick you up from the water as soon as they can. Look at them carefully now. When they come for you, do not try to fight them, thinking them your enemies. They do not look anything like submarines, which are your most likely enemy in these waters, so do not fear them. If you should be in the water for some time, do not give up because of the cold. Keep moving until you are picked up. I believe, however, that we will cross over safely, because the enemy is not aware of our existence.'

With the birdlike boats around us, playing in the water it seemed, it did not look as if we were going to war; it looked more like a gay feast. We watched them entranced, and forgot that we were crossing the water perhaps to die.

We sang songs all the way. The first one was started by a chap called Basson. He turned to watch the cliffs drawing back from us into the mist and sang *Home sweet home*, and we joined in, . . . *there's no-oo-o place like home*. . . .

We landed at Calais within the hour, to be met by French people,

men, women, and girls. All were laughing and shaking our hands.
'*Bonjour, messieurs*,' they cried, '*comment allez-vous?*'

We felt utterly foolish, not understanding a word of their friendly
gabble. Someone shouted for Cassim to come and interpret for us.
This was his chance to be proved a linguist, and we found he had not
been boasting: that fellow spoke French like a native. We later
found he was right about the other thing as well.

After we had eaten, we entrained for Dieppe, where we arrived
at about ten at night, and marched to our camp. The next morning
we were taken to the docks, and we started our work, unloading
ships bearing food, fodder, ammunition, and other supplies for the
front line.

*   *   *

At first our food was reasonable, but after about two months it
seemed that someone from South Africa decided that we were
being treated too well. At our homes, it was said, we ate porridge,
so it was not necessary to give us things like bread, rice, or potatoes
any longer. We tried to see our officers about this, to complain that
when we joined up in South Africa we had no idea that we would be
ill-treated in Europe by our own side. We held a meeting which we
invited our officers to attend to hear our grievances.

I arrived at the meeting some minutes after it had started, and
when I had listened to some of our chaps speaking, I stood up and
made the following speech:

'My people, we must not be surprised: in South Africa, Bantu are
often treated badly. I'm not surprised that this is starting here as
well. We have brought that system with us.

'Look at the confusion that has been caused by the word *Native*;
this word has been written on our lavatories so that Whites and
Blacks need not use the same ones. But in doing this they have
forgotten that here in France it is the French people who are
natives, and they are white, and they are now using our lavatories,
to the utter confusion of the South Africans here. You know how
much wrangling this has caused.

'We Bantu are often treated like dogs here by the white people
from home, yet they forget that we are all here at war against a
common enemy. Actually I made a mistake in saying that they
treat us like dogs, because usually they treat their dogs very well
indeed. They ignore the fact that we have left South Africa for the
moment. We are in Europe, and we are at war, and we were

promised decent treatment as soldiers if we would fight the Germans.'

It was the first time in my life I had made this kind of speech about the lot of the Bantu. I was to make many more.

At that point the minister attached to our two companies got up and left the meeting. He returned soon after, when the meeting was breaking up, with our Sergeant-Major, to whom he said, 'This is the one who spoke so strongly!' He was pointing at me.

'Why do you speak of me like this?' I asked him. 'You know that when I came in several people had already spoken.'

'Lance-Corporal Jingoes,' said the Sergeant-Major, 'do you remember what you were told about martial law?'

'Yes, sir.'

'Then what right have you to speak as you did about your officers and your Government?'

'I stated things that are true, sir—things that are happening in this camp.'

'You are, none the less, subject to martial law, Lance-Corporal.'

I was ordered not to go to work the following morning, but to present myself for a hearing. I well knew that soldiers can be shot under martial law.

That evening before I turned in I went to the place where I used to go to pray. There I prayed to my God and my ancestors, saying, 'If I have committed a sin, by saying that our officers and our Government forget that we are in Europe, and treat us as if we are in South Africa, if that is a sin, Almighty God, then let me die, and receive my soul. But if I was not sinning, then let them not use martial law upon me.'

The thing that worried me most was that I was not on good terms with our Captain, who would be presiding over my hearing; he thought me above myself. We had had a disagreement on the ship, and I knew that he would speak strongly against me.

In the morning, however, it seemed that my God had turned things in my favour, for that Captain had been transferred to the front that very day, and it was the man who had been sent to take his place whom I faced when I walked in.

'You are a lance-corporal. What came over you to make such a grave mistake?' was the first thing he asked me.

'I have committed no offence, sir.'

'You have been charged with making mischief here yesterday. I have to consider your case in terms of martial law.'

'I said yesterday, sir, that in Europe we are not *natives*. Is that an offence, sir?'

'Did you say that?'

'Yes, sir.' Then I plunged straight in. 'Sir, our meals have been changed from the usual rations to mealie-meal, which we are given from morning to night, sir, Monday to Monday, and the mealie-meal we get is bad. There are weevils in it. It is for you, sir, to judge where justice lies in this matter.'

The Captain stood up without a word and walked straight to the kitchen, where he scooped up some porridge and some uncooked mealie-meal in bowls. Both bowls had weevils moving about in them.

My accusers were the minister, the Sergeant-Major, and the Sergeant of our platoon; I had no friends among them. After the Captain had seen this food, he went back to his office and asked them, 'After you had heard this man speak strongly against his officers, and after you had heard the men complaining about their food, did you go to the kitchen to check on whether they were telling the truth?'

They said they had not.

'What did you do, then?'

'We did nothing, sir.'

'Then your complaint is that this man said black people are not *natives* in Europe, thereby implying that Whites are *natives* here?'

'Sir, I am a European, not a *Native*!' one of them exclaimed.

All these terms can be very confusing.

Each was asked to state his complaint. The Sergeant's was that I was insolent.

'Did you report his insolence, Sergeant?' he was asked.

'Yes, sir, I did. Nothing was done about it.'

Then the Captain called them closer to look at the dishes of food on his desk, and they had to admit to seeing the weevils.

'Why do you complain when your men tell you that their food has weevils in it?'

'As *Natives*, we did not think they were telling the truth. . . .'

'What do you mean by this word *natives*?'

'We mean these black people.'

'Reverend, you and I were at Fort Hare together. I saw you preach there to *Natives*. If you preach to people one day about love, and turn around to speak of them like this the next day, do you expect them to respect you or to attend church services where you preach?'

There was silence.

The Captain said that I was innocent of offence, and that he was grateful we had drawn someone's attention to our rotten food.

'Even now', he continued, 'I am afraid that this group of men might fall sick because of the food they have been compelled to eat.'

I was dismissed, jubilant.

At lunch-time, when the men returned from the docks, they were served with meat, potatoes, rice, and bread. They told me they had waited all morning to hear the shots of my firing-squad; seeing that I was still alive, they asked when my hearing was to be held. I told them of our good fortune, and that meal was a joyful, noisy one.

When they had eaten, the men started filing into the Captain's office to thank him. At last he came out to speak to us all.

'My people,' he started, 'I am not here to be praised. I have just returned from the front. Since you people have been in France, our troops have had the time to fight; we are receiving sufficient food and ammunition there now, and our mules and horses are getting their provender. Bear in mind that I will not be with you, probably, for the duration of the war. I have been sick, and I was sent here to this command only to convalesce.'

Because of this incident I foolishly started to hate all white ministers of religion, feeling that they were not the Christians they pretended to be, but my friend Nuoe and another chap told me I was wrong to judge all Whites on the basis of this one clash. They reminded me that among our own ministers there were some we knew who were uncharitable or downright unfit to guide others, and they mentioned one in particular.

'You must believe', they told me, 'that this one you say you hate failed in his Christian duty, and therefore you cannot judge others by him. His God will see him one day.'

Because they were my friends, I listened to them, but I no longer attended that fellow's services.

*   *   *

At that stage of the war Mkiza, the Kaiser, had crushed Belgium, and King Albert of that country had fled to England. The King paid a visit to France to cheer the troops, and one day he visited us at Dieppe. He was a short fellow who seemed very pleasant, and he encouraged us with a friendly speech.

'You people must not believe that you are doing nothing in this war because you are not actually fighting. I say that you are the men who are carrying a large portion of the burden of this war. Before you came, we were hard pressed. This very place, here at Dieppe where I am standing today, this place was once overrun by the Germans. It was behind that hill over there that they were turned back.

'What you are doing here, you are doing not only for your Government and your King: you are also helping Belgium and France and our other allies. Since you have been here, the pressure on us has eased; we have turned the tide of the war. I have every confidence that I shall return to my country, one day, as King.'

We received another visit that really shook us.

We were told one day that some of France's great men would be coming to our camp, among them members of the French Parliament. When they arrived, there was a black man among them, and we assumed that he was simply there to accompany his white masters. We were staggered when these men were introduced, for the pitch-black man held a high position in the Government.

It seemed that Cassim was right again.

When we asked how he had come to occupy such a position when he was black, we were told that there was no colour bar at all in France, and that a person was elected to office because of his education and ability; the man in question had degrees behind his name. We asked whether he had been elected by a white or black electorate, and we were told that the people of his constituency, both black and white, had voted him in.

One of us asked, 'Would such a thing ever happen in our country?' Some replied, 'Who knows?'

But others said quietly, 'It might. . . .'

*　*　*

Although we were not combat troops, we did come under fire. One day we heard the wail of the siren. Looking up, we saw the British soldiers racing to their trenches, and our Captain ordered us to do the same. I was in the shift that was in camp that day. When we were about fifty yards from the trenches, Lieutenant James Berry yelled, 'Stand where you are, and *stand still*! Those who want to can fall down flat, but once you're down, *don't move!*'

A Swazi called Seven—perhaps he only called himself a Swazi, for I've never seen such a cowardly Swazi before—did not seem to hear Berry, for he ran around in circles, screaming, 'Mother! We're all dying. . . .'

As he ran past him, a Xhosa called Matjolo drove his fist into Seven's jaw. He staggered on a few paces and then a Mosotho called Molise grabbed his shoulder and gave him another fist blow. When Seven collapsed they told him, 'You lie here! Don't even blink your eyes!' A man called Pieter, from Kroonstad, threw himself upon Seven and started trying to throttle him, calling to others to help him finish this coward off.

At that instant the sound of planes was heard, and five German aircraft came into view. Everyone froze. The planes started dropping bombs on us. One fell close by, but it buried itself in the sand and no one was hurt. Our soldiers were shooting at the planes until they passed over us and disappeared.

They reappeared shortly after, only three of them this time, diving in low from the direction of the hospital, skimming over the top of the pine and gum trees. The soldiers warned us not to move until they had gone. Then one of the planes was hit and it crashed to the earth while its two companions flew on over the town of Dieppe.

When we found the wreckage, there were three men in it. Two were dead, but the third was still breathing. The Basotho wanted to finish him off, but Captain Geddes stopped us, and the fellow was taken to Dieppe Hospital. We learnt later that when he was told where he was, he asked whether the town had been bombed flat; when he was told that it was still standing, he explained that their orders had been to clean Dieppe off the face of the earth. He said that their aim was to kill the black troops working on the docks because since their arrival the German lines had been pushed back, and the British could not be stopped. He said they had flown over one day and seen how fast supplies were being handled on the docks. They had also tried to bomb a train bearing supplies, but had also had bad luck with that. He did not think they would try for Dieppe again, he said, because it was clear that the town would be prepared for them.

After the bombing, everyone crowded around the unfortunate Seven, and tried to beat him, but the Sergeant-Major stepped in to protect him, saying, 'Gentlemen, you must know that not all men are alike; not every man is brave. Although you all came to war, no man knows how he will react when he sees death at his door; many tremble and say things they did not know they would say. This is what happened to Seven. I always thought he was a strong man. . . .

'Seven,' he went on, 'what are we to do about you? You have just been promoted to lance-corporal, but you have disappointed yourself and us. What kind of N.C.O. will you make? You were screaming like a woman today. You cannot lead men if you cannot stand fast under fire. I don't know what the Captain will say, but as for me, I am disappointed in your behaviour.

'All new N.C.O.s had better listen to me now. When you are promoted from the ranks, you are not placed over men because we like you; you are only promoted because your superiors believe you will stand up well to fighting and hardship, to lead and encourage your men. You are lucky, Seven, that I did not see you from near by when you behaved like a woman, for I think I might have shot you. It is better that you be dead than that you live to terrify the other troops.'

Seven was demoted.

It is very bad luck indeed for a man to cry out as Seven did in the middle of a battle, very bad luck indeed. He was lucky we did not kill him, because he put us all in danger.

From that day we all felt fear stirring in us, because we did not know what would become of us the next day, or whether, like Seven, we might run screaming, 'Mother! We're all dying!' I do not believe that poor Seven was simply screaming because he was a coward; I think he was remembering a propaganda bulletin dropped from the air the week before by the Kaiser's planes. This is what Mkiza had to say to us:

I hate you, Uncle Sam, because I do not know what caused you to come and enter this war. I hate Belgium, and I will crush it, because I have already taken most of it. I hate France. I hate England the most, because she takes other countries into her Empire.

But in this war, I hate black people the most. I do not know what they want in this European war. Where I find them, I will smash them.

Seven must have thought this was the day the Kaiser was going to smash us. Perhaps he was calling on his ancestors. Perhaps he was, after all, simply a coward. We shall never know. We know only that he screamed like a woman, and not like a man. We have a proverb that says a man is a sheep, a woman is a goat. A woman always cries, no matter what you do to her; you can cut the throat of a sheep and it does not make a sound.

*　　*　　*

We worked at Rouen as well as Dieppe until one day there came an order from the Lesotho Paramount Chief, Chief Griffith Lerotholi, saying that all Basotho in France should be placed together, not mixed with men of other nations, so that their work for the war could be seen by all. This was shortly after a group of conscripts had been sent to France from Lesotho under Chief Molapo Maama and Chief Thabo Lerotholi Mojela, representatives of the Paramount Chief. In accordance with this command, our orders came to leave for Le Havre, where the Basotho were to be based.

There were 57 Basotho in our 21st and 22nd Companies; we had come across together, and we felt pain at having to leave our comrades. We were also sad to part from our officers; the one we would miss most was Captain Lionel William Geddes, a fine man.

When he took leave of us he said, 'Here is Lieutenant Edmunds, who will accompany you. He is a Mosotho like yourselves. He will be in charge of you. You know him well, for he was one of your trainers at Rosebank. Go in peace, my people, as we have lived together in peace. If it happens that we meet again, let it be soon and swiftly.

'I have never mentioned this to you, but I feel you should know that about a month ago I received word from Headquarters to say that 21st and 22nd Companies are our finest, in the good work they do. I believe that you will hold high the name of these Companies where you are going now, and never let it be spoiled.

'Mr. Edmunds, don't let this group of yours be mixed up with those who have just been sent from Lesotho; keep them separate, that everyone may know that although they are Basotho, they are men who volunteered in the Union of South Africa.'

We were all standing at attention, and now our Lieutenant saluted the Captain. We picked up our kitbags and went to Le Havre.

When we arrived at the camp of the Basotho, we were a great sight, proud of whatever we did, and acting like soldiers. Mokhahla Senekal from Phiri's village, near where I live today, was among that new group of conscripts, and he can tell you a good story about how splendid our entry was. The new men could not stop staring at us. They copied us in everything, even the way we worked and carried ourselves on parade. We were happy to be among our countrymen, but we missed our friends badly. Four or five months later the war was over for us, and we were free to return home.

*   *   *

In April 1918 we boarded the *Norman Castle* at Southampton, bound for Cape Town, and this time the voyage took only 25 days. At Rosebank we were given our pay for the last time, as well as train tickets to our homes.

I still remember Moferefere Rantuba left the train at Gumtree, while Hope Mosaasa, Khama, Malefane Johnstone (a Coloured), Letsatsi Molukoane, Filemon, Nuoe, and I got off at Ficksburg. The others took the road to Leribe, while Filemon and I walked home. We arrived at midnight.

We stopped outside my father's house, and shouted a greeting to those within.

My parents were up and dressed in minutes. When my mother came out, she was crying, but in a moment she started ululating. We had heard women ululating like that all along our route through the Free State and Lesotho, and had heard exclamations: 'So these men are back! We never thought we'd see them again. . . .'

We were very joyful, close to tears, all of us. I need not describe that night, but we did get some sleep, and the next morning my mother cooked a tasty fowl for us, the first we had eaten since we left home.

At mid-morning I accompanied Filemon to his home, both of us still in uniform. Few people believed we really were soldiers; they thought we had dressed ourselves up to look like soldiers.

'No one can return alive from Mkiza,' they whispered.

Some recognized us and greeted us with shouts of joy, but others said, 'It can't be them. It must be two men who look like them, that's all.'

It was so strange.

We found some of our girl-friends engaged and others married, because we were never to return from Europe, so they had been told. It was a superstition that no black person could cross the sea and return again.

We tasted our second fowl that day. People kept coming to greet us where we sat, reporting that their daughters were engaged or married, all who had been girls when we were boys.

We simply kept quiet and looked at them.

After two weeks my father made a great feast for me, slaughtering an ox. He said he was thanking God for my return, but he was really praising his ancestors.

* * *

Although at that time politics and Independence were a long way off, we were aware, when we returned, that we were different from the other people at home. Our behaviour, as we showed the South Africans, was something more than they expected from a Native, more like what was expected among them of a white man. We had copied the manners and customs of Europeans, and not only copied: we lived them, acted those customs right through.

Home was a little unreal to us. As I have said, we kept quiet and looked at people; we did not know how to tell them the things we had seen.

I am reminded of rumours we heard on Rouen docks about a certain South African colonel who was a survivor when the *Mendi* sank. What we heard was that he was in a dinghy after the sinking, and when drowning men tried to pull themselves aboard, he beat their hands off his boat with an oar. The people who witnessed this gave evidence against him afterwards, for more men would have survived that disaster if he had let them into his dinghy. As it was, more than 600 Africans were killed, along with about a dozen white officers. This Colonel, it was said, was barred from going to the front line, and had to remain on the supply line with the Labour Corps; his case, we heard, would be dealt with after the war. We never discovered the outcome of his case, nor what became of him.

This Colonel was on the Rouen docks one day, so the story goes, when some French ladies arrived to serve the soldiers with tea. The Colonel was a man who upheld the colour bar. It seemed he could not stomach the nasty fact that Africans were served tea before him or that they used the same cups. He was heard to comment, 'If, one day, I arrive in South Africa to find it like this place, I'd rather die than live there!'

Captain Geddes, who had overheard this remark, retorted, 'I'm sorry for you, my dear Colonel. Perhaps you don't understand what you're saying. You hate Africans as if they were not human beings like yourself. Both Black and White were created by one God; their only difference lies in the colour of their skin. What would you say if, one day, you arrived in Heaven to find Africans there— would you refuse to stay there?'

'Yes! Yes! Yes!' cried the Colonel in Afrikaans. He turned to the Bantu standing near him and told them in that language, 'When you people get to South Africa again, don't start thinking that you are Whites, just because this place has spoiled you. You are black, and you will stay black, and there's no room for you in Heaven!'

Well, we did not think of ourselves as white people, but we had learned many things since we left home and in some ways it was not easy to settle down.

You see, we had liked our stay in France. It was our first experience of living in a society without a colour bar. When the time came for us to leave, some of us hid in the houses of our French friends. The military police caught most of us, but there were others who never went back to South Africa. So I returned to my home, but I was a fool; I should have got back to France *somehow*. Ignorance is always the death of a person.

We tried to keep our memories alive, and our determination to return to France, by corresponding with our friends. I kept in touch with Lieutenant Berry at Elliot in the Cape until early in 1919 when I was notified that both he and his father, Captain Berry, had succumbed to the influenza epidemic.

I had met a fellow called William Johnstone of Folkestone on the docks at Dieppe, where he was also working. We hit it off at once and we spent our breaks drinking tea and talking about our two countries, until at last we were close friends. After the war we corresponded for many years, but at last we lost touch and I do not know what has become of him.

* * *

My father sacrificing an ox for me was symbolic of my return to Lesotho: family ties were strong again and I was thrown back into the old, traditional ways. My father thought I had had plenty of time to sow my wild oats, and that I should settle down with a wife. He had a girl lined up for me, too.

While I was in France, he kept writing to me about a girl called Maria Mkuzangwe, Jemina's cousin; she was a Zulu, the grand-daughter of my father's mother's brother. I knew Maria, of course, and I had always thought her ugly, so I kept my letters non-committal on the subject of marriage.

When I returned, I paid a visit to the school at Cana where both Jemina and Maria were teaching, and asked the principal whether I might speak to Miss Mkuzangwe. Instead of calling Maria, he called Jemina.

I knew that Jemina was already engaged by then, to Mofolo Khakala, a brother-in-law of Chief Masupha II. I had heard that she did not really want to marry Mofolo, but that people had put

Genealogy 5 : Jemina and Maria

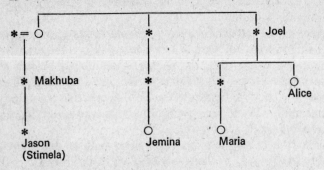

pressure on her, saying, 'What can you do with Jingoes, a mere
commoner? With Mofolo you'll be respected. Even we will come
and pay respect to you!' So, foolishly, as a girl might do, she had
accepted Mofolo.

Jemina came out of the school building and her hand flew to
her cheek; she was so scared to see me.

'No,' I said to her, 'I'm not here to cause trouble. Come and greet
me.'

She was so frightened, and so pleased.

'Is Maria here?' I asked her.

'Yes . . . .'

'Please call her for me.'

While I waited, I thought Maria might have changed in the time
I had not seen her, but when she came out, I still found her un-
attractive.

Well, things had changed. Jemina married her Mofolo, and she
had a very unhappy life until she died, a few years later.

I went home after my visit to the school, determined that, this
time, my father would not have his way. I would *not* marry a girl I
felt nothing for.

Presently my father came to me. 'It's time you married,' he said.

'I have no girl-friend, *Ntate*.'

'I wrote to you in France that my ancestors told me you should
marry my uncle Joel's daughter.'

'Alice is already married, *Ntate*,' I parried, hoping to keep him
off the subject of Maria, but knowing that although he had said
'daughter', it was 'granddaughter' he meant.

'There is another girl . . . ,' he said slowly, spacing the words evenly.

'I cannot marry an ugly girl!'

'My ancestors are my ancestors! I told you when you were in France how Joel appeared to me. You *will* marry Maria Mkuzangwe.'

I said nothing more then, but I went to appeal to my mother. She sympathized with me. We both knew many lovely girls at Tsokung who would do for us, but not for my father; she was powerless to help me. When my father saw that she was trying to influence him, he told her, 'I can see that you are deceiving this boy. If you and he intend bringing the wrong girl into this family, I warn you now . . . I won't have it. I *will not* be bullied by a child!'

My mother came to me and said, 'My child, we cannot do otherwise. Your father has assured his maternal people that whether you like it or not, you will marry Maria. You are going to have to marry her.'

'I'm so sorry, Mother,' I said, 'but I cannot be forced to marry a girl I do not love. If I do have to marry her, you people will suffer, and so will the girl. I will have nothing to do with her.'

My mother said nothing, but she wept.

I turned to my uncle Maguqu for help; he had never let me down before. My father simply refused to discuss the matter with him at all, so there was nothing he could do, even though he was older than my father.

Even my uncle Kabonina, who had instructions to carry through the marriage negotiations, could not help me. He was in our house one morning discussing the marriage with my father. When he came out, I asked him, '*Ntate*, how long will you people keep deceiving this girl? I cannot marry her.'

He turned back, as if to speak to my father, but my father was just then coming out of the *lelapa*.

'Kabonina!' he said, 'what is this boy saying?'

'My brother, this boy has been telling us all along that he does not love this girl. He asked me how long we intend to deceive her.'

'You carry out my orders, Kabonina. I am not going to be controlled by a boy. You go and ask the Mkuzangwes to give us a date for the marriage.'

'These plans of yours are wrong, *Ntate*,' I told my father. 'The whole marriage is a misunderstanding: can't you see that you are misleading those people, because of your stubbornness?'

While I was still speaking like that, my father picked up a stone and hurled it at me; uncle Molonyeni and cousin Letahoa shouted out, 'Stop! What are you doing?' They whirled to face Kabonina. 'Kabonina! Why don't you stop this old man?'

But the old man was wild now, and paid no heed to anybody.

'Go! Go!' he screamed at Kabonina. 'Don't waste time here! Get on your horse and go! Arrange things . . . . These people are trying to thwart me. They have the same mulish streak that my son has.'

And so I was trapped.

But . . . there was still one chance – to disappear into the Union of South Africa. My father, I found, had anticipated this plan; he had spread the word to the authorities that I was a rebellious son, trying to renege on a marriage contract. When I tried, I found it impossible to get a travelling pass to the Union; the recruiting companies would not have me. The borders were closed to me.

There were still the mountains . . . .

I ran away and hid at a cattle-post high up in the mountains, but even there I was found and brought back.

I went to visit Maria and did my best to make her dislike me and refuse to marry me, but she could not be put off.

That was that. I was stuck in Lesotho, to be harnessed with my family's marriage, not my own.

A date was fixed; the marriage negotiations were finalized.

* * *

In those days a marriage party of women left for a wedding several days in advance to brew beer, prepare food, and all that sort of thing. My mother and other women of the family prepared to travel to Cana to the home of the Mkuzangwes in a hired ox-wagon. They were to be escorted by my father, uncle Kabonina, and myself.

The day we set out there was a storm brewing, so my father stopped the wagon at Raletsae's village while I was sent to fetch a tarpaulin to cover the wagon. While they waited, my mother walked on ahead.

By the time I returned with the tarpaulin, the storm was closing in and we struggled to pull the tarpaulin across the wagon against the wind. The oxen were still inspanned, and they started growing restive when lightning flickered near us; the little boy at their head could not control them. I ran forward to bring them under control but before I could do anything they twisted around, knocked the child off his feet, and started to panic.

I shouted to my father and my uncle to unfasten the tarpaulin and get the people out of the wagon. The span of oxen was now beyond control. My father started running around behind the wagon to untie the tarpaulin, but before anyone could get out the wagon overturned.

It had been heavily loaded with supplies for the wedding feast, things like bags of mealie-meal, bundles of wood, and big cast-iron pots; as it turned over, the wagon buried those inside under this load.

We started throwing things out to free them, and people from Raletsae's came running to help us; they tried to lift the wagon while we worked to get the women out. My aunt NoSaka was pinned under one of the wheels; it was resting on her hip. She was lying beside a young girl, MaSegoete. They had both been thrown out and pinned when the wagon came over. We dragged them free.

My aunt NoMzanempi, wife of my father's brother Patane, was the last to be found inside the wagon. When we came to her we found her dead. Her neck was broken.

No marriage could have been fated worse than mine.

I was told to ride on to overtake my mother, who knew nothing of our tragedy, and to inform the people of Cana that the marriage party would not be arriving that day.

When I arrived at Cana, people shouted in high spirits at me, 'Hey! We don't want you here today! What are you doing here! We don't need you yet!' It is against the custom for the bridegroom to appear so early. Unknowingly, they called out to me with bawdy voices.

Without dismounting from my horse, I told them that I had been sent to report that our wagon had overturned, killing my aunt, and that they should not expect the marriage party that day. Then I rode home.

There could be no decision about whether the wedding could go on until the head of the Jingoes family, my uncle Maguqu, arrived. The Mkuzangwes had sent word that they were prepared to let the marriage ceremonies continue as planned; it was up to us to make a final decision.

I thought that Maguqu would seize on this opportunity, as he was my ally in all things, to delay the marriage, but he agreed with them.

'We cannot do otherwise,' he said, 'for the Almighty God wants that, when we go to this marriage, we go crying for the death that has happened. So I say to you, all my people, that we will bury the deceased today, and mourn tomorrow; then we will proceed to the marriage. We cannot stop the hand of the Almighty God.'

I gave up at last, and resigned myself to this marriage.

When the wagon was ready to leave for Cana again, Chabeli went to my father.

'Are you still determined to let this wagon leave without doing anything with *litlhare* to protect it?' he demanded. 'It seems that your faith as a Christian has deranged you. You have seen what has happened. Your brother Patane is grieving. Yet you will not take steps to protect the wagon, the driver, and the leader of the oxen against witchcraft.'

My father turned on his heel and walked away. Chabeli lost no time; he was in a blind rage. He went to fetch his *lenaka* and he scarified the boy who was to lead the oxen. He went to the oxen themselves, to the lead pair, and placed *litlhare* on their heads between their horns. He walked back to the wagon and placed *litlhare* on the reins and the draught-pole. Then he scarified the driver.

This was the day Chabeli scarified me as well, against the wishes of my father, as I have told.

Then he said, 'Now let them go. I will now see what is going to happen.'

Many people, myself included, did not believe that the heavy hand of God had overturned that wagon and killed my aunt. When *lingaka* discover that witchcraft has been the cause of a misfortune, they do not name the witch, because their aim is not to stir up further hatred. A great *ngaka* had told me that my wedding day would be marred by tragedy, and that someone would try to kill me with witchcraft on that day. I had no doubt that my aunt had been killed instead of me.

Reverend Jeanmairet solemnized my marriage to Maria on 9 September 1919. I will not speak further about my first marriage. It was a bitter one, and even now it pains my heart to recall it. My wife and I were unhappy together until the day of her death, in 1950.

*   *   *

I did not spend much time in Lesotho during the following years; there was little to attract me at home. The next years of my life were unsettled, as teacher and clerk in various towns in the Free State and Natal. I was drifting, and I only settled down and gained direction and interest in life when I heard the words of Clements Kadalie, in 1927, and threw myself into working for his movement.

CHAPTER FIVE

Keaubona—I see you

IN 1917 a man called Clements Kadalie was walking down Loop Street in Cape Town. On that day he saw a policeman kicking a black person because he was walking on the pavement when the policeman said he should be walking in the street. Kadalie stopped and watched, and he saw the policeman kick another person off the pavement, this time a black woman. The third person to be pushed into the street was Clements Kadalie himself. He was told that a black man should walk in the street, along with the cars and the trams and the horses; the pavement was for the use of white people.

That day formed things in Kadalie's mind. He decided that something should be done to protect the rights of Bantu in South Africa; a voice was needed to speak for the Bantu, and only an organization could do this. Kadalie went after the two people he had seen kicked and said they must join together to form some kind of body, something tangible, as he put it. He asked them to meet with him later to discuss plans.

Their first meeting was attended by twelve people; these twelve formed the organization known as the Industrial and Commercial Workers' Union of South Africa, or the I.C.U.

We Bantu came to call it the *Keaubona* —I See You. Although its initials stood for a fancy title, to us Bantu it meant basically: when you ill-treat the African people, I See You; if you kick them off the pavements and say they must go together with the cars and the ox-carts, I See You; I See You when you do not protect the Bantu; when an African woman with a child on her back is knocked down by the cars in the street, I See You; I See You when you kick my brother, *I See You.*

I heard Clements Kadalie speaking about all these things in

Bethlehem in the Orange Free State in 1927, and I have described the formation of the *Keaubona* as he told it that day.

I was working in Bethlehem as a clerk when one Keable William 'Mote paid a visit to that town; he was the Provincial Secretary of the I.C.U. in the Free State, and was travelling from town to town, telling the workers to join the new movement which had been started by a Nyasa, Kadalie, a waiter in a Cape Town hotel. I did not attend 'Mote's meeting, but one of my friends, Esau Nhlapo, a teacher, was among the ninety people who joined that day, and he told me about the movement and its aims. He had been elected Branch Secretary of Bethlehem.

'They need people like you to join,' he said to me, 'so that the Bantu can live as people once more.'

Keable 'Mote was an intelligent man who realized that if he was to keep and encourage adherence to the movement, the people had to see and hear Kadalie himself, for he was a dynamic orator, a man who, when you saw him, you recognized as a leader. He arranged for Kadalie to come and speak in Bethlehem.

Kadalie started his speech by telling us how the I.C.U. was born. The twelve who had decided to form the organization wasted no time; they spread the word and held a meeting which about one hundred attended, and of those, seventy joined. Once Kadalie saw he had a following, he moved to legalize the organization. He saw the municipality in Cape Town to register the movement under the name they had decided on; the municipality agreed, but said he needed police clearance as well. Accordingly, he got a letter from the municipality to show he had registered his movement as a *bona fide* organization, and got permission from the police to hold meetings.

After this, they elected a President and other office-holders. The President was Johnson, a Negro from America who was working on the Cape Town docks at the time. Kadalie was General Secretary; the Vice-President was Jabavu, whose older brother was the famous scholar.

When he stood on the platform at Bethlehem, Kadalie spoke of the need of the Bantu to unite, to stop being exploited, to fight to be treated as human beings.

'Just now,' he said, 'as I was coming here this morning, I came to a cross-street; the people who were coming to this meeting were being forced to walk in the street by the police. This is wrong. In the first place, pavements are built by Africans. When they have finished building them, they are told not to walk on them. The person who makes the road safe cannot enjoy its safety. This happens too when we Bantu build houses. Black people are the ones who build houses for Whites, and while they are building these houses, they walk in and out of every door in the house, look out of its every window, and handle every brick. When the house is built, a *motho*, a black human being, when he comes to the house, is told not to use the front door but to go round to the kitchen door. These things must be abolished. We are all human beings.

'This matter does not stop with houses: it is true of all things made by black hands in South Africa. Once we have built something or made something, we are not allowed to use it. Look at the railways. The people there who keep the loads moving, are black; they are the people who are strong, who sing when they work—people who, when they carry a heavy piece of iron, sing because they want to make their heavy weight lie easier on them. Then when hands that are black have laid that railway line, they are told that someone is there before them. Who is that person, that someone? It is a white man. He does not, and will not, recognize that the sleepers and rails were laid by Africans who should share in the profit of their work.

'My people,' Kadalie said to us, 'look at our people on the farms—they suffer. On the farms the people suffer the most. If a man is working in the kitchen of a white *miesies*[1] on a farm, and it is cold and he is thirsty and he asks his *miesies* for coffee, that woman can have that man arrested if she feels like it. She has only to say that the kaffir[2] was being cheeky, or insulting her, for him to be driven, handcuffed, in front of a horse. These things happen not only on farms but even in towns.

'White men expect Africans to work for them for nothing. They ill-treat us and will have nothing to do with us, because they say that we are only Natives and therefore we cannot have what they have.

'What the I.C.U. wants, and I'm telling you today, is that Bantu must share in the profits of their labour. We Bantu must be paid decent salaries; minimum wages must be raised. One day we should have representatives in Parliament, people to listen to our grievances and tell them to Parliament. What the I.C.U. wants is that one day South Africa will be a country where Black and White live side by side, and where we Bantu will have our own representatives to speak for us, and not only white representatives; those Bantu will sit in Parliament and speak for other Bantu.'

Kadalie left, and he left me convinced. I had shaken him by the hand and realized that he was a leader indeed. Soon after, I was elected Branch Secretary, taking the place of Esau at Bethlehem for he had been promoted to District Secretary.

*   *   *

Bethlehem was a wide open field: there were many small towns nearby where the people had never heard of the *Keaubona*, and I saw it as my duty to go out and start branches among these people.

In the beginning things went smoothly. At the first meeting I held, which was at Fouriesburg, ninety members were recruited. I found it very interesting that even the Chiefs in Lesotho had heard about the movement, and had sent their messengers to attend my meeting and clarify for them what they had only heard by rumour. After this easy start I set my sights on Kestell, a small town nestling against the foot of the mountains to the north of Lesotho, with a large farming community.

At Kestell I met difficulties. When I arrived there, on a Saturday morning, I first went to the Town Clerk to get permission to hold my meeting the following day in the location; up to now, this had been a mere formality, and had never interfered with our meetings, but it was our policy never to address a meeting without clearance from the town's municipality. The meeting had been advertised already, and the people of the location and the surrounding farms were expecting me.

I found the Town Clerk just as he was about to lock up his office; it was 12 o'clock. I introduced myself to him, and he said he was sorry to hear that I was Jingoes, for he had heard many things about me. He said he did not want his people in the location spoiled by the I.C.U. He had noticed, he said, that all people who joined the I.C.U. started to disobey their masters; this he did not want in Kestell. Things were working fine in Kestell, and he wanted nothing to change that. If the I.C.U. started there, there would be friction and misunderstanding between the white people and the people of the location. So, he was not prepared to allow me to address his people. Even more, he would not allow me to put up in the Kestell location that night; he wanted me to return to Bethlehem at once.

I looked at him quietly while he spoke, and then said, 'Just let me stay in the location overnight to rest. I've come from Bethlehem today. I'll leave tomorrow.'

'No,' he said. 'I don't want you anywhere near the location. You'll talk to my people for the whole night there.'

'People are expecting me. I won't hold a meeting during the night; I'll stay in a hut the whole night.'

'Well . . . if you go there now, make sure you leave first thing in the morning.'

On Sunday morning while I was having my breakfast, two policemen arrived. The first introduced himself as Sergeant Du Toit. He said, 'I've been instructed by the Town Clerk to tell you that you must not hold a meeting here; you must leave.'

At this point Robert Dumah and Selathiel Molangeni came to join us. Dumah had been appointed District Secretary in the place of Esau, who had been promoted to Provincial Secretary; Molangeni was Dumah's Chairman. They had come to Kestell to help me at the meeting.

'What is the Sergeant saying?' Dumah asked me.

The Sergeant turned to him. 'I've come to tell Jingoes here that he cannot hold his meeting. I am acting on the orders of the Town Clerk.'

'What do you say?' Molangeni asked me.

'I think that the meeting must go on,' I replied.

'Yes,' he agreed, 'that's what I'm thinking also. Let the meeting go on.' Then he turned to the Sergeant again; 'Sergeant,' he said, 'please go and tell the Town Clerk that we are going to proceed with the meeting. If he wants to, he can make a case against us, but we cannot stop now. Look at the crowds that are starting to assemble. Some of these people have come a long way to be addressed; if we call everything off now, there just might be trouble.'

The Sergeant saw the truth in that. 'Yes,' he said, 'these people are too big a crowd to dismiss now, but I'm telling you that I will act as I have been instructed by the Town Clerk.'

We said to him, 'Yes, all right; we understand that. You must issue a summons if you have to.'

'I'll be back at ten o'clock for the meeting,' he said.

So I spoke at Kestell with the police listening. I told the people first that I was glad to be at Kestell; it was the first time I had been there, and I was pleased to see so many people at the meeting. I said I was sorry to have to tell them that the Sergeant of the police, whom they could see for themselves, had told me not to hold a meeting, but that I wanted to speak to them, and speak to

them I would. 'This is the hour', I told them, 'that a black person
ought to join the I.C.U.—the only organization in South Africa
that seeks one day to emancipate the Bantu in South Africa.' I
repeated the things I had heard Clements Kadalie say, and then
tried to turn the presence of the police Sergeant to greater advantage.

'My Sergeant,' I addressed him directly, 'this is the time that
black people must be recognized as people in this country. Generally,
you always see people from farms and towns taken and arrested on
minor charges and enclosed in custody until their case comes up.
Yet this is not necessary. For if a person is charged for a minor
offence you, the Sergeant, can instruct your men to issue a summons
for him to appear before the court; he need not sit in gaol. The
law says that. Only people who break into houses, or who steal
stock, or who kill somebody, only such people, does the law say,
should be arrested and put in custody until their trial.'

The people applauded my words; I could sense their approval.
That day 115 joined, to make Kestell a strong growth-point for the
I.C.U.

I returned to Bethlehem well satisfied, but within a few days a
summons was issued against me to appear at Kestell on a certain
date to answer to the charge brought by the Town Clerk for the
municipality that unlawfully, without permission, I had gone to the
location to hold a meeting there, against the explicit orders of the
Town Clerk.

As soon as I received the summons I went to Mr. Edmund
Ellenberger, our lawyer. Since I had become Branch Secretary, we
had a standing arrangement with him that he would handle our
defence cases for us. I was first advised to see him by one Sergeant
William Lieta, a home-boy friend of mine, who was not a member
of the *Keaubona*, but a black policeman in the South African
Police force.

I placed the summons before Ellenberger and asked him whether
he would defend me. He said he would, and charged me ten
pounds, which the organization paid. Instead of taking the case
himself, he sent his son, Norman. When I came before the court at
Kestell, I appeared before a Mr. Botha.

When Norman Ellenberger studied the newly introduced regulations under which I was charged, he saw a loophole at once: the
Kestell municipality had not yet had these regulations ratified by
the municipal head office in Harrismith, so I could not legally
be charged under them.

In imposing judgment Mr. Botha said, 'Yes, according to what has been said by Mr. Ellenberger, Jingoes has not been lawfully charged by the municipality of Kestell. The regulation has not yet been endorsed by the municipality of Harrismith. I therefore find that the accused should be discharged.'

That same afternoon we went straight to the location again and addressed a jubilant meeting there. By means of this case, we had shown the people what we aimed to do for them through our organization: with skilled lawyers helping us, and with courage, we would define and protect our rights. The rest of the afternoon was taken up with electing a committee to organize the branch at Kestell.

That was the first time I appeared in court for the *Keaubona*. In all, I was charged more than forty times while I worked for them; I was found guilty thrice. Altogether, I spent only five weeks in gaol for the I.C.U.

* * *

My second case came sooner than I expected, and the nasty thing about it was that it was a charge trumped up by my friend Esau Nhlapo, the Provincial Secretary. Despite his rapid promotion, for some reason he was envious of the success I had enjoyed in establishing two branches. It happened like this.

One day Esau arrived in Bethlehem and demanded, in a strange way, a certain amount of money from our branch funds. As Provincial Secretary, he had every right to ask for money from a branch, but we simply did not have any to give him. I told him that we had already forwarded all our funds to our head office in Johannesburg.

'Why did you do that?' he demanded.

'You know we always do it. . . .'

'You've no right! I doubt that the money is really where you say it is. . . . You'll suffer for this now. . . .'

He stormed out and went to the police station, from where one Lebenya, a C.I.D. plain-clothes man, came to fetch me. I went with him. At the charge office I found Nhlapo and Robert Dumah as well—so he had also turned against me. They both gave witness but the Chairman, Molangeni, refused to speak against me, saying he knew me too well, and that he was certain the money had been sent to head office as I said.

In that case I was defended by old man Ellenberger himself. On

5

that day I realized that Ellenberger was truly the son of the *moruti*, the great missionary who instructed, educated, and formed the Basotho nation, and who wrote what I regard as the best book on Lesotho. He suggested in his brilliant defence that the whole case had been set up against me because of jealousy; my two erstwhile friends were most probably envious because I had been more successful than they in establishing country branches. While they had been in Bethlehem they had achieved nothing and had shown no initiative, '. . . while my client here has already opened two branches while he has been in charge'. He pointed out that no representative from head office had appeared to give evidence that the money had not arrived there. As exhibits in court, he produced counterfoils to show that the money had been sent.

I was again discharged.

But I was not happy because I knew that my two friends would not rest until they had discredited me. The I.C.U. suffered because of internal squabbling like this. Nhlapo and Dumah were no longer satisfied to have me in the Bethlehem office—the sooner I got out the better, they said.

'I'll be glad to leave . . . ,' I told them, and I left.

I was pleased when, two days later, I received a wire from head office in Johannesburg telling me to report at Klerksdorp, where there was a new job waiting for me.

* * *

At Klerksdorp I found the District Secretary for the Western Transvaal to be a chap called Jonga. I liked him at once, although by now I was wary of these District and Provincial Secretaries.

There was much to do in the Western Transvaal because Klerksdorp was the only established branch. The Provincial Secretary had been to other towns, but only on visits to address meetings; he had not opened any branches.

I had a hard job to do when I arrived there. I had to go to Wolmaransstad, Bloemhof, and Christiana to organize branches, and I found the travelling too much for me. I found that my headquarters at Klerksdorp were not central enough, so I contacted head office and got permission to base myself at Makwassie; a municipal official named Saayman gave me clearance to stay there. I dug myself in, establishing a sound base from which to spread the word of the I.C.U. in the Western Transvaal.

These were some of the most exciting and vital years of my life. I built up a strong following in the Western Transvaal, and formed branches at Wolmaransstad, Bloemhof, Christiana, Leeudoringstad, Warrenton, and Lichtenburg, and I established links at all the many diggings in the area, for the I.C.U. was, first and foremost, a trade union. Dues were collected monthly. Members paid a two-shilling membership fee on joining, and then a tickey[3] a week, or one shilling a month. The Makwassie branch had the highest membership; we had over one thousand members there. Klerksdorp, although it was a large town, had a membership of only 250; it was a hard town to recruit members in, being an African National Congress stronghold, and that organization was opposed to us.

My name became a byword at the time throughout the Western Transvaal. I was fighting for the rights of the Bantu working there and I spoke out against conditions I thought bad whenever I could and encouraged others to follow my example. I made liberal use of the newspapers, writing hard-hitting letters stressing the needs and rights of the Bantu people. As the Town Clerk of Kestell had said, white employers felt that I was undermining their authority. Whenever I heard of a worker in difficulties, I tried to help him, and I saw to it that any member of our organization who was involved in a court case got decent legal counsel.

* * *

This was the sort of dispute I generally undertook to sort out.

Once when I was addressing a meeting at Ottosdal a man called Klaas 'Mota came and spoke to me; he told me that he was a squatter on a farm belonging to a man I shall call Venter. 'Mota was planning to move from Mr. Venter's farm, but Venter did not want to lose him, because 'Mota was renowned in the district as an excellent hand with animals. Venter said that if he left the farm, he would have to leave behind some of his cattle and some grain, as well as a stallion that he owned. In those days, if you worked for a farmer, he would give you a plot to plough for yourself, and would allow you to graze your cattle on his property. Klaas had arrived at Venter's farm with three head of cattle, but these had grown to a nice herd of about twenty head. Mr. Venter wanted Klaas to leave with only the three cattle he had brought with him. It was strange that Klaas owned a stallion, because farmers always saw to it that the only stud stock on their farms was their own. Usually, only the farmer keeps a stallion, a ram, or a bull; this is common knowledge. But for some reason Mr. Venter had not gelded Klaas's stallion, perhaps because it was a superb animal. He had a great liking for that stallion, and he always used it as his own mount. If Klaas moved, the stallion would have to stay, Mr. Venter stipulated.

'Mota decided to take action against Mr. Venter, and he went to the police. When he mentioned the stallion, they said he was lying— why should a farmer have allowed a Black to keep a stallion on his farm? None the less, they accepted his complaint, and his case against Mr. Venter was due the following day, a Monday.

Klaas told me all this, and asked my advice.

After the meeting I went home with Klaas on his horse-cart. We left at sunset and by the time we reached Venter's farm, the moon was high, and Venter and his wife were waiting for Klaas.

They had been looking for him all day; they had sent to his homestead three times, but the children had been well primed, and told them that they did not know where their father was. Venter knew all about the I.C.U., and he knew that Klaas had a grievance against him, just the sort of grievance that I was always taking up. He knew a meeting was being held that day, and suspected that Klaas would go to me for advice. He also knew that Klaas had taken the horse and cart, and so he must have gone some distance.

As we turned into the farm road I heard a woman's voice saying in Afrikaans, 'Yes, I think it's them.' As we drew closer, 'Yes . . . ,' she said, 'it's Klaas—it's his horse and cart.'

Mr. Venter stepped into the road and stopped us.

'Where have you been?' he asked Klaas.

'I've just come from Leeudoringstad. I went to see my people there.'

'From Leeudoringstad?'

'Yes. . . .'

'Well . . . okay. Who's that with you? Are you sure you haven't been to Ottosdal? We heard there was a meeting at Ottosdal today.'

'I haven't come from Ottosdal, *Baas*.'

'Who's this boy with you?'

'It's my brother, from there at Leeudoringstad.'

'Who're you?' to me.

'I'm Jan, my *Baas*.'

'Jan who?'

'Jan Sekhametsi.'[4]

'Jan Sekhametsi?'

'Yes. . . .'

'You're not Jingoes?'

'*Who?*'

'Jingoes, That *skelm*[5] from the I.C.U. who goes around here and teaches our *volk*[6] to get stupid ideas about all sorts of things.'

'No, my *Baas*, I'm not that man.'

'*Ja*, but there is such a man. He goes up and down putting funny ideas into the heads of our *volk*, so that these days we don't understand each other any more; we don't get on with our *volk* any more. I don't want him on this farm. And I think you are that man. And I think I'm going to shoot somebody tonight!'

'*Baas* Venter . . . ,' I said to him.

'*Ja!*'

'You know perfectly well, my *Baas*, that that person you are talking about, that Jingoes, he can't talk Afrikaans. He only speaks English. Now I'm talking Afrikaans with you. I've got nothing to do with that man and I don't want to hear him when he talks his nonsense.'

'Yes! Yes! What do you think of him, my *jong?*'[7]

'He's a lazy man who walks around and doesn't work. He gives people crazy ideas. I wouldn't follow the path of a man like that.'

'Yes, my *jong*, you're right . . . you're dead right, my *jong!*'

Klaas was growing anxious beside me. He clucked to the horses and lifted the reins, but then Venter's wife spoke.

'No, no. Just a minute! Wait a minute! This boy says he's Jan Sekhametsi, but I don't believe him. This is that man, that Jingoes—I'm sure of it!'

'*Miesies*,' I said to her, 'I can't understand why you think I should be Jingoes. You know as well as I do that Jingoes can't speak Afrikaans. He just speaks English. If I'm Jingoes, where have I suddenly learned to speak Afrikaans?'

'Well. . . .'

We moved off then, and went to Klaas's home.

Klaas warned everyone there not to mention my proper name to anyone, in case we were overheard. We discussed his case for hours before snatching a bit of sleep. At four the next morning we set off for Wolmaransstad where the case was to be heard.

On the way, Mr. and Mrs. Venter passed us. We heard Mrs. Venter saying to her husband, 'I told you he's Jingoes! Where's that boy going now, I wonder?' Then she shouted to us.

'Klaas!'

'Yes . . . ?'

'Stop!'

So we stopped.

'Klaas!' Mr. Venter called.

'*Ja*, my *Baas*. . . .'

'For the last time, *who is this man*?'

Klaas looked at me, uncertain, so I turned to face them and said, '*Ao*, my *Baas*, I told you I'm Jan Sekhametsi.'

'Where're you going?'

'I'm going home. I'll catch the train at Leeudoringstad.'

'Oh, I see. . . . I see, my boy.'

When we got to the court at Wolmaransstad, Klaas outspanned outside while I went in to discuss the matter with Van Blerk, the lawyer I had engaged the previous day to take Klaas's case. Venter was amazed to see me in court—I was no longer Jan Sekhametsi, deferent and bobbing my head. I could see his wife telling him that she was right.

When faced with a skilled lawyer, Venter soon gave himself away. He stated that the stallion was born out of Klaas's mare, but that he had bought the stallion from Klaas; many people could witness that he always rode the stallion. That was why, he said, he would not let Klaas leave his farm with the stallion unless Klaas would refund the fifteen pounds he had received for the stallion. He had no documentary proof of the sale, he continued, because he had always trusted Klaas; he was disappointed to find that Klaas was not a man who could be trusted to keep his word. He also claimed that Klaas was trying to cheat him over the oxen, which he had bought as well. Because he had trusted Klaas, all these sales were verbal agreements—he had no documents to prove his statement.

Van Blerk said before the Magistrate, Mr. A. S. Dunlop, that it was quite clear that the stallion belonged to Klaas 'Mota, because Mr. Venter had admitted that the stallion was born out of Klaas's mare, and Venter was unable to present any documentary proof of a sale. A reasonable man would not enter into a transaction of that nature without recording it. Any reasonable man would have realized that either he or Klaas might die, and that their children would quarrel about the animals. Yet Venter had made no provision of this kind for the future. He ended with a plea that the animals be returned to Klaas as he wanted to move from Venter's farm in the near future.

In passing judgment, Magistrate Dunlop said it was evident that

Mr. Venter was an educated man; the court could not understand why there were no documents relating to these purported sales. Faced with this fact, the court could only conclude that Mr. Venter had not bought the animals in question, and was simply trying to extort them from Klaas. The court ruled that the animals belonged to Klaas, and that he should not be hindered when moving from Venter's farm.

* * *

Not all the disputes that were brought to me involved white people. You must remember that this was an area where people could not go to their Chiefs easily, for the Chiefs lived around Lichtenburg, and members of the I.C.U. often came to our offices asking us to mediate in preference to going to the police. They looked upon the *Keaubona* as a kind of substitute for their Chiefs, some kind of authority they could trust. The Western Transvaal Bantu are no different from those of Lesotho; they believe in witchcraft, and out of this arose an interesting case.

Jobere Mokuoane's child was sick, showing symptoms of witchcraft poisoning. Jobere went to consult Seabata Koaho, a *ngaka*, who agreed to cure the child in return for the usual payment of a heifer. While Seabata was still attending the child, Jobere's wife became sick, with the same kind of sickness caused by witchcraft. Seabata said he would only attend her if he was paid more, and Jobere, who was desperate to have his family cured, agreed. After Seabata had healed them both, Jobere paid him one heifer. Seabata thanked him for the payment, and asked him, 'Where is the money for your wife?'

'I have paid already,' Jobere replied. 'The payment of the heifer was a payment for the whole family; it meant that if anyone of us got sick, you would come and cure us. That is the custom among Bantu.'

The *ngaka* retorted, 'That's not my custom! Our agreement was that if I attended your wife, you would pay me more. And you agreed to this. Your older brother, Jonas, was present, and so was your son-in-law, Monyau. They both agree with me that you said if I cured your wife, you would pay me an additional fee.'

Jobere denied this, so Seabata came to ask me to make peace between them.

Both these men were high-ranking members of the I.C.U. Jobere was the Chairman of the Leeudoringstad branch, while

Seabata was a member of the Executive Committee of Makwassie. I assembled my committee to hear their case.

After Seabata had stated his grievance before us, Jobere still insisted that he could not scrape up the necessary money, and that Seabata was mistaken. To substantiate his claim, Seabata called as witnesses Jonas Mokuoane and Monyau, Jobere's son-in-law, and they corroborated the fact that Jobere had promised payment for the curing of both his child and his wife; they had been present when the agreement was made, and they were sorry to see that their kinsman was turning against his word. If Jobere did not pay, who knows what further disasters might befall his family?

Monyepeng, Chairman of the I.C.U. branch at Makwassie, asked Jobere to bring a witness who would back up his version of the story.

'No,' said Jobere. 'What can I do, when my own brother and my son-in-law have turned against me? I will have to pay. . . .'

He agreed to pay a heifer or a *tollie*[8] to get shot of the whole matter.

This satisfied everyone, and within four days Jobere brought us a good brown *tollie* to pay Seabata. Seabata was called and he took the *tollie*, and the case was over.

That is how the I.C.U. was often called upon to mediate and make peace between its members.

Because of the influence we had over our members, at the end of every month we had women coming to ask us to force their husbands to give them money so that they could support themselves and their children.

One such woman was MaMabebe Mokhosi. *Helele*! I remember this well! We used to threaten these men to make them toe the line; we would say, 'You pay up the money, or we'll go and spoil your work. . . .'

MaMabebe came to my office one day crying and complaining, desperate for lack of money. I knew her well because both she and her husband were members of the *Keaubona*. Ben, her husband, was working at the Makwassie hotel, earning good money, but he did not bring his money home: he had another woman, a girl called Moroesi.

At the end of the month Moroesi would slip around to the hotel early, at the time she knew Ben would be paid. As soon as Ben received his wages, he would place the money in her hands. She was eating the money that Ben should have been using to feed his family.

MaMabebe's story made me angry. These were common cases. I called Ben before the office.

He swaggered in when he came, trying to be nonchalant, saying that no woman would ever control his money. He was tired of his wife anyhow, he said casually, and she herself was a whore, running around with other men, and he had never said anything about that to her. Why should she try to control his life?

'That your wife is a whore is your own fault,' I said to him. 'You should have spoken to her about that before. At the moment we're not talking about her habits; that's your problem. Whatever she is, she's your wife, and she needs money. You haven't divorced her. She's known as your wife, and she has to look after your children. Why do you take your money and hand it over to that other woman, Moroesi?'

He looked shamefaced, and I sent him out to fetch Moroesi, who was also a member of the I.C.U. They arrived together and stood before me and my fellow committee members. Leo, the Vice-Chairman, asked why Moroesi took money from Ben.

'Because I am in love with him,' she replied. 'And I don't make him give me the money, either! He gives it to me freely.'

'Where's the money for this month?'

'I've used most of it,' she explained, 'and at present I've got only one pound ten left.'

'Give it here,' I said.

'Here it is,' she said, and put it on the table.

Then we asked Ben how much he had given his wife MaMabebe that month.

'I've given her nothing, because she cheeked me,' he replied. 'If she'd been civil to me, I'd have considered giving her something at least.'

We told him severely that he had better give her something every month or get out of the *Keaubona*. The committee decided to give MaMabebe the one pound ten Moroesi had produced, and everybody started looking happier. It was a strange set-up, really, because even Moroesi seemed satisfied. Her last words, as they left, were, 'Well, MaMabebe, we're both Ben's wives now. So I suppose you too ought to get a share of his money. . . .'

A lot of our time was taken up with this sort of case.

There were many other details to occupy us as well. If a member lost his job and was having a hard time making ends meet, we would try to give him one pound ten a month while he was unemployed.

If an employer approached us to find someone to fill a vacancy, we did our best to find a suitable worker for him. This sort of thing. But always the foremost aim of our organization was to protect the worker, and this meant, in South Africa, interceding most often between Black and White.

* * *

When a man had a dispute with his master, or reported a grievance to us, we did not rush headlong to turn it into an issue in a court of law. We would first approach the master and talk to him to try to discover the truth of the dispute and seek a solution. But if the master was in the wrong, and we could not make him see reason, or if he did not want to discuss the question with us, we would put the matter before the police in the charge office; at this time the police had many cases brought before them to be settled that never went near the courts but were sorted out right then and there in the police station. Only if the employer was adamant or persistent in his stubbornness did the matter go further. If he paid attention in the charge office and was reasonable, the police often ended the matter there. But there were many cases that could not be settled in this way and I nearly lost my life as a result of one of these cases.

A man called Jonas Mathibe came to us one day complaining that his master, whom I shall call Landman, was refusing to pay him for some grain. We told him to start at the beginning and explain the matter in detail, and this is what he said.

He was one of Landman's *volk* and, as was the custom on farms, Landman allocated him fields to plough for himself. Mathibe was a skilled farmer, and he reaped very good crops which Landman always sold for him through the farmers' co-operative. It happened that Landman had not paid Mathibe for his crops of the last two seasons, always fobbing him off, saying he had not yet received a cheque from the co-operative. When the I.C.U. came to the Western Transvaal, Mathibe realized that we were an organ through which he could express his grievances and obtain the money due to him.

We advised him not to be hasty; perhaps the co-operative had indeed been slow in paying. He should go, we said, to speak to Landman reasonably, and tell him that he needed the money.

Mathibe did as we advised, but Landman told him he was mad: how could he claim the amount he said was due to him? Natives never reaped such crops. He was sure, he said, that Mathibe had been stealing from his crops to swell his own harvest.

Mathibe asked him, 'How can you say I stole from your crops? We live on the same farm. I would have been seen, and you would have noticed your loss.'

To this Landman simply said, 'How can I see what you do at night?'

Mathibe came back to us and related his interview with Landman, and we advised him to go to the police. Sergeant Van Heerden called on Landman and advised him to pay Mathibe what he owed him, but he refused. Most of the farmers of the district supported Landman, saying that if he paid, the Natives would get used to having their own way.

Sergeant Van Heerden decided to make a civil case of it, and Landman was served with a summons and came to court.

This was a big case because Landman was an important man in the area. If you go into that town today, you will still see the large clock donated to the church by Landman. Most of the Whites in the area were solidly behind him and looked upon it as a test case. By that time the I.C.U. was a force to be reckoned with in that district, and the Whites wanted us to make fools of ourselves in court.

We engaged Mr. Levy, a lawyer from Lichtenburg, to appear for Mathibe.

I still remember that one of Landman's witnesses said before the court, 'It's a surprising thing that a respected man like Mr. Landman should have to appear in court accused by a Native. I cannot understand why a Native's word is being taken before that of a European.'

The Magistrate said to this witness, 'I must inform you that the law is there for Black and White alike. Just because a man's skin is black, it does not mean that he should not be heard and believed. All are equal before the law.'

To make a long story short, the Magistrate said in judgment that the court was sorry to notice that there were some white men who did not think that Bantu were entitled to the fruits of their labour. Landman had admitted that he always gave his *volk* acres to plough; he had agreed that Mathibe, as an old inhabitant of his farm, had more acres than the other Bantu; he stated under cross-questioning, too, that Mathibe was a skilled farmer who had once been at an agricultural school. The Magistrate instructed Landman to pay Mathibe for the crops he had sold for him.

The sum of money involved was considerable. This judgment

aroused terrific resentment among the white farmers. As I came out of the court they pointed at me, saying that since I had come to the Western Transvaal they had had trouble with their labour; someone said, 'We should get rid of him. . . .' They said that a white man of Landman's standing should not have to defend himself against kaffirs; it was unthinkable that a White's integrity should be called in question by a kaffir. They said a good many things and, seeing the mood they were in, I must confess their remarks made me a little nervous.

I used to leave my horse to graze just below the railway station, but when I went to where I had tethered it I found that it had pulled up its peg and wandered off. In my search for it I passed an Indian store where I was told that the horse had passed along that way, dragging its tether. I followed the tracks of the horse in the dust of the road. Behind me, I heard a horse and cart approaching. I knew the two men in the cart: the first I shall call Fourie, a man I knew to be a member of the South African Party; the other was Mr. Williams, who was a National Party member.

I stopped them and asked them to give me a lift, explaining that my horse was somewhere on the road ahead, having broken free.

'Climb up!' Mr. Fourie said amiably, and I got into the back of the cart. We had not gone more than a dozen yards when Williams grabbed hold of my shoulder and said, 'Yes! I've got you now! You've caused enough trouble in this community. Tonight you die. . . .'

Mr. Fourie gave an embarrassed smile. I did not pay much attention because I was sure Williams was joking. Then we came over a rise and I saw my horse ahead, grazing beside the road. I thanked Fourie, and he stopped the cart, but when I swung my legs over the side to jump down, Williams said, 'Don't! I meant what I said. You and I have got business tonight!'

I did nothing. I just sat, waiting to see what Fourie would do, but he only said, 'Let's go,' and we went on.

When we came to Fourie's house, Williams jumped down from the cart and shouted, 'Where are the kaffirs? They must bring me a *riem*.'[9] Mr. Fourie looked embarrassed; I think he was scared of Williams.

Williams grabbed hold of me, dragged me to the ground, and took me to the kitchen of the farmhouse, shouting to Mrs. Fourie to bring him a gun, that he was thinking of shooting a man, a man who had been causing trouble in the district. Mr. Fourie told the man that there was no gun in the house, but Williams ignored him and shouted again for the *volk*, yelling for a *riem* with which to tie me up.

In the kitchen, Williams took his hat off his head and placed it on mine. He said, 'If this were my farm, I'd put my hat on your head, shoot you and carry you outside, and say that you had been stealing from my house.'

I kept quiet.

All this time Fourie was looking ashamed, shuffling his feet and glancing towards the door, as if to tell me to run for it. His wife was also indicating with her eyes that I should make a break for it, and when Williams left the kitchen to look for a gun inside the house, she whispered, 'Go on! Get away!' I got out and ran. My horse was tied behind the cart, and I was on it and off.

* * *

Well, you can gather that the farming community, and especially members of the National Party, did not have much time for me. Once a politician called me a 'black snake' when addressing a meeting at Wolmaransstad, and warned people to be on their guard against me. We had our disagreements, and they called me many names, but the real trouble started when the meetings I addressed caused people to strike for better wages.

I had held a meeting at Lichtenburg, and was on my way back from there to Makwassie when the labourers of Lichtenburg struck to have their wages raised from one-and-six a day. I understand the police thought I was still in the location, organizing the strike, but when they went there to search for me, they were told that I had already left. I only heard about this trouble later. The strike was broken when the workers were promised a minimum wage of two shillings a day.

On another occasion, at Klerksdorp, when I had left the place after holding a meeting, trouble broke out and again the police searched for me, even as far as the railway station, but I was no longer there.

The third incident was the one that caused a total clamp-down on my movements. This was at the Leeufontein diggings, where the miners held a strike. This time I was present, and this strike I saw. They nearly came to blows; men were discarding their jackets to fight, but the authorities calmed the workers and violence was averted. My presence there must have been reported in higher circles than I had realized because I was summoned to Wolmarans-stad to meet a certain Captain McNaught.

Travelling by car, I arrived late in the evening. When I went to his office, McNaught handed me a long envelope with red seals on it, dated 9 March 1932. It was opened, and when the contents were read to me, I realized that I was being served with a type of banning order. In effect, for twelve months from the date mentioned, I was not allowed to be in a group of more than five people. This effectively debarred me from addressing groups of workers. Specifically, I was told that I might not place my foot near any mines or diggings in the whole area from Johannesburg to the Western Transvaal. It was signed by Oswald Pirow.

For the next twelve months I was on my own. Whenever possible, the I.C.U. gave me a bit of money, but I eked out a living by working for an Indian as a clerk. I chafed under the banning order, however, and held secret meetings on farms at night. I noticed that I was followed wherever I went.

One day I was expected at a farm near the Boskuil diggings, and when I got on the train at Ottosdal, I noticed that a policeman was watching me, and saw me taking the line to Makwassie. At Makwassie Station there were two detectives I knew who were watching the train, one Van Rensburg and his assistant, a Mosotho called Masiu. I stuck my head through the window and when they saw me, they seemed to lose interest in the train; so I knew they were checking on where I was going.

By now it was night. I went on to Boskuil on the train. Because I did not know the way from there to the farm where I was expected for the meeting, I was afraid that I would get lost in the dark, so I went to a hut on a farm near the Boskuil diggings and asked them to put me up for the night. My delay here caused the police to catch up with me; if I had kept walking, they might have missed me, but I was not to know that; I was sure no one had seen me leave the station and head for the diggings.

Early in the morning, the police arrived. They had been searching the diggings for me most of the night. One of them was called Marais. I could hear them talking as they came towards the hut where I was. I was certain Marais was a witch because he was so hot on my trail when the others wanted to give up. Marais kept saying he was sure I was in the neighbourhood. When they came into the hut I was still in bed; I scarcely breathed. The bed-springs were sagging and the mattress was very old and soft, so that I had sunk down deep into the middle of the bed. I had pulled the blankets neatly over my head, so they did not notice me. They went outside, but Marais came back—I am sure that man practised *litlhare*, to know where I was—and he found me this time.

He asked me what I was doing there.

'I've done nothing wrong,' I replied. 'I'm not on the diggings.'

'Yes, that's true, but you're very close to them—don't play with words. You know well that you're not allowed anywhere near here. How did you get here? Didn't you walk around by the diggings?'

Laughing, I replied, 'You didn't see me. Maybe I flew!'

He arrested me and took me to the police station at Makwassie. This was a Sunday. On Tuesday I appeared before the Magistrate. I told him I needed time to see my lawyer and was allowed bail of five pounds, which I paid. Then I went to Ottosdal to see my lawyer, Mr. De Villiers, who had defended me in the past. I was a friend of his, but this time he let me down; he would not touch my case.

At first he said he would defend me, but a week later, when I was actually waiting for him to accompany me to the court, he did not turn up. I went to his office and asked him what was going on. He said he had no choice, and could not help me. He was clearly scared. He suggested that I go to the police, because my case was due to be heard in Wolmaransstad that very day and I had made no alternative arrangements to get there.

The police took me to Wolmaransstad. Before the Magistrate—A. S. Dunlop again—I suffered this time. I based my defence on the fact that I was not actually at the diggings when I was arrested, and accordingly the court travelled to inspect exactly where I had been arrested. It was found that the farm was a little more than a mile from the diggings. None the less, the banning order stipulated that I should not go on or near any diggings, and I was found guilty. I was sentenced to six weeks' hard labour with no option of a fine.

I was released after five weeks, with one week's remission for good behaviour. I did not enjoy any part of those five weeks and do not intend to say any more about them.

After this I was often arrested again, for more trivial matters, like being in certain locations unlawfully, but I squashed these charges myself. I did not use lawyers any longer, because I was fed up with the whole fraternity; by now I was more experienced in legal matters and never went to gaol again for being a troublesome member of the I.C.U.

*   *   *

By the time I was free to address meetings again there was already strong dissension within the I.C.U. The split went back as far as the 1920s, when Clements Kadalie went overseas to attend a labour conference at Geneva. While he was in England attending various meetings to explain what the I.C.U. was, he met a man called William George Ballinger, a trade union organizer, who volunteered to come to South Africa as an adviser to the I.C.U. Kadalie assured him that he would not regret his decision; the I.C.U. had sufficient funds to pay an adviser handsomely.

Most of us only learned about this through the newspapers while Kadalie was still abroad, and we approached some of the higher officials at head office to discover whether they knew anything about this scheme. It seems they had discussed the matter with Kadalie before his departure and all had agreed on the necessity for an adviser from overseas. We made an effort to have this decision reversed and to stop Ballinger from coming out, but we were too late.

Those who were in favour of an adviser from overseas felt it would defeat the aims of the I.C.U. to recruit an adviser from among the Whites of South Africa, while those of us who opposed Ballinger's appointment did so because we felt that a South African would be best informed on our problems and therefore best equipped to advise us.

The need for having an adviser at all perhaps stemmed from the fact that rival organizations like the A.N.C. and the Communist Party were starting to boast about their white advisers. There was thus a petty feeling among some that we could score over these groups by recruiting an adviser from England, for theirs were local people.

When Kadalie returned he tried to ascertain the feeling of various branches of his movement about Ballinger by sending letters around asking for comments and views. I heard on the grapevine that most of the branches were not in favour; why not have a white South African favourable to our cause, one who knew the conditions and laws under which we lived?

When the General Secretary saw that there was opposition to his plan, he decided to hold a conference at Kimberley to thrash out the matter. I myself suspect that Kimberley was chosen as the venue with an ulterior motive: it is in the Cape, where different liquor laws prevailed from the other provinces and, as you will see, liquor had an influence on the outcome of the conference.

When, on the second or third day of the conference, the question of the adviser was raised, we were still strongly opposed, and we were in the majority. The session was then adjourned until seven o'clock in the evening; it was noon when this happened. Most of the members spent the rest of the afternoon drinking brandy.

When the conference discussion was resumed at seven that evening, within less than ten minutes nearly everybody was asleep. Some of us went around, trying to keep them awake, but when we shook a man he said, 'Yes . . . what is it? Leave me, man! Leave me . . . I'm sleeping . . . ,' or else, 'Yes, man! I'm listening!' and then, slurring, they drifted off to sleep again, quite overcome by the afternoon's brandy.

When it came to the vote, no more than thirty raised their hands against the adviser from Europe. The ones in favour of the project were crowing: 'We need a European adviser—from Europe! We need Mr Ballinger! We need Mr Ballinger!'

In the morning when the minutes were read, then things started.

Those with hangovers were aghast to learn that only thirty had voted against.

'No!' they cried loudly. 'No! Such a thing never happened! When was the vote taken?'

We told them, 'Well, we were right here, and so were you . . . . This happened between eight and nine last night. When we tried to wake you to tell you what was going on, you said we should leave you to sleep.'

This whole thing caused a lot of trouble.

Well, Ballinger came out to South Africa, but he had not been around long before he started making trouble. First he moved against the General Secretary, Kadalie, saying that he was a drunkard and a useless organizer and all that sort of thing. He said many things.

Kadalie said to him, we understand, 'I brought you here as an adviser, but now you're throwing your weight around as if you owned the movement. There is the President; you don't seem to recognize him; you never say a word to him. There is the Executive Committee; you have never said a word to them either. What is it that you're trying to do now?'

Champion, the Provincial Secretary of Natal, backed Ballinger in a move to expel Kadalie on the understanding, we thought, that Champion would take his place as General Secretary.

This quarrel was continued in Johannesburg; I was not there, but this is what I heard about it. Jo'burg, as you know, is a place where one can obtain anything at all, and where brandy is king. I understand that there was a meeting held there where most of the people had been drinking very heavily; a lot of them said that they were tired of Kadalie and that they wanted a new General Secretary.

So Kadalie was kicked out of the I.C.U., and the Provincial Secretary of the Cape, a man called Lujiza, was made acting General Secretary until the next general conference.

Feeling cheated, Champion seceded from the I.C.U. and organized the Zulu of Natal into an independent I.C.U. movement. Kadalie also retained a following that remained effective.

Consequently there were now three distinct groups. Anyone could see that what had once been a strong organization was now nothing; it had split into nothing. Still, we held on. I remained in the original I.C.U. under Lujiza, and tried to hold the Western Transvaal network together. But I am not ashamed to say that some of us were disgusted with Ballinger and saw him as the primary cause of the trouble.

He did some things which I consider downright stupid. For example, he wrote me a serious letter saying that if I wanted to follow Kadalie, I was free to get out. I replied to his letter in the strongest terms, saying, 'You have just come to the I.C.U., and I notice that you have forgotten that you were brought out here only as an adviser. You seem to have changed from an adviser to the owner of the organization; more than owner—you have become its *BAAS*. Now, as you consider yourself our *Baas*, let me tell you that you cannot control all the people. One day, if you are not aware, you'll find yourself out of South Africa without any friends here, without knowing what to say or do.'

I heard that after this letter was received at head office, Ballinger showed it to Lujiza and Joel Kokozela, the Administrative Secretary, who told him he was making a mistake in alienating branches in this way.

At this time there was a big meeting organized at Makwassie that was to have been addressed by Kadalie. Since Kadalie had broken away, they sent down someone called Solomon Crutse in his place. This chap was a Secretary from head office. When he arrived, he did not tell me what he planned to discuss at the meeting, nor did I ask him, but when he stood up to give his speech, he pulled my crumpled letter to Ballinger out of his pocket and started reading it to the gathering. The people, not fully understanding what was going on, but sensing that Crutse was involving me in a serious dispute, started shouting at him. He was howled down. People got up, muttering aloud, 'We've no time with people like you!' and 'Go! Go! Go! We don't want you here!' The meeting closed in disorder.

Crutse came back to the office with me and demanded that we hand over to him the funds that had to go to head office. This was his biggest mistake. I told him to get out.

Still, Sol Crutse was a gentleman. He went back to Kokozela and reported honestly what had happened at Makwassie, saying that the people had utterly rejected him and were solidly behind me. I still see Crutse occasionally in Maseru where he is now living. When he told Kokozela and the others all this about Makwassie, they said to him, 'Oh-oh, Crutse, it was a mistake to ask Jingoes for the money after you had tried to discredit him in public.'

Then Kokozela was sent down to see us.

At this stage head office did not know for sure whether we would break away to follow Kadalie or stick with them and the original lot under Ballinger and Lujiza, and they were more or less running around in circles, salvaging what they could.

Do you know what the poor Kokozela did? He was coming from Johannesburg by train with another fellow; they knew that the train was scheduled to arrive at Makwassie at ten o'clock at night, so they got off at Klerksdorp, so as to arrive at Makwassie the following morning in daylight. He was scared stiff to arrive in the dark. Crutse had told him, 'I don't think anyone who goes there will be accepted . . . the people are so angry . . . you'll be kicked out . . . .'

In the morning I was in the office when I saw a man coming up with another man and a woman. I thought I recognized Kokozela, but I could not understand why he should have come without letting us know in advance. When they entered the office I found it was Kokozela after all, and he told us he had come to discuss new events in the movement with us. I told him coolly that I was not prepared to discuss anything at all with him until I had gathered my committee, some of whom lived on farms outside the town.

By about three o'clock all the members of the committee had arrived. Before Kokozela could speak, one of them said to him,

'We cannot give you anything if you are here on behalf of Crutse, the fellow who was here. He told us that someone would be sent from head office to replace Jingoes.'

'Yes . . . .' Kokozela encouraged them.

'We have no time for people who want to kick out our General Secretary, Kadalie, without reasonable cause. Now we understand that you also want to chase Jingoes away from here. We have suffered a great deal together with this man, and he was the one who paved the way for the I.C.U. in this district. Now that he has set up a sound organization here, you want to move in your own people. No! We won't have it!'

Kokozela managed to placate them somewhat by saying that he did not agree fully with Kadalie's expulsion, and that all he was trying to do was to get funds for their head office to continue its work.

When the committee had left, he said to me, 'Jingoes, I must tell you the truth. Lately, after this split . . . .'

'Yes . . . ?'

'There are only five branches left now, supporting the original head office . . . .'

'*Five?*'

'We had more than two hundred branches, and of them, only five remain. This is the fifth one. This is the strongest one left. We are afraid, you know. If our organization dies, we ourselves will become nothing . . . .'

I gave Kokozela the money and he left.

It was after this that I received a letter from Ballinger telling me lots of things, like, 'If you meet hardships or temptation, remember that you are the captain of your soul. . . .'

Yes . . . 'the captain of your soul', and what else?—the 'fate' of something or other; I don't remember exactly. Ballinger and I got on better after that.

When he paid a visit to Makwassie to address the branch, there was an amusing incident in the pub before the meeting started. Apparently Ballinger was having a quiet drink at the hotel when a group of local Whites started discussing him and his visit and the I.C.U., not knowing that the man listening to them was Ballinger himself. They were saying things like, 'I wonder how a chap from Scotland can come and advise our Natives here? How can he advise people when he has never lived with them, as we have? He's obviously not qualified to be an adviser.' Anyone who knows a South African pub can imagine the conversation.

Ballinger joined in the discussion without revealing who he was, but he made little headway when trying to convince them that Ballinger was capable of advising a trade union movement. People were astonished when, to satisfy their curiosity, they attended his meeting, and discovered who it was they had been arguing with. He did quite a bit in Makwassie towards giving the white population a better idea of the aims and ideas of the I.C.U.

So Makwassie remained in the original I.C.U. under Ballinger until at last we kicked him out as well and remained with Lujiza to lead us. We wanted Kadalie to return to us, but he would not. He said that he was afraid to throw in his lot with us again because those who had remained in the original I.C.U. were the ones who had not wanted to secede with him.

*   *   *

The whole I.C.U. gradually ground to a halt because of this internal wrangling. By the time I left it, in 1937, it was a useless shadow of itself; it had lost its vitality and the tremendous sense of urgency and excitement that had drawn me to it in the first place. Its real purpose had become obscured and clouded with side-issues. It was not really that I had grown tired of it, or disillusioned; even now when I meet up with old members, we talk of nothing but the *Keaubona*. It was rather that another chapter of my life had drawn to a close; it would have been like flogging a dead horse to have stayed on.

Besides, my Chief at home, Chief Boshoane, wanted me to go back and work for him in his administration, and my ancestors were becoming insistent that I return home.

It became apparent that it was time to leave the Union.

When I was home, I received many letters from Clements Kadalie, who was then living in East London, encouraging me to start an I.C.U. in Lesotho. By then I was involved in other causes, and the idea did not tempt me.

Kadalie died in East London in November 1951. When he died, a great man and a great politician was lost to South Africa and to the Bantu.

NOTES

1. *Miesies* is an Afrikaans term approximating the English 'mistress of the house'. It is a polite form of address used by Blacks towards white women, and by Whites when referring to a woman of their own colour in the presence

of a Black. It is a 'loaded' status term. In the way in which it is used in this book, it has ironic overtones.

2. *Kaffir* derives from the Arabic *Kafir*, meaning 'infidel', and, its meaning corrupted, the word came into usage in South Africa in reference to black people. Although it is still used, it is now a term of abuse, in much the same way that 'Yid' is a derogatory way of referring to a Jew.

3. A *tickey* is a threepenny coin.

4. *Sekhametsi* means 'drawer of water'. Mr. Jingoes used aliases like this one to poke fun at some widely-held views in South Africa. Some white South Africans still believe literally that black men were created to be 'hewers of wood and drawers of water'.

5. *Skelm* is an Afrikaans word meaning 'rascal'.

6. *Volk*, an Afrikaans word generally meaning 'people', in this context means the black farm labourers and their families dependent on a white farmer.

7. *Jong* is an Afrikaans term of address used towards servants. It corresponds to the English 'boy' used in the same context.

8. *Tollie* is the Afrikaans term for a young ox.

9. A *riem* is the Afrikaans word for a thong made of hide.

CHAPTER SIX

The story of a Chieftainship

WHEN I came back to Lesotho after my years in the Union, my fate became linked with that of a Chieftainship, the Makhabane line of Mats'ekheng. The years I spent in their service coincided with a period of turbulence for the Chiefs of Lesotho, stormy events that shook the Chieftainship to its roots and left their mark on all of us, Chiefs and commoners alike. To describe my own life without describing the lives of my Chiefs would be meaningless; my whole life was bound up with theirs.

In the part about my ancestors, you will have heard that my grandfather Ngolozani was a man respected by Chiefs. To understand the position I occupied, as close adviser to a succession of Chiefs, one must go back to the past to see how Ngolozani first won the trust of those men.

* * *

Makhabane I was the full, younger brother of Chief Moshoeshoe; he lived at Ntlo-Kholo, a mountain adjacent to Moshoeshoe's Thaba Bosiu. His line has always been a powerful one in Lesotho, for they are aristocrats of royal blood.

Makhabane was killed during a raid into the Cape Colony, and we have always believed that Moshoeshoe was responsible for his brother's death, because he did nothing to help him when word came that Makhabane was surrounded by his enemies and needed reinforcements desperately. We have been told that Moshoeshoe did nothing to rescue his brother because he was jealous of him, for Makhabane was a great and popular warrior.

This is why Chief Peete referred to his people as 'orphans' before the *lekisoa* ceremony I have described.

Makhabane left a young son, Lesaoana, whose praise-name was Ramaneella, and this boy was raised by his uncle Moshoeshoe along with his own sons of his first house, Letsie, Molapo, Masupha, and Majara. As could be expected, Moshoeshoe favoured his own sons, and when they came of age, he gave them territories over which to rule while Lesaoana remained without a chiefdom. At last Lesaoana's counsellors told their young Chief that it was clear to them that Moshoeshoe did not intend to install him as a chief, and that he should leave Thaba Bosiu to carve out his own future.

Lesaoana pushed northwards, taking his followers with him, to settle to the east of Fouriesburg in what is now the Orange Free State, at Clarens, which we call 'Makalane.

I cannot say exactly how, but grandfather Ngolozani threw in his fortune with that of Lesaoana, and moved to 'Makalane with him.

You must remember that at this time in the history of our nation, the Boers were clashing with the Basotho in a battle for territory and cattle. It happened that Lesaoana was attacked by the Boers in his village at 'Makalane, and he and his people were forced to flee to a nearby cave, where they could hold the Boers off. Ngolozani was the last man to enter the cave. When he looked among the women, he noticed that the aged Chieftainess Sebina, mother of Lesaoana, his Chief, was not among them. He asked where she was and was told that she was too old to move, and they had had to abandon her in the village; it was no use: she would have to be left to die there.

'I cannot rest,' Ngolozani said, 'when I know she is not here. We might bring bad luck upon ourselves.'

He scrambled up to the village again and put the old lady on his back. The Boers had spotted him, however, and when he was returning, they started firing at him. Some yards from the cave, it is said, a bullet went through both his calves. One Motsupa, of the Bafokeng clan, rushed to help him, and he carried the Chieftainess into the cave while Ngolozani, lying on the ground, kept up a fire against the Boers. When the others were safely in the cave, he crawled back to safety himself.

There were no hospitals or white doctors at that time, but the Basotho were skilled in the use of herbs, and Ngolozani's wounds must have been treated on the spot by a *ngaka*. He walked with sticks for the rest of his life, but his legs were saved.

On this day Ngolozani made a name for himself, a name that

brought honour to his descendants as well, and secured them the
favour of the Makhabane Chieftainship.

Ngolozani is an arrow in flight,
You cannot eat him.
The boy who had only a first name
When he should have been known to the people
As one of a great clan.
He is Baqetene, The-one-who-finishes-people.
He is known by the Boers who are west of Qeme;
Even at 'Makalane, the Boers know Ngolozani.
You Basotho, especially you, Lesaoana,
You do astonishing things:
You abandoned Chieftainess Sebina,
Your mother,
In the village.
Mhlabase's brother ran like a bullet from a gun
When he went to rescue Sebina.
Chieftainess Sebina! When you come to praise your people,
When you praise, say first the name
Of the one who says, 'Let them kill each other!'
About bulls.
Do not forget to praise also the Mosotho
Known as Motsupa.
A Boer warrior shot the legs of Baqetene
While Baqetene was carrying Sebina on his back,
Sebina, Chieftainess of the Mats'ekha.

While they were pinned in the cave, Lesaoana sent a message for
help to Moshoeshoe, who sent back word that he himself was surrounded by Boers and fighting for his life; Lesaoana was on his own.
His cousin Masupha wanted to go to Lesaoana's assistance, but he
was called upon to help his father. At last word was got to Lethole,
Chief of the Makhoakhoa tribe, who broke the Boers' siege and
allowed Lesaoana and his followers to slip out of their cave and make
for safety.

After the skirmish the Boers were still pushing him hard, so
Lesaoana crossed back over the Caledon River, heading for his
father's stronghold at Ntlo-Kholo. When night fell, the party had
reached Koeneng, where one of his advisers told Lesaoana to stop
and speak to his ancestors.

In the morning, Lesaoana told his people, 'My ancestors told
me not to be vengeful and not to repay evil with evil, but to be just.
My uncle Moshoeshoe did not rescue my father; he did not rescue

us. But Moshoeshoe is now surrounded by Boers, and I must go to his assistance.

'I know that you are tired, my people, but the men and boys must push on with me while the women and children remain here.'

He turned to Ngolozani and said, 'You, old man, are lame, wounded in the leg. Return to the Caledon River and stay there; send word to me at once if the Boers cross the river.'

On his Chief's instructions, then, Ngolozani went to settle at the place west of Ficksburg known as Maholiallang, which means 'where the pied starlings cry'.

* * *

At Maholiallang, Ngolozani became known among the Chiefs across the river, because he helped protect them from the Boers. In those days the Basotho would sally out across the Caledon into Boer territory, raid their cattle and then flee back to the safety of the mountains across the river. Ngolozani was often involved in the furore that followed these raids, for the Chiefs would contrive to cross the river near Ngolozani's village. Then when the Boers followed their cattle tracks to the banks of the Caledon, Ngolozani would confront them and ask what they were after, pointing out that they were about to enter the territory of the Basotho. When the Boers showed him the tracks of their cattle, that they wanted to follow across the river, Ngolozani would explain to them that cattle came down to the river to drink, and that the tracks they were pointing out to him were made by Chief Molapo's cattle, for by then Chief Molapo was living in Leribe. The Boers always turned back then, convinced by the reasonable old man.

Chief Masupha was a famous raider, and his descendants have always liked and remembered my family because of Ngolozani's protection and aid.

It is said that when Chief Masupha had crossed over the Caledon and the Phuthiatsana Rivers, going to his home, he would always stop at the place that has since been named Sebalabala, which means 'counting place', to divide up his spoils. He would send a few head of cattle to his father Moshoeshoe and some to his brothers Letsie and Molapo. With these cattle he would send the following message: 'Tell them that their servant is back from the hunt.'

* * *

Lesaoana and his son Peete, who was then a youth, fought bravely to relieve Moshoeshoe at Thaba Bosiu while their womenfolk waited for them at Koeneng, and in gratitude Moshoeshoe allocated the area of Koeneng and Mapoteng to Lesaoana as his chiefdom.

Before he did this, Moshoeshoe summoned Molapo and Masupha and, in the presence of their older brother, Letsie, who would one day be Paramount Chief, he discussed the allocation with them, for each would have to surrender a portion of his territory in order to give Lesaoana his ward. Although the two were not overjoyed, they consented, as Lesaoana had been so brave at Thaba Bosiu.

I have heard it said that Moshoeshoe used the following words, 'You two are already installed. Because my brother's son has been driven from 'Makalane by the Boers, I will take a certain portion from each of your areas so as to install Lesaoana as a Chief in his own right. Had it not been for him, we would, all of us, have died on top of Thaba Bosiu.'

Letsie then said, 'Take not a small portion from each of my brothers, my father, but a *portion*. We have been treating Lesaoana badly, but he did not look for revenge.'

Although he consented at last, Molapo warned his father that disputes might well arise out of this installation and allocation of land. He was right: the Masupha and Makhabane Chieftainships are even now fighting about boundaries.

After years of discord, some sort of peace was established by the British between Moshoeshoe and the Boers, and the official boundary between them was fixed at the Caledon River.

Then Ngolozani was free to end his vigil at Maholiallang and rejoin his Chief. He moved first to Makhobalo's, near Koeneng itself, but when he found that this place lacked sufficient ironstone for him to ply his trade as a smith, he moved to the village of Tsokung, where he lived out his days, and where I was born.

* * *

When Ngolozani moved to Tsokung there was nothing there but bare veld, with only one or two scattered households. Chief Peete, son of Lesaoana, had asked Ngolozani to go there as headman, to protect his boundary (the Futhong stream mentioned in descriptions of my childhood).

Ngolozani was honoured by his Chief's offer of a headmanship, 'But', he said, 'I am old now, as you will agree. The administration of a village needs a person who can move about freely, on horseback or on foot. You know, my Chief, that I am a cripple who cannot keep moving about, even on your orders. Please take Sotshangani, my friend, to be your headman there. I will accompany him to live there, and I will advise him to the best of my ability. This I will do, Chief.'

Chief Lesaoana was still alive then, and he gave his consent to this arrangement, but he reminded Sotshangani, 'You were picked by the Chief to be Ngolozani's adviser; it was Ngolozani himself who asked for you to be made headman in his place. You must respect him always, and listen well to all the advice he gives you.'

The arrangement worked well, even in my father's days, with Sotshangani and his descendants ruling Tsokung as a whole, and Ngolozani and his descendants ruling their own village within Tsokung, but in my time Sotshangani's descendants resented that they had been given the headmanship at second hand, as it were, and made trouble for us whenever they could.

*   *   *

Even though we did not accept a headmanship, the Chiefs honoured our family in other ways, and this honour stemmed mostly from Ngolozani's great skill in the working of iron. He was widely known as a man who could make spears, hoes, gunpowder, and ammunition for guns; I have even seen a gun he constructed. He also made the brass rings that warriors wore in battle to deflect stabs to the throat. A man of this trade was valuable to Chiefs, and Ngolozani was one of the few smiths living in that area of Lesotho.

In some ways the old man was strange, because he did not pass his knowledge on: none of his sons took over his work or acquired his skills. When Lesaoana or Peete sent men to study under him, Ngolozani would discourage them. Whenever people crowded around his forge to watch him, he would stop working. It is said that Chief Molapo and Chief Masupha tried to send some of their own subjects to learn from Ngolozani, but Lesaoana refused to allow this and told Ngolozani not to teach them.

'You know well', he said, 'that the two Chiefs Molapo and Masupha are my enemies. I have fought them in battle several times about land. Now they are sending men here to learn things to increase their strength so that they might invade me by means of things they had learned from my own man. I forbid you to instruct these men. I do not want', he concluded, 'to be killed by my own sticks, or my people to be killed by their own sticks.'

Ngolozani obeyed his Chief's orders. Lesaoana also refused to allow one of the Paramount Chief's men to learn from Ngolozani, fearing that his knowledge would be passed on to his enemies.

I have heard, too, that my grandfather Ngolozani was a strong *ngaka* who could make deadly spears. I have seen some of them. One type of spear he made is called a *koebe*; it is barbed. When such a spear is praised, it is called 'the feather of a quail that rips tatters' because of its light balance and its deadly barbs that will tear a man's flesh.

Some men would ask for a spear that had been treated with special *litlhare*, and they would pay a goat for it. I understand that if you were stabbed with this type of spear you became paralysed. Many people desired these spears, and so the old man grew rich.

I heard these stories from uncle Maguqu and cousin Chabeli. Chabeli, himself a *ngaka*, told me that he had tried to get my grandfather to tell him what type of *litlhare* he used to fortify his spears. Ngolozani would always say to him, 'My child, you are still too young, and so I cannot teach you about this mixture. I say this because you youngsters are always fighting. Once I teach you this type of *litlhare*, you might use it on your sticks, and that would cause trouble for you because people would call you a witch.'

Another *ngaka* in our family, Malambule, also tried to learn the secret of this *litlhare*, and he was told, 'Your heart is bad: if you know things like this you will witch people.'

To my great regret, I myself know very little about this *litlhare*; all I know is that the spear tip need be treated with it only once, the metal being left in the infusion of herbs for one day. Then Ngolozani would say that the *litlhare* had penetrated the metal, and would never need to be renewed. I know also that the words he intoned when working the spear were, 'Please work and injure the one who fights me . . . .'

When I was a small child, I used to see my grandfather fashioning iron, but I was very small indeed then, and I do not remember the things about his trade that I should like to know now. I used to see him sitting down with a bellows made of hide with sticks fitted to serve as handles; in the front, a horn was fixed into the hide as a nozzle. The two handles were pumped alternately to keep a constant flow of air. He used a type of sedge called *motolo*[1] for coal; the roots of this plant are slow burning and give off great heat.

Our family believes that Ngolozani's skills aggravated the dissension already existing among the three chiefdoms of Makhabane,

Masupha, and Molapo. You will recall that when Lesaoana was given his ward, Molapo warned his father that there would be trouble. Their chiefdoms were then fairly recently established, and they were starting to test each other's strength and boundaries; there were many arguments and many battles. Moreover, each of the Chiefs was trying to recruit to his area men who were specialized in certain trades which would help them get firmly established.

Ngolozani had already helped Masupha and served him well in the matter of the cattle stolen from the Boers, and Masupha tried hard to lure Ngolozani to his area; he would be gaining an astute man, whose many sons were brave warriors, and who had skill in his hands.

This dispute, of which Ngolozani was one of the causes, resulted in our bloodiest battle with Masupha's. This is what happened.

*   *   *

One day Masupha asked Lesaoana to let him have Ngolozani as a subject. Lesaoana refused curtly, and they grew heated. Finally Masupha told Lesaoana he was an arrogant fellow.

'You instructed your son Peete to violate my boundaries,' he said. 'You're trying to provoke a quarrel with me . . . .' Lesaoana knew he had done no such thing, but this was a grave accusation, so he summoned Peete at once and repeated to him the allegation Masupha had made. Peete replied that he had never in any way failed to respect their common boundary, and since Masupha could produce no proof to back up his statement, he had to be satisfied with Peete's assurances.

Some weeks later, however, Masupha summoned his son, Lepoqo, who had been placed at MaMathe's, and together they planned a strategy whereby they could provoke a showdown with Lesaoana. They placed Moeketsi, a son of Masupha in a junior house, at Menyetleng in Mapoteng, that is, in Peete's territory. This Moeketsi was a famous warrior.

If Peete ignored Moeketsi's presence, Masupha would gain land to extend his territory; if, on the other hand, Peete chose to come to blows about Moeketsi, Masupha could gain terrific prestige by defeating him.

This sort of strategy is still used today by Chiefs and headmen who are trying to extend their areas; they allocate lands to their own subjects within a neighbouring headman's area and wait for him to charge them in court, where the battles are fought today.

When Lesaoana learned that Moeketsi had settled at Menyetleng, he knew that his strength was being tested; if he backed down he would become a laughing-stock and Masupha would continue his encroachments, so he ordered Peete to drive Moeketsi out.

Peete sent word to Masupha, remonstrating with him, but Masupha replied that Moeketsi had every right to Mapoteng, and that it was Peete who was the intruder there, for the land belonged to the Masupha Chieftainship. He was turning against the agreement that had been drawn up by Chief Moshoeshoe, and not living up to the words he had spoken at that time.

Battle followed. Chief Peete and his brother Seshophe defeated Lepoqo and Moeketsi that day, burning Moeketsi's village and sjambokking their men like boys. Ngolozani himself was too old to fight in that battle, but his two sons, Maguqu and Makhuba, were there that day.

When Lepoqo and Moeketsi were defeated, they went to report to their father Masupha, telling him, 'Your brother's sons have thrashed us . . . .'

'Did you think you'd be fighting nothing, you people?' retorted Masupha. 'Those are superb fighters—they break people's heads. You can do nothing to them. I'll go for them myself.'

After this Masupha did not leave matters to his sons; he planned to handle Lesaoana and Peete himself. He sent word to Chief Jonathan, the son of his brother Molapo, that he was planning a raid on Mats'ekheng, and that he did not want to travel there along the direct, and therefore expected, route. To take them by surprise, he would make a detour through Jonathan's territory and come upon them from the north-west; he asked Jonathan to grant his men safe and secret passage. In addition, he said, he would be returning after the battle with Ngolozani, who had helped him against the Boers and whom he claimed as his subject.

Jonathan sent back the message that Masupha's men were free to cross his land, but that he himself wanted Ngolozani as payment for their safe passage. He told Masupha that although Ngolozani had called himself a subject of Lesaoana while he lived at Maholial-lang, that place was, in effect, in Molapo's territory at that time, and therefore Ngolozani belonged to the Molapo's.

The raid went off as planned, with Masupha and his army taking Lesaoana by surprise in the middle of the night. Many of our people were killed there. Lesaoana could not turn to Molapo's for protection because Masupha had struck from Molapo's area and had obviously arranged an alliance with him, so he turned and fled to Mapoteng, Peete's village.

Masupha broke through into Seshophe's area, burning villages as he went, and at last crossed the Futhong, heading for Tsokung, to capture Ngolozani. He was leading one spearhead of warriors. The other, under Lepoqo, went on to Mapoteng, to Peete's village. They burnt that village and killed Chief Ramakoro, Lesaoana's son. This was their cruellest blow.

But Chief Lesaoana had not forgotten Ngolozani, his prized smith. Amidst the havoc of battle he sent three of his toughest warriors to guard Ngolozani. They were: Mabonte Madlikivani, a tall, black man; Mbhambho Mabaso; and Siphinga Masimini. Each took up his position in the rocks surrounding Ngolozani's village, forming a rough triangle, with the old man's house at the centre. Ngolozani himself was not idle: in the deserted village he prepared powder and shot which was carried to the three men by two plucky little girls acting as runners. The children, women, and old people of the village, together with the village cattle, were concealed in some caves nearby.

When Masupha reached Qoboloto's village, the three men opened fire; four of Masupha's men dropped there, and seven of his horses were killed.

'No!' cried Masupha. 'You told me there was only one old man living on that rock; yet there is a good-sized group there, of very brave men. That place is too dangerous. If we go for Ngolozani today, we'll be killed.'

He signalled to his men to turn their horses, and they retreated back down the slope, driven on by Ngolozani's bullets which his three defenders sent after them. One of Masupha's men turned around in his saddle and yelled, 'Ngolozani! *Ngolozani*! The Chief says we'll come to fetch you one day, and on that day we'll take you!'

The veterans of Lesaoana's army were the Maanya, the companions of Chief Makhabane I. They gathered at Mapoteng together with the Litlhakola, as Chief Peete's companions were called. We are told that the slaying of Chief Ramakoro, the young brother of Peete and son of Lesaoana, made them mad with grief. They buried Chief Ramakoro, and then they called Lesaoana's regiment, the Mats'ekha, to make their plans of battle.

'We cannot be killed like flies,' they cried. 'We ought to die like men today.'

Their plan was ingenious.

Ntate Semema Marabe (the man who had attended school with my uncle Maguqu) was ordered to ride out to cut across the path of Masupha's army, which they could see gathering between them and Tsokung, for Lepoqo had joined his father to make a final attack. *Ntate* Semema was given a plaited grass thong that had been smeared with *litlhare* and made potent; this thong would lure Masupha into an ambush. Acting as a decoy, *Ntate* Semema rode out, dragging his thong along the ground behind his horse. Masupha's men would follow him, enticed by the *litlhare* on the thong which would mislead their minds and make them vulnerable.

When *Ntate* Semema rode out on his dangerous mission, the Mats'ekha, Litlhakola, and Maanya started preparing their ambush. They built a low stone wall, leaving a gap in the middle, in a narrow pass through which Masupha's men would have to pass if the *litlhare* on the thong brought them. They hid their horses down behind a hill and lay down as still as lizards behind the wall with their weapons ready.

Ntate Semema doubled back towards the defile with Masupha's men sniffing at his trail. The plan worked. As the Masupha's strung out to pass through the gap, they ran into a rain of bullets and spears, suffering utter defeat.

We sing of that day:

> Masupha, you and your sons
> Have killed Ramakoro,
> And burnt Peete's village.
> What did you think the Maanya would do?
> What did you think the Mats'ekha would do?
> The Litlhakola are mad
> At the burning of MaLoela's *lelapa*.
> Peete, your people changed
> To become lizards at the wall;
> They killed the people
> Of Masupha cruelly.
> Ramakoro's single head
> Was repaid with many.

Chief Lesaoana, our great Ramaneella, died not long after this battle, on 14 August 1888; it is said that he sickened because so many of his people were killed.

* * *

If anyone thinks I am telling tales about the worth of my grandfather, listen to this.

6

One day here at MaMathe's village where I live today, I was sitting in the hot sun outside the court of Chieftainess MaMathe when Chief Moorosana Masupha arrived in front of the packed courthouse. Moorosana, who died in 1971, was the last surviving son of Chief Masupha I; when he died, he was over one hundred years old.

'MaMathe! *MaMathe*!' he shouted for the Chieftainess.

'Grandfather . . . ?' she replied.

'I am thankful to you, my child. My father wanted to get Ngolozani, but he failed. Today, although—how sad it is!—there are no more wars among us, still we do battle with our tongues.

'You, who are now the Chief of Masupha's, have succeeded in capturing one of Ngolozani's grandsons. You have Jingoes here now as an adviser. Please hold him fast. He makes weapons with words like his grandfather made spears. Don't let him go back to Mats'ekheng again. We all know that there were battles between Masupha my father and Lesaoana. I know my father was fighting only for Ngolozani, because Ngolozani was a smith who could make good weapons.'

> What are Masupha and Lesaoana fighting for?
> They are fighting over The-one-who-separates-bulls,
> The son of Jingoes.
> Tsokung's men are adamant;
> They say, 'Chief Masupha, you cannot
> 'Make Ngolozani your prey—
> 'He is not an animal!'
> Tsókung's men are Mbhambho of Mabaso,
> Siphinga of Masimini,
> And Mabonte of Madlikivani.
> These men will not relinquish Ngolozani.
> They say, 'If Ngolozani is taken by Masupha,
> 'Where shall we get bullets?'
> You people of Ngoyiyana,
> People of Ngolozani's wife, you rejoice:
> Your daughter NoMadlozi's husband
> Knows how to dance in war,
> And yet he is an old man.
> Hold fast to your spears and your guns,
> Because Chief Masupha is now angry.
> We have no more Ramakoro Lesaoana. . . .
> Masupha has killed him. . . .

*   *   *

My grandfather Ngolozani, then, was mainly associated with Chief Lesaoana and with his son, Chief Peete. My father was born the same year as Chief Mitchell, the son of Chief Peete, and became one of his advisers when Mitchell came of age and started to rule his own area as a Chief under his father the Principal Chief.

I myself was the contemporary of Chief Boshoane, Chief Mitchell's first son; he was my true friend, and we never quarrelled until the day he died. It was through Chief Boshoane that I, in turn, like my father and his father before him, came to serve the Chieftainship of Mats'ekheng.

We were born on the same day, Boshoane and I, within a few hours of each other. This I learned from MaBoshoane, his mother, when I was ten, when my father Makhuba went to pay his respects to her and took me with him to show her his first-born.

'Yes,' Chieftainess MaBoshoane said to him, 'I know this boy. I know the day he was born, for that was the day of Boshoane's birth. I remember well the day, ten years ago, when you sent a report to Mapoteng, to tell Chief Peete of the birth of your son; it was afternoon, and it was then that Boshoane was born.

'My father-in-law, Chief Peete, said that day, "Boshoane has now found his *letona*, his right hand. From today you must all know that Makhuba's son, Stimela, will be Boshoane's *letona*. Wherever Boshoane goes, he will be accompanied by this boy. Tell Ngolozani I am pleased about the birth of his grandson."'

That was how Boshoane and I were brought together.

I grew up with Chief Boshoane, and accompanied him every-where in his youth, just as Chief Peete had said the day we were born. Boshoane was a Chief and so, from an early age, I came to know the tensions and intrigues that beset a Chieftainship.

* * *

Succession to the Chieftainship is a terrible thing in Lesotho: it causes hatred and violent disputes. The law says that the first son of the first wife is heir to his father, but in reality this is a legal fiction, because so many successions are disputed by claimants.

When Boshoane and I were boys, the Principal Chief was Chief Peete, who lived at Mapoteng with his second wife, Chieftainess MaLoela, whose son, Mitchell, was heir to the Principal Chieftain-ship.

Chief Mitchell's second son, Nkuebe, was born about six years after his brother Boshoane. By the time Boshoane and I were young boys, there was already speculation about which one of them would succeed his father.

Boshoane and Nkuebe were brought up together with another young Prince; this was Gabashane Masupha, son of Chief Masupha II and MaNkhabe, daughter of Chief Peete and Chieftainess MaLoela. At the age of about four, Gabashane was sent to his maternal grandparents to be reared.

These three young Chiefs spent their early years together with their grandmother, Chieftainess MaLoela, and I spent months at a time with them at her *lelapa* at Mapoteng. Each of them had his own companions, boys picked by his parents from the families of commoners who had the confidence of the Chiefs.

Chieftainess MaLoela was the daughter of Chief Letsie I, the son of Moshoeshoe, and she was very conscious of her royal blood, always going on about how things were done at Matsieng, the place of the Paramount Chief.

But Boshoane's mother was a Mofokeng, a commoner, and this caused MaLoela to hate the boy. She made up her mind that Boshoane, because of his mother, would not succeed to the Principal Chieftainship.

Nkuebe's mother, on the other hand, was the daughter of Chief Joel Molapo and a great-granddaughter of Moshoeshoe, and was thus of royal blood. MaLoela, the old aristocrat, determined that it would be Nkuebe who would succeed his father instead of Boshoane. To her, blood was all.

MaLoela, in a way, was merely following a precedent that her own life had set: she herself was not the first wife of Chief Peete. His first wife, MaLeeto, was a commoner, and although she bore Chief Peete a son, Leeto, this boy never had the chance to rule. It was Mitchell, born of the daughter of Paramount Chief Letsie, MaLoela herself, who took Leeto's place and whose descendants would always rule Mats'ekheng.

This made life very difficult for Boshoane in Chieftainess MaLoela's *lelapa*. Nkuebe was treated like a prince by his grandmother, and by her actions MaLoela made it clear to Boshoane that she considered him of commoner stuff than Nkuebe. Gabashane was also given precedence over Boshoane, because he would succeed his father one day as the Principal Chief of Masupha's ward. Boshoane was treated harshly. He was given the least food, for example, and this humiliated him because the sons of Chiefs are expected to feed their companions from their own food, and he never had enough to give us a meal fit for the companions of a future Chief. It was always made clear to him at his grandmother's place that, although he was Chief Mitchell's first-born son, it was Nkuebe who would rule one day, because of his mother's ancestry.

Chief Peete, his grandfather, however, was a kindly man; he noticed that Boshoane was lonely and unhappy in MaLoela's *lelapa*, and so he sent him to a place called Thaba Ntlenyane, where the late Chief Lesaoana had once lived. There, he put him in the care of some trusted people. Chief Peete had good reason for doing this: he had noticed how his wife, MaLoela, was treating the boy, and it had become obvious to him that MaLoela did not want Boshoane to succeed Mitchell. Chief Peete *did* want Boshoane to be Principal Chief one day, and he wanted him to be brought up as a Chief, not to have his confidence knocked out of him at an early age by his grandmother; he knew Boshoane would not be a good Chief if he doubted that his claim to the Chieftainship was a valid one.

It was soon after Boshoane moved to Thaba Ntlenyane that an incident occurred which revealed some of the tension that was inherent in the Makhabane Chieftainship, and indicated a pattern to the events that were to follow.

* * *

Although MaLoela did not make him welcome, Boshoane was obliged from time to time to visit his grandparents, Chief Peete and Chieftainess MaLoela, at Mapoteng. It was during one such visit that MaLoela lost patience with Boshoane over some trivial matter— I do not recall now how it started—and snapped at him.

'It seems to me', she said, 'that you are just like your father, Mitchell: badly brought up. One day you will defy your father, just as he once defied his father. You Mats'ekheng children are undisciplined and bad-tempered. Why aren't you like Nkuebe? He does not behave as you do.'

Boshoane was used to being scolded, but never before had he been insulted like this: he had never heard of his father having defied Chief Peete before, and imagined horrible things. We ran outside, Boshoane close to tears with humiliation.

'What does she mean?' he asked me.

Although I was fascinated even then by court cases and disputes within the Chieftainship, and gathered information whenever I could, I could not enlighten my friend; I had never heard of the incident when Chief Mitchell defied his father, but it had obviously left a very bad impression on his mother, MaLoela.

'I *must* know . . . .' Boshoane said to me.

So we set off at once for Bela-Bela, where Chief Mitchell lived, to ask him. It was late afternoon when we arrived at Tsokung, which was on our way, and we decided to spend the night there, and to ask my father what Chieftainess MaLoela had meant.

Boshoane plunged straight in: '*Ntate* Makhuba, don't think me insolent . . . . Why does my grandmother MaLoela hate me so much?'

'Why do you ask that?' my father asked slowly.

Boshoane told him what his grandmother had said to him.

To his eternal credit, my father spoke to Boshoane as an adult, and did not try to fob him off with half-truths.

'I'm sorry,' he said, 'but I cannot give you an answer now. I might be able to tell you tomorrow. Although I was preparing to go elsewhere, I will stay here and see to it that I reply to you in the presence of the Chief, your father.'

The following morning my father took us to Bela-Bela, where we found Chief Mitchell on the point of leaving the village. My father told the Chief that our business was important, so we went into the *lelapa* and my father told Chief Mitchell about Boshoane's question to him, and related all we had told him.

The Chief was silent for a long while, but seeing Boshoane weeping, he said at last, 'Boshoane . . . my son . . . I wish you did not have to keep going to visit your grandparents, because you always return from there unhappy; yet the custom exists, and so we have no choice.

'What your grandmother was referring to was this. I was once involved in a dispute with headman Makhetha, because your mother's brother, Matjeketa, wanted to have an area of his own to rule as headman. To give him such an area, I decided to deprive headman Makhetha of some of his land. My father Peete overruled my decision in his court, and upheld the appeal Makhetha had brought before him. Against the advice of Makhuba here, the father of your companion, I wanted to help Matjeketa fight his case in the Paramount Chief's court, but my mother, MaLoela, stopped me by telling me that if I did that, I would be defying my own father.

'I did not realize that this case made such an impression on her and that there is still rancour in her heart because of it. I was not really trying to defy my father, you must understand; I acted as I thought right. . . .

'I cannot continue with this now—it upsets me. Go back to Thaba Ntlenyane, and try to put it out of your mind.'

Chieftainess MaMpoi, the first wife of Chief Mitchell, intervened at this point. As the senior wife of Chief Mitchell, Chieftainess MaMpoi had considerable influence over Chieftainship affairs. She herself had borne only a daughter, so none of her offspring was directly involved in the competition for the Principal Chieftainship, but her word would have to be taken into account in any quarrel about the succession if she chose to make a stand. It was at this moment that she made her stand.

'Whose child is this?' she asked her husband, looking at Boshoane.

'He is my child,' he replied.

'Who is the mother of this child?' She was weeping. All of us were weeping.

'You are my first wife; he is your child as much as mine.'

'Then why do you say he must return to Thaba Ntlenyane?'

'Because my father, Chief Peete, instructed me to send him there. . . .'

'Are you happy with the way Chieftainess MaLoela spoke to this child? Don't you see that words like that will distort the mind of this boy, who is my child now?'

By doing this, Chieftainess MaMpoi was showing, publicly, that she was taking Boshoane under her wing, into the first *lelapa* of Chief Mitchell. Her action would tell everyone that she considered Boshoane to be Mitchell's successor and heir. Although she had not given birth to Boshoane—his actual mother was MaBoshoane—she was extending to him the status and protection accorded to a son born to a Chief in his first house.

Then Chieftainess MaMpoi turned to Boshoane.

'Boshoane. . . .'

'Mother?'

'Boshoane, my son . . . you will stay here with me. I would not like to hear again the words my mother-in-law, Chieftainess MaLoela, used against you. My Chief, as your wife, I ask you to instruct men to go and report to Chief Peete, to ask his permission for Boshoane to live in my *lelapa*. I don't want him to be brought up by anyone else. I know he must be trained by men, but he will get food from my hands.'

MaLoela was very angry and dismayed when she heard that

Boshoane was living at MaMpoi's *lelapa* and she sent her message forthwith: she had not realized, she said, that MaMpoi despised Nkuebe, and she was surprised that MaMpoi would slight Nkuebe publicly by favouring Boshoane with her protection. She thought MaMpoi ought to be reminded that Boshoane would never be Chief after the death of his father, Chief Mitchell, because his mother, MaBoshoane, was a commoner.

Chief Peete realized that, once he and his son Mitchell passed away, there would be a terrific dispute about who would succeed Chief Mitchell. He did not want this to happen because conflict of that kind usually rives a Chieftainship into opposing factions whose rancour takes a long time to die down. Accordingly, he decided to make a public announcement, a sort of verbal will, stating without equivocation whom he wanted to succeed to the Principal Chieftainship after his son's death. Such a will would discourage competition for the Chieftainship and, in the event that a dispute should, after all, develop, his will would have to be taken into account by the hearers of the dispute.

It was at this time, when Boshoane was about eleven years old, that his own mother, MaBoshoane, died. Her funeral at Mapoteng was attended by people from all over Mats'ekheng, and by most of the Sons of Makhabane.[2] A funeral is an important event because its ceremony is conducted with strict attention to custom and rank. At a ceremony of this kind, to give an example, junior brothers cannot precede their seniors. Everyone was watching with keen interest to see who would take precedence, Boshoane or Nkuebe.

It was at this funeral that Chief Peete chose to make his will known.

When all the speeches at the graveside were over, he called one of his men to bring Boshoane to him. Lifting the young boy high above his head, Chief Peete said in a voice that carried to the farthest person in the crowd, 'Do you all see this young boy? This boy is Boshoane. *He is my heir.*'

There was movement in the crowd.

'He will rule', concluded Chief Peete, 'after my son's death.'

When I heard this story after the funeral, I was proud and moved. My best friend would become my Principal Chief, one day.

*   *   *

Boshoane and Nkuebe were still boys, and the position they

wanted to succeed to was one of wealth and power; it was inevitable that there should be bad feeling between them because of this. But neither of them showed it openly, for both were reasonable and generous by nature and, besides, they were most often accompanied by a company of men specially appointed to look after them and rear them. These men would not have tolerated cheap behaviour from two young Princes.

But there were covert ways in which they could compete for dominance, and one of these was to create situations in which their companions would have to choose between them. This made life difficult for me. I loved them both, and I hated having to chagrin the one by choosing the other. They would do things like this. Each would say he was going somewhere on a certain day, and each would ask me to accompany him.

At first, my choice was easy: I was Boshoane's *letona*, appointed by Chief Peete on the day of our birth, and so I always accompanied him.

Then it happened when they were older that, according to custom, Nkuebe was given a village of his own where he could live, and which he could rule, if he chose. He was given Tsokung, where I was living then.

Nkuebe decided not to live in Tsokung, but he stabled his horses in our stable and I was given the task of caring for them. Whenever Nkuebe went anywhere, he had to be accompanied by the headman of Tsokung and by me as well.

* * *

Chief Peete died at Mapoteng in July 1921; he was buried at Thaba Bosiu. His son, Chief Mitchell, succeeded him as the Principal Chief of Mats'ekheng, destined to rule for less than one year.

Chief Mitchell was as anxious as his father before him to ensure that no internecine conflict followed his death, and he determined to name his successor. He was aware that, despite the law of first sons of first houses being heir to their father, it was not the custom in the past for Chiefs' sons born of commoners to rule, even if they *were* first sons of first houses. Customs of this kind have more force when applied to Chiefs than to commoners, and so Chief Mitchell knew that, whatever the law said, and despite what Chief Peete had said at MaBoshoane's funeral, few people at Mats'ekheng had any doubt that Nkuebe and not Boshoane would succeed his father.

The most Chief Mitchell could do was to make it clear at a large gathering that Boshoane was his heir.

This he did at Leribe, where he attended a gathering of most of the Chiefs of Lesotho. With him were his two sons, Boshoane and Nkuebe; I accompanied them, together with the Chief's retinue.

When food was served at the gathering, Chief Mitchell, in front of everybody, called Boshoane first to receive his meal; then he called Nkuebe. This was a symbolic act that could not be overlooked by anyone present, and its meaning was clear to all: Boshoane was Chief Mitchell's heir.

*   *   *

Chief Mitchell died at Koeneng on 24 July 1922.

This was the moment of crisis, the time that had been anticipated years before, the decision for which the Chieftainship had been paving the way. All that had gone before was so much background: MaLoela's favouring of Nkuebe as a tiny child; MaMpoi's symbolic adoption of the child Boshoane; Peete's 'He is my heir' at the funeral; Mitchell's placing Boshoane before Nkuebe; behind it all, the silent figure of MaBoshoane, mother of the Chief's first son, herself born of commoners.

Now the old procedure would take its course: first the Sons of Makhabane would make their decision; then their choice would have to be endorsed by the Paramount Chief.

It is customary, when an important Chief dies, to report his death to the Paramount Chief with what we call hloho, which means 'a head', represented by a certain number of cattle, and, at the same time, to present to the Paramount Chief the heir of the deceased.

The Sons of Makhabane must have realized that they themselves would not easily reach agreement on who would succeed Chief Mitchell, and so they tried to evade the issue by leaving the decision in the hands of Paramount Chief Griffith.

Chieftainess MaMpoi, as the senior widow of Chief Mitchell, and Chief Seshophe, as the oldest surviving male of the Makhabane line, went to Matsieng to report with hloho of five head of cattle. They took both Boshoane and Nkuebe with them.

Chief Seshophe said, before Paramount Chief Griffith, 'Your Chief Mitchell has passed away, and he has left two eggs,' referring to the two young men. 'It will be for you, our Chief, to decide who is the heir of Chief Mitchell.'

Chieftainess MaLoela, however, had not been satisfied to leave the decision entirely up to the Paramount Chief. She and her ally, Chief Nkutu, wanted to be sure that Nkuebe's name was mentioned as their choice. So they sent two representatives to the Paramount Chief, to arrive at the same time as Chieftainess MaMpoi and Chief Seshophe.

These two men waited until Chief Seshophe had spoken, and then they, in turn, reported the death of Chief Mitchell and gave Chieftainess MaLoela's message: 'He has left two sons, but according to our custom, we bring you the name of Nkuebe'.

Before Paramount Chief Griffith could reply to either group, Chief Hlajoane, the son of Chief Seshophe, stood up.

'My Chief,' he said, 'I am a *letona* at Mats'ekheng, and I always give advice in matters affecting the Chieftainship. I am astonished that members of our family have brought such a matter before you without having come to a definite decision at home. I have not been consulted yet about the succession; the Sons of Makhabane have not been summoned to sit together and decide who will accede to Chief Mitchell's position. I am lodging a protest about the way this matter has been laid before you, my Chief.'

Paramount Chief Griffith then sent them back to Mats'ekheng to sit together and reach a decision; on a date he mentioned they should come before him again so that he could hear what they had decided, and on that date he would give them his own views on the Makhabane succession.

Although the Sons of Makhabane met, no clear-cut decision could be reached at home. They only agreed on one point, that each side should prepare its case and present its views before the Paramount Chief, whose decision they would all accept as final.

I was a teacher at that time, and all this happened during the school holidays. Both Boshoane and Nkuebe sent for me in turn and asked me to attend the case that was to be heard by the Paramount Chief. I was not prepared to have to choose between my two friends in public by attending the case with either one of them, so I made the excuse that I would have to be back at school on the date the case was to be heard.

On the appointed day there was a great dispute before the Paramount Chief. MaLoela led the group supporting Nkuebe, and she based her case on the fact that Nkuebe's mother was the daughter of Chief Joel Molapo and was thus of royal stock. Chieftainess MaMpoi and her party rested their case on the fact that both

Chief Peete and Chief Mitchell had named Boshoane as his heir and that he was, after all, the first-born son of Chief Mitchell.

The Paramount Chief's court found it very difficult to choose between law and custom, and so it gave an open decision:

'Nkuebe, you must know that Boshoane is the son of Chief Mitchell; you ought to consult him in whatever you do. Boshoane, remember that Nkuebe is the son of Chief Mitchell, born of the daughter of Chief Joel.'

Both parties appealed against this noncommittal judgment. Their appeal went before the court of the District Commissioner of Teyateyaneng, a Mr. Sims.

Each side stated its views once more. MaLoela's side referred to the precedent of Chief Peete's first son, Leeto, who had not succeeded his father because his mother was a commoner; they mentioned the Sesotho proverb 'One cannot cut a shield without a pattern.'

MaMpoi's witnesses relied on the two incidents when Boshoane was publicly named as the heir and successor, and they stressed a very important point: although many of the Sons of Makhabane were present on both occasions, no one had spoken out then in protest against the actions of Chief Peete and Chief Mitchell. If there were objections, they asked, why did Chieftainess MaLoela wait until after the death of Chief Peete and Chief Mitchell to raise them?

After an adjournment of two days, the court's decision was in favour of Chief Boshoane, and he became the Principal Chief of Mats'ekheng.

Most of the people of Mats'ekheng were surprised and disappointed when they were told the news; they had fully expected Chief Boshoane to lose. Despite the custom, in my heart I had always wanted Boshoane to win, first of all because we were companions, born on the same day; also because Chief Peete and Chief Mitchell had chosen him as their heir; also because Chieftainess MaMpoi, for whom I had great admiration, had taken Boshoane as her son; most of all because I loved him.

*　　*　　*

Boshoane was married by the time he succeeded to the Principal Chieftainship, to a granddaughter of Chief Molapo. Their son, Makhabane II, was born in the early 1920s.

In 1927, while I was working as a clerk for Messrs Ross and Co. in Bethlehem, I was called to the police station one day, where I was told that Chief Boshoane urgently wanted me back at Mats'-ekheng. For one thing, I had to appear in his court on the charge of having eloped with some girl.

I was at Bela-Bela before the court on the appointed day, and my case was dismissed. When I left the courtroom I was told that I was wanted at the *lelapa* of the Chief, where Chieftainess MaMpoi would speak with me.

'When are you going to return?' she asked me at once after I had greeted her. 'You grew up with Boshoane. You ought to come and rear the child Makhabane for us.'

'I am sorry, Mother,' I replied, 'but I cannot deceive you by promising to come home at once. I have not given notice at my work. But I do promise that when the time comes, I will come home and serve the Chieftainship.'

While we were still talking, my beloved uncle, Maguqu, came in.

'I am glad, Chieftainess,' he said, 'that you are telling this boy where his duty lies. I was the one who brought up Chief Mitchell, your late husband, and it is my nephew's duty to bring up Makhabane. Among all of Ngolozani's children, he is the one I am choosing to inherit my position in the Chief's administration. He must be Chief Boshoane's adviser because they grew up together, and because they like and trust each other. I cannot understand why he keeps going to the Union of South Africa. Among Ngolozani's sons, I was the one who inherited Ngolozani's position of trust; this boy Stimela, here before you now, son of my brother Makhuba, must inherit that position from me. We have always served the Chiefs and trained their sons.'

Something touched my blood when my uncle told me these things in the presence of Chieftainess MaMpoi, but I was a man after money and there was no money in working for the Chieftainship. I did not want to return home then.

That same day Makhabane, a little boy of five, was called to be introduced to me. He was light of complexion, with mischievous eyes. He reminded me of his mother's people. He greeted me shyly, putting out his hand as a young child does, with a slack wrist. I liked the child at once, and could not foresee the sad day when he and the Chieftainship would turn against me and hold me responsible for their tragedy.

I returned to Bethlehem then and before the end of that month I started working for the I.C.U., the organization that claimed my time and energy until 1937. I was too caught up in the events of those years to return to the parochial world of a Lesotho Chieftainship. During those years my family and the Chieftainship tried in vain to reach me.

When I returned home at last in October 1937, Chieftainess MaMpoi charged me before the Bela-Bela court for having despised her orders, the orders she had given me ten years before, to return to work for the Chieftainship. The court fined me two goats, which I paid.

Chief Boshoane wanted me to work in his administration at Koma-Koma, from where he ruled as Principal Chief, but Reverend Maja of the African Methodist Episcopal Church came to an arrangement with the Chief that I should be allowed to teach in his school for a while as he was desperately short of teachers. I was a teacher until February 1940, when at last I became a clerk to Chief Boshoane at Koma-Koma. A large part of my time, during those years, was spent in looking after and instructing the youth Makhabane—seeing that he lacked nothing at boarding school and that he received the right training to become a Chief.

*   *   *

My long association with Makhabane II started the day Chieftainess MaMpoi, his grandmother, called him and his companion, Makotoko,[3] before me.

'My children,' she said to the boys, 'I have noticed that your behaviour is not what it should be. I have called this man, *Ntate* Jingoes, from his work as a teacher, and I have made him leave his school, to come and take charge of you. From today you must know that you are under the care of this man. Whatever you need, you must ask *Ntate* Jingoes for; wherever you want to go, you must tell *Ntate* Jingoes. I am giving you into his hands; he has power over you. If you continue in your bad ways, this man has the power to thrash you.'

With their first request from boarding school, the boys decided to test me. They asked for pocket money to attend a school sports meeting at Morija and added, '*Ntate*, please remember that we are Chiefs' sons.'

I asked Chief Boshoane to give me four pounds, an enormous sum, to send them, and I got it. With this wealth the boys were able to make a bold show at the sports gathering, and they were very grateful to me; the ice was broken between us and I had succeeded in winning their trust. Makotoko is now a Doctor of Medicine, having graduated from the Witwatersrand University, and he still remembers me with affection and respect.

The rearing and training of a Chief's son is a complex matter. A Chief's son is not like other boys because he has the spirit of ruling in his heart. His temptations are greater than those of other boys, because his companions and the boys of his village must respect him and carry out any order he gives.

The son of a Chief must learn responsibility at a tender age. For this reason, he must have at least one man to look after him; he should not be allowed to remain in his mother's *lelapa* among women; he should be fed by men only. If a commoner's son commits mischief or damages someone's property, his father can be held to account in court for his son's behaviour. A Chief, however, cannot be humiliated by being held responsible for the errant behaviour of his sons; the man who looks after them will be held totally responsible for any misdemeanour they might commit. If a young Prince causes damage to anyone's property, like leading cattle to graze on someone's land, the commoner who owns the property cannot charge his Chief in court and demand compensation from him: that is just not the custom. What is done is that the Chief will fine the man looking after his son, and then that fine is taken to recompense the commoner. The Prince's guardian, who had to pay the fine, is then free to give the naughty child a hiding without having to account for it to the Chief.

For example, Chief Boshoane's guardians were his two materanl uncles. A boy and his mother's brother have a specially warm relationship to start with; in Boshoane's case this was a deeper bond than usual because Boshoane was a special person, with great charm. His two uncles found it quite impossible to punish him, and they paid many goats as fines for the pranks of Chief Boshoane and his companions, who felt themselves immune to retribution and licensed to misbehave as they chose.

Once Boshoane and his companions—including myself—stole into the land of a man named Philip Molete, where we broke off mealie cobs and roasted them right in the land. We thought we would be protected because we were with Boshoane, the son of a Chief, and we took as many mealies as we could, far more than we could eat. Philip complanied to the Chief, and Boshoane's two uncles were fined a goat apiece to recompense Philip.

A Chief's son often plays games that imitate the duties of the Chieftainship. I have known some who held court, fining their companions cattle which had to be paid in stones. The men of the village would not mock youngsters engaged in these activities, but would watch them carefully, encouraging the boys, pretending to give witness in their court, acting as assessors in their cases; in fact, entering as much as possible into the spirit of the game. Later, at the men's *lekhotla*, you would often hear a man saying, 'I saw the Chief's son playing at court today. They were trying a case about a land in dispute. That boy has the makings of a good Chief; he seems to know the law and procedure involved in a land case.'

I think that of all the duties of the Chieftainship, knowing the law and knowing how to preside over a case without bias or favour are the most important. The first thing the Chief must know is how to deal with cases. This is no easy thing to teach a person. There is no age limit concerning court attendance in our country. Boys start attending the men's *lekhotla* from an early age, and for a Chief's son attendance must be encouraged. It is from the way a young Prince behaves at the men's court that one can judge what sort of Chief he will make.

Today Chiefs are no longer trained by men. Nowadays they are just people who sit behind desks and use rubber stamps. In my days, Chiefs were still brought up by men; when I was bringing up Boshoane's sons, they were still instructed by the tribe. Today this is finished. Sons of Chiefs often work now as clerks in urban centres; they are brought up by their mothers like ordinary people. In Lesotho today, women have gained a great deal of power; more women than men vote in the general elections, and there are many women acting as Chiefs and headmen.

*　　*　　*

Chief Boshoane died on 23 December 1940.

Makhabane was still at school when his father died, and so Chief Boshoane's wife, MaMakhabane, became regent for her son.

With the death of Chief Boshoane, my relationship with the Makhabane Chieftainship entered into a new phase. The deep friendship that Chief Boshoane and I had formed as boys had made working for him an easy task; there was never any strain between us as we trusted each other absolutely. Things were destined to change when his wife took over as regent. I continued to work for Chieftainess MaMakhabane as I had for her husband, and in the beginning we got along well. It was when her son Makhabane wanted to return from school to claim his father's position that discord began between me and the Chieftainess.

In my lifetime I have always seen that trouble starts in a Chieftainship with a regent. In the old days, we Basotho used to appoint as regent a boy's uncle if the boy was too young to rule, but this often led to the uncle trying to usurp the Chieftainship and hold it for his sons. To get around this problem, we have started to appoint the heir's mother as regent. But power seems to be a terrible thing, and in Lesotho today you often find mothers who fight desperately to cling to power, and who are most unwilling to relinquish their position to the rightful heir. This is what happened in the Makhabane Chieftainship. Chieftainess MaMakhabane did not want to give up her rights to rule. I supported Makhabane in his quest for the Chieftainship, and so fell into disfavour with his mother. Makhabane's quest began in the following manner.

One day I received a letter from Makhabane saying, 'Please, *Ntate*, expect me home at any time, and tell my grandmother, Chieftainess MaMpoi, that I am about to return home. I am tired of school.'

I went at once to Chieftainess MaMakhabane and showed her her son's letter.

'Why does he write to tell *you*?' she cried. 'Why doesn't he write to *me*? You are the one encouraging him to leave school and come home—I can see that!'

I did not take her accusation seriously because she was in a rage and had to vent her anger on someone.

Then I went to see Chieftainess MaMpoi, as Makhabane asked me to do in his letter, and told her what her grandson had written.

'If Makhabane feels that he cannot manage school any longer,' she said to me, 'he must be allowed to come home.'

I explained to her that it was important for Makhabane to get his matriculation exemption and possibly to go on to the University, but the old lady said reasonably, 'That won't achieve anything, Jingoes. If Makhabane has made up his mind not to study further, he's made up his mind. We'll only be throwing away money because he won't pay attention to his lessons.'

I wrote back to Makhabane, asking him if he were finding his studies too difficult for him. 'What is the real reason behind your wanting to return home before you have finished school?' In reply, he wrote to me, 'The lessons are not all that difficult, but I just don't like school any more,' and he asked me to reply as soon as possible to give him my opinion. When his letter arrived at Mats'ekheng it fell into the hands of Chieftainess MaMakhabane, for it went to her office; she recognized Makhabane's handwriting and opened the letter and read it. She was outraged.

'I have always told you people', she said to her advisers, 'that this child is not mine! He does not love me. He is Jingoes's child in spirit. Just listen to what he is discussing with Jingoes here; he talks to him about things he does not even mention to me. This man will spoil my child. I'm getting tired of him!'

I heard the Chieftainess had my letter from Makhabane and went to claim it. One of the many things she said to me was, 'Why do you teach my child to leave school and come home?'

'I'm not such a fool', I retorted, 'as to advise the child to leave school at this stage of his education.'

'You make me sick!'

'I'm just as tired of you with your unfounded accusations as you are of me!'

In disgust she tossed the letter to me, saying, 'This child is going to grow bad because of the way you teach him. You are teaching my son to come back *and take the Chieftainship from me*!'

Makhabane left school; he was not cut out to be a scholar anyway. On his arrival at home he went straight to his uncle, Chief Nkuebe, and reported to him: 'I have returned from school for good; I'd like to stay at home now. What are your plans for me? I am in your hands. . . .'

When Chief Nkuebe went to report this to Chieftainess MaMakhabane, she said, '*You* seem to be the one who told Makhabane to leave school! You and Jingoes are in this together it seems. What business has Makhabane to come home and tell *you* that he is at *your* disposal? I will show you people that *I am MaMakhabane, a Chieftainess*! I *will not* be controlled by you people!'

Nkuebe told her flatly, 'I have come here to report to you—not to be abused. What I am saying is lawful. What Makhabane has done, by coming to report to me, is the custom. I am his father's brother. Tell me, who else could Makhabane have gone to report to?'

'Why didn't he come to see *me*? I am his mother!'

'Do you know what you're saying? Was Makhabane wrong in coming to report to me?'

'I don't say that. . . . All I'm asking is why he didn't come to see me first. I would have called you, of course. . . .'

'It seems to me that you and I won't reach agreement on this. I think we had better call in the Sons of Makhabane to settle this matter.'

'If *you* want to call them yourself, fine! *I* won't call them!'

'Please, instruct your secretary to call them together. I want to lay this matter before them.'

'I am not prepared to do so!'

You must remember that Makhabane was by now old enough to rule, and that it was tacitly accepted throughout the Chieftainship and the district that he had returned home to take over the reins of authority from his mother. Nkuebe saw at once that his sister-in-law, the Chieftainess, had become fond of power and was not going to give up her position without a struggle. It would have been a breach of custom for him to call the Sons of Makhabane, for he was not Principal Chief. Yet he knew that without them the dispute would never be resolved. Without further discussion, Chief Nkuebe turned to the Paramount Chief for arbitration, and Chieftainess MaMakhabane received a letter from Matsieng instructing her to call the Sons of Makhabane to hear Nkuebe's complaint against her.

Chieftainess MaMakhabane called the meeting.

At the gathering, Chief Nkuebe described the impasse he had reached with Chieftainess MaMakhabane, and continued, 'Sons of Makhabane, I want you to advise me: some of Makhabane's companions have already been installed as Chiefs; it was only because Makhabane was still at school that we have delayed his installation. The day the Chieftainess became regent, she knew that, one day, Makhabane would claim his Chieftainship.

'At the present moment, however, we are not here to discuss the Chieftainship of Mats'ekheng; I called you to come and make peace between me and Chieftainess MaMakhabane.

'The Chieftainess refused utterly to hear what I wanted to tell her that day; I had intended to advise her that Makhabane's turn to rule had come; that he ought to be given his position as Chief Boshoane's heir. I wanted first to reach an agreement with her before calling you, the Sons of Makhabane, but we failed to agree. So now I am including this in my case against the Chieftainess: Makhabane is home—what do you, the Sons of Makhabane, say about his presence?'

When she replied to Chief Nkuebe's complaint, the Chieftainess said that she realized fully that one day Makhabane would claim his position; she had never disputed the fact that he was Chief Boshoane's heir and the Principal Chief of Mats'ekheng. When the day came, she would gladly hand over to him. Her only objection, she said, was that Makhabane had ignored her and gone to Nkuebe.

Then the Sons of Makhabane revealed their views by means of the questions they put to the Chieftainess.

Chief Mangoato, son of the late Chief Peete's brother, was the first. 'Chieftainess,' he asked, 'do you admit that Nkuebe came to see you about Makhabane's return?'

'Yes.'

'What does the law say about that?'

'I don't understand what you mean. . . .'

'I say: what does the law say about Nkuebe and Makhabane?'

'I still don't understand your question. . . .'

'Chieftainess, my question is this: was Makhabane wrong in going to see his uncle, Chief Nkuebe, to report that he had come home?'

'Yes. He was wrong.'

'But what does the law say?'

'Makhabane ought to have come to me first; after he had reported his presence to me, I should have summoned the Sons of Makhabane, through Nkuebe.'

'Chieftainess, don't you know the section of the Laws of Lerotholi[4] that refers to an heir? It says that if the father of a minor son dies, the uncle of that son is the one to look after the widow and the heir. The uncle or uncles of the boy will often go to the regent to ask about the inheritance of the boy, how it is being used, and so on.'

'Yes. . . . But I still contend that Makhabane ought to have reported to me first!'

Chief Dyke, the full brother of Chief Nkuebe, was the one to continue. 'Do you want to tell us, Chieftainess,' he asked, 'that Makhabane was wrong in seeing Nkuebe, his uncle, first?'

'*Yes*! He should have seen *me*. . . .'

'Can you point out the law that says Makhabane should have seen you, his mother, before he went to see his father's brother, his senior uncle?'

'I cannot point out such a law, but according to custom, he should have come to me first.'

'According to custom?'

'Yes.'

'Tell us, Chieftainess, does Makhabane visit you often?'

'Yes, he does. He was here the day before yesterday.'

'When he was here the day before yesterday, according to the custom, who prepared his food?'

'The man called Taole cooked for him. . . .'

'Why didn't you cook for him?'

'Because his food must be prepared by men.'

'Why didn't you claim that, as he is *your* child, *you* ought to cook for him?'

'I have always found that to be the custom: men cook food for the sons of Chiefs.'

'So what is the difference between Taole cooking for Makhabane, and Makhabane reporting to Chief Nkuebe?'

'You have confused me now. All I know is that I did want my son to report to me first. . . .'

Then Chief Ntina, son of another brother of the late Chief Peete, took over the questions. He said, 'Chieftainess, it seems that you are trying to snatch Makhabane away from us.'

'No, my uncle. . . .'

'Then what *are* you trying to do?'

'Well . . . I thought I was right. If I am wrong, then I'm wrong. Let's proceed!'

'Did you say, "If I am wrong"?'

'Yes.'

'I want to hear you say you *are* wrong, not "*If*". . . .'

'Yes. I am wrong. I see that I have made a mistake. . . .'

At that point Chief Malefetsane Khomaleburu, a grandson of Chief Seshophe, interrupted: 'The Chieftainess has admitted that she was wrong. I think we should not press the matter any further.'

The rest agreed with him.

One of them suggested that since they were there, they ought to push things to a conclusion and settle the matter of Makhabane's accession, but Chief Molikuoa, a descendant of the brother of the late Chief Lesaoana, demurred.

'I think it is not for us', he said, 'to take away the rights of Chieftainess MaMakhabane and Chief Nkuebe. It is for them to reach a decision first. After they have discussed the matter, they will call us again and give us the date of Makhabane's installation.'

This was also agreed upon, and the meeting dispersed.

The faith of these Chiefs in Chieftainess MaMakhabane's

willingness to hand over to Makhabane was ill placed, however. Nkuebe could not bring her to name a date on which they could discuss the matter. Every time he went to see her, she stalled him with some excuse; either she was not feeling well, or she had to go to some place or other urgently. Each time she promised to summon him as soon as she was able. In this way, months sped by, and still Makhabane was at home doing nothing, and still Nkuebe could not make Chieftainess MaMakhabane see him. It was clear to all that she wanted to hang on to the Principal Chieftainship until her death.

*   *   *

Chieftainess MaMakhabane tried in many ways to delay giving up her regency. Her first ploy was to insist that Makhabane could not be installed as Principal Chief until he was married. She stipulated, too, that he should marry a girl of her choice. Makhabane objected to his mother's choice on the grounds that the girl was fat and would cost him a lot of money in clothes. Then the Chieftainess suggested another girl from the District of Leribe, and again Makhabane refused to consider his mother's choice of a wife for him, because the girl's father had once expressed disrespect towards his ancestor, Makhabane I.

Then Makhabane picked his future wife himself; she was Nkhala, the daughter of a Chief of Leribe. When his mother was told of his choice, she blamed me: 'I know that you are the very person who encouraged the youth to reject the girls I chose for him; I know that Makhabane will do nothing against your wishes. I expect you to make all the arrangements for this marriage, you and Chieftainess MaMpoi, my mother-in-law, because you and she seem to approve of Makhabane's future wife. As for me, I'll be having nothing to do with it!'

I ignored her accusation as nonsense; she was wrong.

This was a difficult marriage to arrange because Chieftainess MaMakhabane was unwilling to contribute cattle for a marriage that went against her wishes. Makhabane complicated matters by going to Pitseng, where Nkhala lived, and eloping with the girl before any cattle had been paid for her bridewealth; he took the girl to his grandmother, Chieftainess MaMpoi, at Bela-Bela.

When news of the elopement reached Chieftainess MaMakhabane, she paced up and down without cease, very angry indeed.

'Yes, I know all about it!' she raved. 'Jingoes is the one who instructed Makhabane to go and elope with this girl. Have you heard that Jingoes's daughter-in-law is now at Bela-Bela with Chieftainess MaMpoi?'

Raletsukana, one of her advisers, asked the Chieftainess, 'Why do you call Makhabane's bride the daughter-in-law of Jingoes?'

'Makhabane respects Jingoes more than he does you, yet you are a Chief of Moshoeshoe's blood,' she replied. 'Makhabane also respects Jingoes more than me. That's why I say Nkhala is Jingoes's daughter-in-law. He will have to see that he goes to pay her bridewealth at Pitseng—I myself intend to have nothing to do with it.'

Another adviser reminded the Chieftainess that the people of Mats'ekheng would pay the cattle; she herself would need to contribute nothing towards Nkhala's bridewealth.

'Oh! You and Jingoes are in this together, I see! You are assisting him!' was her response to that.

'No, Chieftainess. I am telling you the custom and the tradition of the Basotho.'

Since Chieftainess MaMakhabane really meant what she said about having nothing to do with the marriage arrangements, Chieftainess MaMpoi took charge. She sent out circulars to all the Chiefs, sub-chiefs, and headmen of Mats'ekheng, informing them that their Prince, Makhabane, had eloped with Nkhala of Leribe. She urged them to hasten to supply her bridewealth, as they knew it was their duty to do, as she did not want the Chieftainess to be charged in court by Nkhala's family for having failed to pay.

Within one week, the people had brought in 55 head of cattle for their Prince's marriage payment.

A group of Chiefs with Chief Dyke and Chief Buller at their head were to drive the cattle to Pitseng. Meanwhile Chieftainess MaMakhabane was making plans of her own to stop the wedding. She collected some Chiefs she could trust and armed them with rifles, instructing them to go and head off the cattle being driven to Pitseng.

'Follow the cattle and bring them back to me,' she instructed her men, 'and if that group tries to fight, don't waste time, just shoot them. They're a rough lot!'

Even at this late stage, Chieftainess MaMakhabane was hoping to prevent the marriage. Her men were successful, for when Chief Dyke saw that he and the herd were surrounded he was ready to fight, but Chief Ntina and Chief Buller said to him, 'Don't fight! We cannot kill each other for cattle. . . .' Besides, Chief Dyke's men were armed only with pocket revolvers. So Chieftainess MaMakhabane's men drove the cattle back.

When Chief Dyke later told Chief Nkuebe and me this tale, we all roared with laughter. When Nkuebe laughs, his eyes disappear, because he is a very big man. The Chieftainess was a worthy opponent, we decided; it is not often that marriage cattle are turned back on the whim of a woman.

The Chieftainess had the cattle kraaled at Koma-Koma, in her own kraal. Chief Nkuebe rode over the next day to take issue with her on the matter. He asked her on what authority she had sent armed men to waylay the bridal cattle of a Chief's marriage. She replied that she was the Principal Chieftainess and that the cattle were being driven to Pitseng without her consent; they were sent to Pitseng on the orders of Chieftainess MaMpoi, she said, and Chieftainess MaMpoi was her subject, even if she was her mother-in-law.

'Makhabane is not your child,' Nkuebe told her. 'He does not belong to you alone: he is the son of the people of Mats'ekheng. The cattle you stopped from going to Pitseng were not your cattle, they were the people's cattle. Chieftainess, you must watch out. Would you like to have the people of Mats'ekheng—your subjects —turn against you? I am telling you that the people are angry about this, and there has been muttering and complaining about your rule. I stopped the people from coming here in a mob. I have a good mind to report you to the Paramount Chief for the way you have gone against the instructions of Chieftainess MaMpoi, the grandmother of Makhabane, and the will of the people of Mats'ekheng.'

Chieftainess MaMakhabane was starting to feel scared now, and when a man arrived from Pitseng on behalf of the bride's people to charge her before the court for having failed to pay elopement damages for Nkhala, she gave in.

Pitseng finally demanded only 35 head of cattle as bridewealth. The balance of the original 55 head was given to Makhabane as a gift from his people. And so Makhabane was married to the girl of his choice and was ready to assume the Chieftainship.

I must point out now that a great rift had come between Chieftainess MaMakhabane and myself. Whereas before she had included me in all her plans and taken my advice on every subject, she now hated me and saw me as Makhabane's man who had stabbed her in the back. In some ways this was very lucky for me.

*   *   *

Because of his position, a Chief is especially vulnerable to witch-craft; many people hate or envy him and would like to see him brought down. Consequently, Chiefs search continually for power-ful *lingaka* and for potent *litlhare* to hedge them with protection. This is so, even now. It has long been believed in Africa that human flesh makes *litlhare* of uncommon power and I, as a *ngaka* myself, although I abhor the practice, cannot say that this is not true.

Chieftainess MaMakhabane could feel her power slipping from her. Most of the people in her own district wanted their Prince, Makhabane, to rule, and even old friends, like myself, were opposing her ambitions. She allied herself with a *ngaka* to commit a tragic deed.

We had noticed for some time that she had been holding secret meetings with a group of men who were not her regular advisers, but although we suspected her of some new ruse we could not guess at the depth of her desperation, nor at how ruthlessly ambition had seized her.

* * *

The story starts at Maqotsa's village near Koma-Koma on the day of a wedding feast for one of the headman's sons. In the evening Chieftainess MaMakhabane arrived in the village, where the feast was in full swing. She was with three women and three men. The men were Chief Raletsukana, Mabokosana Mohlokacana, and Setene Sebajoa. The Chieftainess had her presence announced to Dane Rachakane and Pholo Rachakane, the headman, who sum-moned some other men. We later learned that when this group had gathered, the Chieftainess said to them, 'I am here. Now we must do what we all decided to do long ago.'

While they sat there, people from the feast came up to greet the Chieftainess. One of them was Mocheseloa.[5] After he had greeted her, Chieftainess MaMakhabane said to him, 'I want you. I must make a *lenaka* out of you. . . .'

Mocheseloa pleaded with the Chieftainess and her group, and offered his big black ox to take his place; he said he would pay for his life with the ox, but they ignored his plea.

When they grabbed him, he screamed to his uncle, Pholo, who was in the group, 'My uncle! Please leave me! I will pay with my big black ox. . . .'

'We do not want your ox,' Pholo told his nephew, 'we want you.'

All this took place near the cattle kraal of the village, and no one saw or heard except some herdboys. When the Chieftainess and her companions left the kraal with Mocheseloa, they did not go unobserved. When the little boys of the village heard that the Chieftainess had arrived, they rushed to see her, and their curiosity was aroused when they saw Mocheseloa caught and dragged off, struggling, into the dark. The party hurrying away with their victim noticed the boys following, and one called Mzimukulu picked up stones and flung them at the youngsters, telling them to get away. Most of the boys fell back, but Malefetsane Lebetsa still followed after them, stealthily keeping to the shadows, and always behind and to one side of them.

The Chieftainess and her group entered a shallow cave or overhang under some flat rocks. Growing above this cave was a *mosilabele*[6] bush under which the boy Malefetsane crept, squirming right into it until he was quite hidden, and he spied on them by the light of the lantern they had lit. He could hear Mocheseloa still pleading, and he saw Mosala, the *ngaka*, approach him. Mosala's task at this point was to drug Mocheseloa so that his screams would not be heard from afar. The little boy said later that he stayed above the cave because he was so paralysed with fright that he could not have moved. He said the *ngaka* lit some herbs and made Mocheseloa inhale the smoke.

After that they began cutting his flesh, while Mocheseloa was still alive and too drugged to struggle. The one to cut him first was Dane Rachakane, who cut away his lower lip. While he hacked at the lip, he was talking: 'With this, your lower lip, I am cutting it to make me stronger so that when I talk to people and headmen they ought to understand me and pay attention to what I say. When I mix your lower lip with my *litlhare*, I must be understood and respected.'

The second to cut was Pholo, the victim's uncle. He wanted the tongue. He also spoke about how he wanted the tongue to work for him. The boy lying in the bush watching all this said that while this cutting was taking place Chieftainess MaMakhabane was sitting on a rock nearby with Mosala next to her and a tin in front of her. The pieces of flesh were placed before them in the tin, and Raletsukana was pointing out where the pieces should be placed.

When her turn came, the Chieftainess asked Mzimukulu to cut for her. He did so. Mzimukulu was a butcher in the village, and when he was about to cut, he looked up and said he had never cut a man's joints before, and did not know how.

'Like a cow!' he was told. 'It's just like cutting a cow!' and so he cut.

While Mzimukulu was cutting for the Chieftainess, these were the words she spoke: 'Oh mercy, Mother Maria, for you know I am committing a sin, but I am doing this because I want to be known. I pray to Thy Holy name, that You do not count this as a sin, because I want to keep the Chieftainship of Mats'ekheng, and not to have it taken by Makhabane. Even after my death, Makhabane must not take the Chieftainship; it must fall on the shoulders of my younger son, Posholi.'

When Dane went to cut flesh from Mocheseloa for the second time, he said he was now cutting so that he would be lucky and successful on the mines as a compound *induna*. 'I must not fail,' he said. 'The one who has taken my place as *induna*, when I appear, must be dismissed. I must be lucky, too, and get the headmanship of Tsokung, and do away with the present headman, my older brother, Lehlobi.'

When Raletsukana's turn came, he did not speak as the others had done; what he said was simply, 'I want to be honoured by the people and the Chiefs.'

The last one to cut was Mosala, the *ngaka*, the son of my uncle, Malayisha. He said, 'I am the youngest in the house of Malayisha, but I would like to be head of them all: not only of that house, but of the whole lineage. . . .'

The pieces of Mocheseloa's flesh in the tin were taken to Koma-Koma to the Chieftainess's place. The body—for Mocheseloa had died at last when his throat was cut away—was wrapped in an ox hide and taken to the house of Setene.

The other details of how Mocheseloa was cut I do not want to talk about. He was related to me, and beloved of everyone, especially of the Chieftainship and of his uncle, Pholo.

* * *

The following day word went out that Mocheseloa was missing, and people started searching for him. We were working in Chieftainess MaMakhabane's administrative offices when the message came. My fellow clerk, Koenyama Cheba, said, 'We must not waste any time here, but must go and search at once.'

'What do you think . . . ?' I asked him.

'I've been telling you. . . . How can you be so dense? I have been telling you to be careful, as there is something going on in this village. Remember the group that always holds meetings in secret with the Chieftainess? Mocheseloa is now missing. . . .'

'Do you suspect something then?'

'Yes. I suspect a great deal. We won't find Mocheseloa alive. . . .'

We had not been searching for thirty minutes when we found Mocheseloa's corpse right near by, below some cliffs under the village. We were amazed that he was so near, and that he had not been found before. It was quite clear that his corpse had but recently been placed there by someone when news of the search had gone out. When someone cried out, 'Here he is!' we went to the spot and found Dane Rachakane there already. Dane lived at Tsokung, so far away, but *he* was there, beside Mocheseloa's corpse.

'Here is the child of my mother's brother, sleeping here! *Joo . . . oee*! How cruel are the people who have done this!' he cried.

All I noticed then was that Mocheseloa's teeth were grinning bare: he had no lips.

Koenyama did not waste time by going to report first to the Chieftainess, but rode straight to the Mapoteng Post Office from where he telephoned the police at Teyateyaneng. Then we went to the Chieftainess and told her Mocheseloa had been found.

'You'd better telephone the police,' she said.

'I already have,' Koenyama replied.

'Who ordered you to do so?' she snapped.

It was I who replied. '*Liketso*,' I said, 'deeds. It was the deeds of Mocheseloa's murderers that ordered Koenyama to phone the police. . . .'

*   *   *

There cannot have been many people in the district who did not know who was responsible for Mocheseloa's death. But people do not like to talk about ritual murders, and especially those committed by Principal Chiefs. But the murder had been seen by a child, and who can stop children talking? Rumours about the murder spread first from the school.

One little boy, the son of Setene Sebajoa, told his friends, 'In my home, my father and some others came in with Chieftainess MaMakhabane. They placed something rolled in cowhide on the floor. They said it was Chieftainess MaMakhabane's parcel, and must not be touched by anyone. They told us not to enter the hut it was in. I cannot understand why they said it was a parcel, when Mocheseloa is missing. . . .'

This particular story spread fast, and it is said that when Setene heard it, he nearly killed his son.

'Do you want me hanged?' he shouted.

With stories like this one going around, the murder could not be hushed up, and soon the police knew the whole story of that night.

*   *   *

So Mocheseloa died because people like to be Chiefs, and not only that, but because Chiefs favour certain of their offspring. I cannot say why Chieftainess MaMakhabane wanted Posholi rather than Makhabane to succeed her. Perhaps it was because Makhabane was like his father, assertive and masculine; his food was cooked by men, and not women, while Posholi used to eat MaMakhabane's food, or food cooked by women. We did not like that. We used to mock Posholi, saying that he belonged to his mother's people and not to the Mats'ekheng Chieftainship. We used to insult him to wean him from his mother's *lelapa*.

*   *   *

You must remember that this murder came as the result of continual pressure by Chief Nkuebe and myself to have Makhabane installed as the Principal Chief. By the time of the murder, Makhabane had been home for three years, his rightful claims still blocked by the Chieftainess. Eventually we were forced to see Chieftainess MaMpoi for permission to call the Sons of Makhabane again to discuss this matter. By that time, the people of Mats'ekheng were impatient and grumbling; some headmen and sub-chiefs flatly refused to obey Chieftainess MaMakhabane in anything. The Chieftainess herself would not take the advice of the Sons of Makhabane. Finally we went to see Paramount Chieftainess MaNts'ebo for help and, under her express orders, Chieftainess MaMakhabane fixed a date for the installation ceremony. This happened at about the same time as the ritual murder.

It should have been a time of rejoicing, for at last Makhabane was to rule his people. But the dark spell of the ritual murder was hanging over us. Chieftainess MaMakhabane had been taken into custody, and had been released and allowed to go home, pending further investigation.

I was with the party of Chiefs who accompanied Makhabane to Matsieng, the seat of the Paramount Chieftainess, to report with oxen that Makhabane was ready to take his position as Principal Chief. The Paramount Chieftainess's representatives accepted the cattle, and then their head, Chief Theko Makhaola, addressed Makhabane:

'My brother's son, you are taking the Chieftainship in hard times. The Chiefs of today have turned against the people; they are no longer ruling their people, but using them as animals. If you become one of those who commit ritual murder, I will say that you were not installed by me to do such things. Makhabane's people are not animals. Your fellow Chiefs want to slaughter the people of Moshoeshoe, the Basotho nation. I have advised the Paramount Chieftainess to strike from her roll of Chiefs any Chief who is a ritual murderer. I am tired of these Chiefs who are eating the Basotho people like the cannibals of old.'

He then instructed Chief Nkuebe to take home a message for Chieftainess MaMakhabane: he would be at Mats'ekheng on a certain day to install Makhabane in the presence of his people; the Chieftainess should summon the women and men of Mats'ekheng to be present on that day. Remember that the Chieftainess was at home still, having been released from custody while the police made further investigations into Mocheseloa's murder. So, ironically, she was in charge of the preparations for her son's installation.

*   *   *

On the day appointed for the ceremony, a large group of us rode with Makhabane from his place to Koma-Koma, where Chieftainess MaMakhabane awaited her son.

Although she was a murderess, that woman was still a CHIEFTAINESS.

When we came in sight of Koma-Koma, the people there recognized us because our horses were dancing. When we dismounted, Makhabane turned to go into his mother's *lelapa*, but Chief Raletsukana stopped him; that day his place was not in any woman's house, but at the *lekhotla* of the men.

When we entered the *lekhotla*, three Chiefs carried in the meat of an ox and placed it before us; it was half cooked. Then the Chieftainess entered with Chief Ntina; each carried a sjambok. Their faces were set and fierce. We felt like boys from an initiation school caught up in a strange ritual. Chief Ntina snatched a piece of meat, and threw it towards us.

'Eat!' he commanded. 'Don't say the meat is raw!'

Someone caught the meat. We did not use knives, but tore the flesh with our teeth. Then they started flinging lumps of meat at us. We had to catch them and eat them without letting them fall, or they slashed at us with their sjamboks.

'Don't use knives!'

We ate and ate, red blood from the raw meat dripping from our chins.

'Come on! *Eat*!'

We were like girls playing, catching meat from the air all over the place. We ate all that raw meat. As I ate, I thought of the *lekisoa* ceremony I had witnessed when I was a boy, when the warriors of Chief Peete devoured the bull raw to strengthen themselves. We were like them: if we had met enemies that day we would have fought until we were all dead.

Then we rode to Mapoteng to meet the Paramount Chieftainess's representatives; Chieftainess MaMakhabane followed us, also on horseback.

At the installation ceremony Makhabane took his place in front of his people, but his mother, the Chieftainess, hung right back until Chief Nkuebe said to Makhabane, 'I think it fitting that the person who has been regent for you should be at your side now.' Then Makhabane turned round and beckoned to his mother, and he drew her forward and placed her at his right hand.

The Paramount Chieftainess's representative spoke, addressing himself initially to Chieftainess MaMakhabane.

'I am glad', he said, 'that you have eventually consented to Makhabane's being installed. We thank you. As for you, Makhabane, the Paramount Chieftainess told you while you were at Matsieng that people are not animals. I repeat again: *people are not animals*. Do not become a cannibal to the people. The Paramount Chieftainess instructed me to tell you to respect people, for then they, in turn, will respect you. Respect the Sons of Makhabane. Respect the people of Makhabane. Then you will be respected by the Paramount Chieftainess.

'Administer your area well, and work together with the British Government, and they will work in peace with you. Don't associate with thieves. A Chief is exposed to temptation. Your subjects will come and greet you, and say, "I've been hunting, and I have found this for you. . . ." On their hunt, as they call it, they may have "found" a sheep or a horse. Don't accept these bribes; they are trying to spoil your name.

'Make your people pay their poll tax. Be impartial when it comes to the collecting of poll tax: do not overlook your friends—people are all alike when they have to pay tax.

'Do not come drunk to hear cases in your court. Do not throw poor people out of your courts. Once you behave like that you are no longer a Chief. If you behave like that the Paramount Chieftainess will strike you from her roll of Chiefs.'

So Makhabane became Principal Chief.

The Basotho have two proverbs 'The one who builds a fountain does not drink from it' and 'The builder of a shelter does not enjoy its shade'. I say this because no one ever thought that one day there would be bad blood between myself and Makhabane, Makhabane whom I had trained, whom I had made a Chief.

*   *   *

It was not long after Chief Makhabane's installation that Lieutenant Castle of the Teyateyaneng police and a party of seven constables arrived one morning at the Koma-Koma *lekhotla* and asked to see the Chief.

I went to call the Chief, and found him with his mother, who said, 'They have come for me today, and yet I did not commit an evil act.'

I have always loved the Chieftainship, yet I felt no pity then for the Chieftainess; I only wanted justice at that time. It was only later that I started to feel pity for her. Her rule had been bad for the Chieftainship, even though she had been a competent ruler, and her striving ambition had made me angry with her, and had turned her people against her.

I conducted the Lieutenant to the Chief's quarters. After they had greeted each other, Lieutenant Castle requested a private interview, for he was a fine man, and sensible of the gravity of his task. I turned to go out but was stopped by the Chief.

Then the Lieutenant said, 'I am sorry, my Chief, but I cannot do anything to help. The law is forcing me to do this. I never thought or dreamed that one day I would raise my hand against the Chieftainess, your mother, but today matters compel me to do it. I have come to arrest Chieftainess MaMakhabane for the murder of Mocheseloa Foso. It is quite clear, after our investigation, that

Pitso (Maseru, 1947) for the British Royal Family

At Malimong inside the cave of Rakotsoane, the cannibal leader who captured and devoured Moshoeshoe's grandfather, Peete. The platform in the middle is said to have been the cooking area

Mr. Jingoes (seated) in the 1940s on the introduction of Treasury Courts in Lesotho. Chief Dyke stands immediately behind him

Mr. Jingoes in the 1950s　　　　　Mr. Jingoes in 1969

the Chieftainess was responsible for his murder. Perhaps the law will take pity on her, but I have to take her.'

The Chief asked me to fetch his mother from her *lelapa* where we had left her, and to bring her to his office. When I found her, I told her only that the Chief wanted to see her, because I was afraid that if she knew she was about to be arrested, she might run outside and throw herself over the cliffs right by the village.

'I am to be arrested,' she said to me in a wondering tone, 'and I have never committed an evil deed. . . .'

'No,' I said, 'you are not being arrested. You are only wanted by the Chief, your son.'

After the Chieftainess entered her son's office, we left her alone with Lieutenant Castle and Chief Makhabane. After a few minutes, they set off for the Teyateyaneng police station. And so Chieftainess MaMakhabane left Mats'ekheng for the last time.

Of the fifteen accused, two were discharged. Other sentences ranged from seven to fifteen years imprisonment. The Chieftainess and Dane Rachakane were sentenced to death.

*   *   *

The death, by hanging, of Chieftainess MaMakhabane altered forever my relationship with her son. There was a lot of talk at Mats'ekheng around this time that I, who was so closely linked with the Chieftainship, must have had something to do with the ritual murder. Makhabane himself firmly believed that I was, somehow, responsible for his mother's death; either I had omitted to warn her about the consequences of such an act, or else I had informed on her to the police, or perhaps I was the one who encouraged her to kill Mocheseloa in the first place. I have never been sure exactly how he blamed me, but blame me he did. He could not believe that I had known nothing whatever about the murder until it was discovered.

Chief Gabashane Masupha, the Principal Chief of Masupha's ward, had often invited me to settle under him on the strength of our friendship as boys. He had grown up with Chief Boshoane and myself and had heard of the service our family had rendered the Chieftainship at Mats'ekheng. Although Chief Gabashane was hanged in 1949,[7] his wife became regent for their son Chief David, and she would not hear of my settling anywhere else in Lesotho; so I moved to MaMathe's village, the village of the Principal Chief of Masupha's, and I have lived there since 1952.

7

Time has healed the breach between me and Makhabane, and he and other Chiefs of Mats'ekheng have asked me to return. As you know, my ancestors have also told me to go back home, and I would like to die in the place where my fathers lived and died.

NOTES

1. *Motolo* is the sedge *Scirpus burkei*.
2. The *Sons of Makhabane* are members of the Makhabane lineage, who form a consultative body in the regulation of chiefly affairs.
3. Dr. Seth Peete Makotoko was for some years national leader of the ultra-royalist Marema-Tlou-Freedom Party, and was later appointed President of the Senate.
4. *The Laws of Lerotholi*, originally drawn up by the Basutoland Council, ratified by Paramount Chief Lerotholi and published in 1907, are a summary of the principal traditional laws of Lesotho. The original publication has long been superseded by subsequent amended re-editions.
5. There is some discrepancy in the spelling of names between Mr. Jingoes's version and that of G. I. Jones, *Basutoland Medicine Murder*, H.M.S.O., London, 1951, pp. 11–12 and 97. In the latter, Mocheseloa Foso, Rachakane, and Setene are given respectively as Mochesela Khoto, Rachakana, and Steve.
6. *Mosilabele* is the tree *Rhus viminalis* or karee tree.
7. Chief Gabashane Masupha and Chief Bereng Griffith, son of Paramount Chief Griffith Lerotholi, were hanged for ritual murder.

CHAPTER SEVEN

A Chief is a Chief by the people

IF the Basotho ever lose their Chiefs, they will cease to be the Basotho as I know them; they will become a faceless nation, like the people of the Thaba Nchu[1] Native Reserve, who are Basotho, it is true, but who are somehow a formless crowd, whose Chiefs are puppets. I am not saying that a nation cannot be a nation without an hereditary ruling class, but what I mean is that every nation has a traditional style that makes it unique, and for the Basotho that style is given substance by the Chieftainship. It does not necessarily follow that every Chief is a good Chief who has his people's interests at heart, nor that the Basotho are incapable of adapting to a Western style of government, but it is true, for us, that the Chieftainship is like the father of a household: strict or loving, kind or severe, his children can expect his backing; he gives a sense of stability and order. It takes a long time to grow accustomed to the feeling of having a father elected by democratic vote, even if his rule promises greater freedom and prosperity.

My years with the Chieftainship at Mats'ekheng were the years of change, when, under the British, I saw the Chief's role change from that of father to administrator. Those were the years when the essence of Chieftainship—a Chief is a Chief by the people—was lost. What is meant by this is that the Chief and the people served each other; they both stood to gain by their relationship. I cannot give you a picture of this in cold words. The best way is to show you how it worked.

*　　*　　*

Take the question of gifts to the Chief. Today in Lesotho there is bribery. If you want a land—and land is in short supply—you take money, or a shirt, or a watch, to the clerk of the Chief and you say to him, 'There is a nice field over there. . . .' He will arrange, at the next allocation, that the field you pointed out be allocated to you, even if it already belongs to someone else, even if there are widows and orphans who are landless. This is bribery, and it exists.

What a bribe is, is clear: it is direct exchange of favour for favour. For example, if you have a case in progress before the Chief's court, and you give the Chief a gift, it is not a gift, but a bribe.

The gift to the Chief, which we call *teboho* or gratitude, was a different thing. With it, one was thanking the Chief for his protection and favours in the past and, in addition, one was insuring one's future. No reasonable Chief would have refused you a favour when you had fed him.

I remember men at home who were known as good farmers; their crops were always early and bounteous. I used to see these men, in early summer, carrying baskets filled with peaches, carrots, beetroots, cabbages, mealies, and sweet cane in bundles. They would take them to Chief Boshoane and say, 'We have brought you these crops, as they are the first to be eaten. We found it our duty to bring you these gifts.' You must remember that these men did not have cases before the Chief when they brought him their gifts, and they were not short of land.

I also remember one Jim Ncepe, a rich man at Mats'ekheng. In the winter he would take a sheep or a goat to the place of the Chief and say, 'Please, Chief, slaughter this animal for your children when it is cold, because it is winter now. Let them have rich gravy for their porridge.' *Ntate* Ncepe was not the only one: I have seen many people bringing gifts in this way.

My present wife, NoMaqhesha, still gives gifts like this. She is a skilled spinner and weaver of mohair. She once sent a girth woven of fine mohair to the King for his famous horse, Abel, and she takes gifts of hand-made handbags to the Chieftainess of the village where we live today.

Yet it is not all that easy to distinguish between a gift and a bribe. In the old days, if you wanted something from the Chief you would take him a large gift, like a cow, and say, 'Please, Chief, I notice that you do not have sufficient milk for your children. Here is a cow —please milk it for your children. . . .' Then you would leave.

When you went back to ask him for whatever you wanted, the Chief would not hesitate to let you have it. His advisers might protest, but the Chief would simply tell them to give you what you were asking for. If, by chance, the Chief did hesitate, his wife would tell him to give you what you wanted, 'For he is the person who knows when I and my children are hungry,' she would say.

If what you desired from the Chief in return for your gift was a land, you would get it. You must remember, though, that land was not as scarce then as it is today; the Chief would not be depriving anyone in giving you the land you asked for.

Now this is *not* bribery. In those days, the Chiefs were not paid salaries; they were not civil servants. They lived on what the people gave them, and you were feeding your Chief, quite literally, when you took him a gift. His income was from the people, for what he did for them. If, today, a Chief accepts a gift for giving someone a land, he is taking a bribe because he is being paid a salary by the Government for his work.

Still, it was true in Lesotho in the old days, as it is even now throughout the world, that a rich man had a better chance than a poor man of getting good fields and favours from the Chief. But in those days the Chiefs and the people were dependent on each other; they served each other.

* * *

The old custom of *letsema*, by which the people used to cultivate their Chiefs' lands, is a good example of how the Chief and his people served each other. It worked like this: when the time came to plough or hoe, the Chief would send out word to his subjects that he wanted a certain land ploughed. Then men and women would gather in a large work-party; those who had oxen brought them to make up spans, for the people had to use their own ploughs. They also had to provide their own food while they worked.

The people were bound by custom to work like this only on three lands of the Chief. The first was the *ts'imo ea lira* or the land of the enemies. It was called that because if the Chief and his warriors needed provisions while on the march, they would send back word and food would be taken to them from the grain of this land. It was usually maize, ground and roasted—what we call *lipabi*—which is highly nourishing. People used to believe that the order to go and plough the Chief's *ts'imo ea lira* would break droughts, and they often sent deputations to their Chief to ask when he would give the order to plough. When people went to make a *letsema* on this land, they went gladly, and they never expected food, beer, or water from the Chief while they worked, because they knew that when the winter came, and they were hungry, they could go to their Chief and ask him for food; they would be given what they needed, and that grain came from the *ts'imo ea lira*. So when they went to plough or hoe this land, they were pleased to do it; they knew they were cultivating their own land.

Grain sold from this land was also used to pay for journeys undertaken by messengers of the Chief. I remember how I, when I accompanied the Chief on a journey, had to sell grain from this land to buy supplies. The first time was when I accompanied Chief Boshoane to Matsieng on a case, and the Chief had no money to feed the staff of advisers and grooms he took with him. He ordered me to get three bags of grain from the *ts'imo ea lira* at Mapoteng, the land that had belonged to the late Chief Peete.

'By getting our food from that land', he told me, 'I am praying that Chief Peete will be with me in this case.' By this he meant that his ancestor would bless him and help him in the case he was about to undertake. I sold the three bags for £7.10.0. and bought provisions for our journey.

The second time was when I had to go to Matsieng to represent Chieftainess MaMakhabane in a case and, as we had just sent money to Makhabane at school, and the Chieftainess had no ready cash, she told me to get my provisions for the journey from the *ts'imo ea lira* at Mapoteng. Although there were such lands at Koma-Koma and Bela-Bela as well, our Chiefs liked to use the one at Mapoteng for important occasions because it was the oldest.

This was not just a whim. In England, in times of crisis or when a great event occurs, like the installation of a new monarch, although they have beautiful motor-cars and modern machines, they go back to the ways of their ancestors: the Queen rides in an old carriage, drawn by horses, as her ancestors used to do, and she is followed and guarded by men on foot carrying old-fashioned weapons.

The Chiefs had two other lands on which people were bound to work, although here they did not work with such alacrity as on the first. These were the *ts'imo ea borena* or the land of the chieftainship—and the *ts'imo ea lelapa* or the land of the family. With the produce of these lands, the Chief supported and clothed his family and himself; he was not bound to feed his people from it.

A Chief's lands were far better and bigger than a commoner's, perhaps twenty times bigger, but they were still the lands of the Chief, about which we say, 'They cannot be measured.' Even so, the people did not begrudge their Chief his lands because we say that the Chief is the child of the people, and people ought to work gladly and joyfully to see that their child lacks nothing.

Consider the matter carefully, and you will see that the Chief was not exploiting his people, even when he made them work on lands from which only he and his family would profit. The Chief had no time to leave his duties to farm his lands or to work for money like other men; he was always expected to be at the service of his people. The Chief had to have sufficient income to put him above bribes and other temptations.

Chiefs also owned minor lands, and if they wanted work done on these, they would have to order their wives to cook food and brew beer and so invite people, by means of a feast, to plough for them. People were free to refuse to work on minor fields, and they did if they felt the Chief was starting to exploit them.

I remember one day we made a *letsema* to hoe a *ts'imo ea lira* under the supervision of Chief Mitchell. When we finished, he asked us to hoe two more lands, one belonging to Chieftainess MaMpoi and the other to Chieftainess MaNkuebe, Chief Mitchell's wives. We finished these two lands long before sunset. Then Chief Mitchell pointed out two other minor lands belonging to his wives, and asked us to hoe them as well.

'Oh, no!' someone shouted. 'We were only asked to hoe one *ts'imo ea lira*. We did that *and* the next two fields, although we were not bound to, as a favour. That's enough! Where does the food from these other fields go? Not to us!'

Chief Mitchell turned his horse at once and rode away, but his son Boshoane, still a youngster, was not so wise. He rode in among the people wielding his whip and threatening to thrash anyone who refused to hoe for the Chief.

'Just try!' the people shouted insultingly. 'Just try, and we will beat you! Do you think we're going to work on your mothers' lands without getting food for our work? We are not your slaves. Go and tell your mothers to bring us food, and then we'll work! If you don't, we're off home now.'

That was the end of our work for that day.

Now there are always lazy individuals, and the Chiefs sometimes had to enforce the custom of *letsema* by fining won't-works in their courts. I remember the case of Moloi Makoa, my cousin, who was fined while I was working as a clerk for Chief Boshoane. When he was instructed by his headman to join a *letsema* at the land called Sekants'ing, the *ts'imo ea lira* at Koma-Koma, Moloi flatly refused, saying he had already rendered his due by ploughing and hoeing the Chief's land at Mapoteng; why should he have to work twice over? Besides, he boasted, his cousin Stimela Jingoes was working in Chief Boshoane's own office and was an intimate of the Chief, so nobody could touch him!

The *letsema* took place without Moloi, and he was summoned to Chief Boshoane's court to account for his absence. From the moment he entered the Chief's village on the morning of his case, he pretended to be a lunatic, to escape punishment.

'Who doesn't know that my cousin works here?' he bellowed as he walked through the village. He caught sight of Chief Boshoane standing outside the court and said to him, without even a semblance of respect, 'Boshoane! Don't you know that you are younger than me?'

'I have never disputed with you about our age,' the Chief said gently, smiling at Moloi.

'So what are you doing now, calling me before your court?'

'I have not called you—it is the law that summons you.'

'Why and what for?'

'Go into the court and you will learn what for.'

Moloi swaggered into the court, waving his arms about and trying to create a scene, but he was quietly told to sit down and wait until his case came up; he would be attended to in due course. When his turn came, he was charged by the court for having failed to work in a *letsema*.

'But I've just worked in the *letsema* at Mapoteng!' he protested. 'So why should I have to go to the one at Koma-Koma? What are the rest of Boshoane's subjects doing—sitting in the shade?'

The court asked him whether he pleaded guilty or not guilty, and he said he was certainly not guilty. But the evidence against him was clear, and he was fined one goat, which he told the court they had no hope of getting from him.

From the court Moloi came straight to my office.

'I have been charged, found guilty, and fined here,' he told me. '*You* allowed these people to do this to me, so *you* are the one to pay this fine of mine.'

I said facetiously, 'I'm sorry, cousin, but I don't happen to have a goat with me right now!'

'Yes. . . . But still. . . . You ought to pay for me. You are the child of my maternal uncle; how *could* you let these people take steps against me? Why didn't you stop them?'

'The law is there. Had I gone against the law, I would also have been charged.'

'Can *you* also be charged, if you do wrong?' He was incredulous.

'Yes, indeed,' I assured him.

'So now what do I do? Will I have to pay this goat then?'

'Oh yes! You had better pay it! If you don't pay, you will cause lots of trouble.'

'I don't *want* to pay it! I *won't* pay it!'

'Tomorrow the Chief's messengers will be at your place to collect that goat, if you have not brought it down here yourself. They don't like having to fetch fines like that, and will tell you to cover their costs and inconvenience with another goat. You will end up by paying two goats.'

'What? *TWO*?'

'Yes.'

So Moloi decided to pay his fine at once.

As with all customs, *letsema* was abused by some Chiefs, and it could happen, for example, that a man would spend the crucial weeks of the ploughing or hoeing season working on various lands of the Chiefs and not get his own cultivating done. But, having worked on the Chief's lands, you could not die of starvation in the winter when the snow lay on the ground; nobody went from village to village begging, as people do today. A good Chief did not allow people to go hungry or to wear rags in his village.

Look at the case of Likotsi Leohla, a man who was shot during the battle between Chief Hlajoane and the men of Thota-Moli. Likotsi was a cripple because of his wounds. As often as the seasons changed, Likotsi would send someone to Chief Boshoane to say that his land had brought him nothing because he was unable to hoe properly, and that he was poor and had nothing with which to clothe himself. Then the Chief would arrange to give him a blanket and a pair of trousers, brand new, from the Mukunutlung store.

I can remember many other such people. There were two widows, one at Bela-Bela and one at Koma-Koma, who had no one to support them. They used to go to the Chief for assistance whenever they were in need, and they were never turned away empty-handed. All the Chiefs, sub-chiefs, and headmen used to report cases of need in their areas to the Principal Chief. When Chief Nkutu kept sending a certain woman to Chief Boshoane for support, the Chief told him, 'Nkutu, you are not a sub-chief or a headman: you are a Chief. So don't keep sending this person to me; see to it that you give her what she needs yourself.'

I say that when the old system was working well, people were fools who said they were being exploited by the Chiefs. As things changed, and the Chiefs rendered back less and less to the people, I can understand why there was growing bitterness about working for the Chiefs and getting little in return. But when a Chief was still Chief by the people, the people had no right to resent the *letsema* custom or the gifts their Chiefs expected of them.

*   *   *

At Mats'ekheng, we commoners never thought of the Chiefs as a force above us. We used to say that they were our children; we said that we paid for their wives with our cattle and that therefore their children belonged to us all. In return, we expected certain things from our Chiefs. We have often, literally, thrashed our Chiefs for having failed us in some way. We Mats'ekha like to think of ourselves as people who are not easily taken in; we cannot believe that simply because people are Chiefs they are right or true.

The first time I saw a Chief flogged with a whip was when I was a youth. Chief Peete called a *pitso* at Mapoteng one day and informed his people that the Paramount Chief had made a request of them. The request was that they should go and hold a *letsema* to hoe the lands of Chief Jonathan Molapo of the neighbouring chiefdom. This request, the Mats'ekha thought, was ridiculous. We were not bound, in any way, to work for any Chiefs other than our own, and besides, we felt we would be humbling ourselves to do so.

When Chief Peete had finished giving the Paramount Chief's message, he turned at once and scuttled into his house, not giving anyone time to argue or protest. He knew as well as we did that no one would like the idea of working for the Molapo Chieftainship.

His brother, Chief Seshophe, and his son, Chief Mitchell, were left facing the people at the *pitso*.

'Chief Seshophe!' someone shouted. 'Go and tell your brother that we are Mats'ekha. We have never bowed to Chief Molapo or Chief Masupha. We shall never bow to Chief Molapo or Chief Masupha. If this is our day to die, then we will die, but we *will not* hoe Chief Molapo's lands.'

Without a word, Chief Seshophe turned and entered his brother's *lelapa*. The crowd waited, muttering, but he did not come out again.

Then the people turned to Chief Mitchell and said to him, 'Chief, go and see what is keeping your uncle, Chief Seshophe.' When Chief Mitchell returned from the *lelapa*, he said, 'My father and my uncle say they cannot do otherwise—they are simply complying with an order from the Paramount Chief. . . .'

That was enough.

'Mitchell!' someone said—not 'Chief' or anything else, but just 'Mitchell!' 'Mitchell! Go and fetch your father and your uncle. Tell them to come out here to face us.'

Chief Mitchell entered the *lelapa* again, and this time he was gone for a long time. When at last he reappeared, he said, 'My father and my uncle say they cannot alter the Paramount Chief's word. . . .'

He got no further, for two men stepped up and whipped him with their sjamboks, while the rest surged forward. A man called Maqebo stepped in front of the people and gave the traditional greeting we usually reserve for Chiefs, '*Likhomo*, Mats'ekha! Peace!' but they whipped him as well. His attempt to create order had given Chief Mitchell time to slip inside the *lelapa*.

That was the day I realized how wild the Mats'ekha can be. They were striding up and down, shouting, 'We'll beat you, you boy! You cannot do what you please with us—*you are a Chief through us!*'

Chief Mitchell must have had some fine bruises to show his parents. After a long time Chieftainess MaLoela, the wife of Chief Peete, appeared before us.

'*Oho*, Mats'ekha . . . *Oho!*' she started, trying to pacify the men before her, but once the Mats'ekha are angry, they are angry.

'We don't want you!' someone shouted at her. 'We want Chief Peete. We want Chief Seshophe. We want the boy Mitchell.'

'You have already used your sjamboks on my child. Please, pay attention to what I am saying!'

At last the Chieftainess quietened the mob, and there was silence.

'My people,' she said quietly, 'I also agree with you about this thing, but don't do things in anger. My advice to you is to tell Chief Peete that you cannot agree to grant the request of the Paramount Chief, and then Chief Peete will pass your message on to the Paramount Chief.'

'We understand you, Chieftainess,' said the people, 'and we want to see Chief Peete now to tell him exactly that. Please tell him to come out with his brother and his son.'

When Chieftainess MaLoela came out of the *lelapa* again, she brought a message from her husband: 'I will not come out. I don't want to be sjambokked by the people!'

Well, the incident was closed. Nobody was ever asked again to work on a *letsema* for a Chieftainship other than our own.

Some people ruling nowadays think that to be a Chief is to be a tin god.

I have shown you a little of what the Chieftainship was like when Chiefs and people still respected each other. Lesotho was a land of order then. But in my lifetime, I saw this order and respect change, and Chiefs and people become foreigners to each other.

*   *   *

The period between 1938 and 1948 was a time of turmoil in Lesotho, when the trust between Chiefs and commoners was put to severe test, and when the Chiefs misguidedly signed away most of their powers. I was working as a clerk in the Chief's administration during this time, and I could see the old system crumbling.

The trouble started with the simple fact that there were too many Chiefs in Lesotho. There had been generations of Chiefs since the time of Moshoeshoe; this meant that there were many people of royal blood who expected, and who were given, areas over which to rule. By the 1930s the situation had reached the stage where these numerous petty Chiefs were involved in continual squabbles, trying to maintain and enlarge their territories; it was virtually impossible for them to find land over which to install their children. If you realize that each of these petty Chiefs had his own court, as well as the power to allocate lands and sites, you can see that a system like this created too many centres of power.

The British wanted to stabilize the existing political structure by recognizing only a limited number of Chiefs, sub-chiefs, and headmen. They put this proposal to the Paramount Chief and the Principal Chiefs, who consented to radical changes in the placement system. In essence, these changes meant that headmen, sub-chiefs, and Chiefs who were not gazetted were not officially recognized, and the right to gazette was placed, in effect, in the hands of the Principal Chiefs, who would act in consultation with the District Commissioners. This last had little meaning, because the D.C.s usually agreed with the Principal Chiefs simply because they were not as familiar with the people and areas concerned as the Principal Chiefs. The consequence of this was that the Principal Chief's power was increased enormously: he could appoint subordinates according to his own whims—a right he had never held in the traditional system where he was held in check by his subordinate Chiefs and relatives. Think how Chieftainess MaMakhabane was reprimanded by the Sons of Makhabane when they thought her actions arbitrary and senseless. The Principal Chief now had the backing and sanction of the Government, rather than the people, for his actions.

For the petty Chiefs, and especially for the headmen who were commoners, this was a blow. If they fell out of their Principal Chief's favour, and were struck from the gazette, they lost a major part of their income, the revenue from their courts, for Proclamation 62 of 1938 limited the number of courts to those authorities who were officially recognized.

*   *   *

The first the commoners of Mats'ekheng knew about the changes was when, in 1938, Proclamations 61 and 62 were made known to them by Chief Boshoane at a *pitso* he called at Koma-Koma for this purpose. These two Proclamations spelled out the changes that I have mentioned above. At this *pitso*, a man called Josiel Lefela of Mapoteng protested strongly against the reforms; he spoke for the people when he predicted the consequences that were in store for Lesotho. He saw, in the destruction of automatic hereditary rights to office, the beginning of the end of the Lesotho Chieftainship. I remember well his impassioned words.

'Now you have done away with Lesotho, you Chiefs. You have sold Lesotho. The people will suffer from today. Chiefs will not be respected as Chiefs any longer, because I can see that these Proclamations destroy the whole point of Chieftainship. You Chiefs, are you prepared to sell Lesotho? Are you sell-outs, you people? Why didn't you call the people when you gathered to discuss this reform?

'I, Lefela, tell you that I foresee the end of Lesotho in this thing because it will start events that will take away the Chiefs' power bit by bit. In these Proclamations it says that Chiefs will be known as Chiefs only if they are gazetted; this goes for sub-chiefs and head-men as well. This is to say the Lesotho Chieftainship will cease to be a Chieftainship by birth.

'What *is* going on? The day Moshoshoe was building this nation, he said a Chief is a Chief, a headman is a headman: they are to be respected because they were born to be rulers. But now, today, as you say the only people to be recognized will be those who are gazetted, you are saying that if *you* don't like a Chief or a headman, he will be struck from the gazette. The Chief could even take an ordinary man like myself and gazette me to rule, if he chose. . . .

'Are you prepared to abolish Moshoeshoe's customs and laws? Are you prepared to accept this *khubelu*—this book with red covers?[2] If not, take this book to the Paramount Chief and tell him to take it and place it before the British Resident Commissioner, and say to him, *The Basotho people say they are not prepared to accept this* khubelu, *because this book says that those who will rule Lesotho and those who will have power and authority in Lesotho will be only those who are gazetted*. Even those who are Sons of Moshoeshoe, even those whose parents were Chiefs or headmen, they will not rule by birth any longer.

'I appeal to you, my Chief, Chief Boshoane, if you are afraid to go and tell the Paramount Chief these things, please send *me*, and I will go.'

It was Chief Nkuebe, I recall, who stood up to reply to *Ntate* Lefela's speech.

'I know *Ntate* Josiel,' he said, 'and I like this old man. He disciplined me in my youth, and he never led me wrong. He used to be a man of some sense, but today he talks wildly. Today he does not know what he means. The Proclamations are correct. Today, as you all know, there are too many Chiefs and too many headmen in this country. These people are disputing with each other continually about territories and boundaries, and bringing hardships to the people. We, the Chieftainship, believe that if we follow these Proclamations things will turn out well, and Lesotho will be a more orderly place, worthy of respect.'

I am sorry to say that my friend, Nkuebe, was mistaken. As a commoner, I knew the bitterness that would follow when headmen were deprived of their power by the reforms. Many headmanships had been won by faithful service to Chiefs by men like Sotshangani and Ngolozani. These small headmen were struck hardest by the changes that placed so much power in the hands of the Principal Chiefs. Lesotho was built by such men; they were the ones who fought for Lesotho, and they were the ones who died for its people. Now they were the ones who lost most, for they could be demoted or gazetted subject only to the decision of their Principal Chief and the D.C. A Chief was no longer a Chief by the people, but by the Government.

*   *   *

You might be thinking, *What difference does it make? Succession to office was hereditary anyway, so the people themselves had no choice in who would rule them.*

This was not so.

The position was only hereditary in that a particular family or lineage retained the right to rule. The choice of the actual ruler was subject to the people's approval, even though the custom was that the first son of the senior house should rule. If that first son was, say, an idiot, the people would help decide who would act as ruler in his place.

An example that comes to mind is the village of Letsoela, whose headman was Moqeetsane. When he died, he left two sons: Mohapi was the elder, and Potfol the younger. It had happened that while their father was alive, Mohapi spent very little time at home as he worked as a policeman at Leribe. Whenever he was home, Mohapi was impatient with the people, ignorant of the affairs of the village, and unwilling to identify himself with the everyday life of the villagers, whom he considered peasants. The younger brother, Potfol, on the other hand, worked with his father in running the village, and he served the people with friendship and concern. So the people drew aside and looked blankly at Mohapi whenever he was home, for they knew he relied on his position as Moqeetsane's first son, and his power as a policeman, to carry him to the position of headman when his father died. By contrast, the people trusted Potfol and carried out his orders, for he was the one who stayed with them and who knew them all.

After the death of Moqeetsane, the people of the village accompanied the two sons to the court of Chief Mitchell, to report their headman's death, and to name his successor. Before the Chief, Mohapi claimed that he was the heir of Moqeetsane, and the villagers agreed happily with him; nobody was going to dispute that.

After Mohapi had spoken, Potfol stood up and said, 'I agree that my brother Mohapi is our father's heir, but I am the one who has been doing my father's work in the village all along, taking his orders and carrying them to the people. Nobody ever came from Mohapi to assist me in this work. Are you going to do away with me now, you people?'

Before the people could say anything, Chief Mitchell said, 'No-no-no-no-nooo! Potfol, you are wrong! The people are here to have their new headman installed. It is well known that Mohapi is senior to you, and it is the custom that he must take his father's position.'

'I do not deny, my Chief,' Potfol replied, 'that Mohapi is older than me. What I am trying to say is this: I was the one who sweated for these people of my father's village. You have seen me before your court several times. Whenever I appeared before you, I would say that I was there on behalf of my father, Moqeetsane, and you never contradicted me then, you never said I was wrong. You accepted me as Moqeetsane's representative because I was working for him. My Chief, did I ever say that I was representing my older brother? Did you ever tell me that I was representing him?'

Then Potfol turned to face the people and said, 'You people of Letsoela's village, if I ever said I was acting on behalf of my older brother when I was working for you, you must tell me now.'

The Chief did not give anyone time to speak, but said simply, 'People of Letsoela's village, your headman, Moqeetsane, has passed away. His first son and heir is Mohapi. Here is Mohapi now —your new headman. . . .'

At this the people said, 'We are sorry, Chief. . . .'

'What do you mean?'

Their spokesman said, 'My Chief, one day when we were at the *lekhotla* at home, Mohapi was there on a visit, and his father called him to be present at the hearing of cases. Mohapi had spent hardly any time in the court before he walked out, saying that he could not go on sitting in Sesotho courts because they irritated him. Now you, my Chief, want to give us this man who said he had no time to sit with us in our court? What kind of headman will he be?'

'Is there any truth in this?' demanded the Chief.

All the people shouted that it was indeed true, and that Mohapi would not deny it.

So the younger brother, Potfol, became their headman. However, he and his family never failed to show respect for Mohapi and his line, even though Mohapi moved away from Mats'ekheng. When people asked them why they always went out of their way to show deference to Mohapi's family, they would say, 'We were born Mohapi's servant, and we will die Mohapi's servant.'

In the traditional system, then, the people had extensive rights in choosing and recognizing their rulers. The Proclamations were framed without reference to the people, and deprived them of their rights.

*   *   *

But the Proclamations led to even worse abuses. Many Principal Chiefs saw to it that their favourites were gazetted, while many efficient and respected men went unrecognized.

From my position in Chief Boshoane's administration, I could see that the people were growing bitter, and I picked up strong under-currents of resentment from many quarters. All this found vent at a *pitso* which had been called for a trivial circular concerning stray animals; the people used the *pitso* to make their grievances known to the Chief.

Josiel Lefela was one of the men who spoke. Their drift was that there were many exemplary headmen with large, well-run villages who had not been gazetted, while lesser men had been recognized. I recall they talked about people like Nthoba, Sekoati, Malefetsane Khomaleburu, Ramaema, and Lihoapa Lejaha, men who had been passed over although they were sound administrators. They asked the Chief by what standards he judged men fit to be gazetted.

'Our task today is not an easy one,' Chief Boshoane said in reply. 'We are not gazetting everyone who is a Chief or headman ruling a large village. We are gazetting only people who have proved their worth, men who can set a good example to others. Having many tax-payers is not an automatic qualification for being gazetted.'

The people at the *pitso* were not satisfied. They asked the Chief to allow them to send a deputation before the Paramount Chief. Chief Boshoane said they were free to do so. They then elected a committee on the spot to compose a letter to the Paramount Chief, and when the letter was written Chief Boshoane endorsed it. His endorsement did not mean, necessarily, that he approved of the contents of the letter, but was merely to show that he was aware of the letter and that his people had passed through the proper channels with it.

The deputation proceeded to Matsieng to deliver the letter to the Paramount Chief. The Paramount Chief's clerk, Molise Tsolo, first read the letter and then took it before Paramount Chief Griffith, who asked where the deputation was and had them brought before him. He ordered his clerk to read the letter, and then asked, 'Is *this* the letter you have brought here?'

'Yes, Chief,' they replied. 'That is the letter we were sent to bring here before you.'

'Who sent you?'

'We were sent by the people of Mats'ekheng.'

'Have you the right to call a *pitso*, you people, and write such a letter?'

'No, we have no right to call a *pitso* ourselves, but there is a person at Mats'ekheng who does have the right to call a *pitso*—Chief Boshoane.'

'Why did you discuss *this* matter at that *pitso*?'

'We are Chief Boshoane's people. We have the right to talk at his *pitso*. After he had finished reading your orders about stray stock to us, we asked him whether he was finished with the business of the *pitso*, and he said he was. Then we told him we had something to talk about in his presence. We are his people. He let us speak.'

'Did he agree to *this*?' holding up the letter.

'My Chief, he did not agree. We only expressed our opinions to him. If Chief Boshoane agreed with our views, we would not have had to come before you today.'

'Is it your intention to alter what I have done, I and the Government?'

'Chief, as we are your subjects, we have the right to point out things we do not like, or things we notice will bring ill fortune upon you.'

The Paramount Chief became very angry indeed, and Chief Griffith was known to be terrible in his anger.

'I can blow you out!' he said. 'I can have you expelled from Lesotho NOW!'

'My Chief, if you blow us out of Lesotho, where will you ever find us again? We are your own Basotho, your loyal subjects. If we do wrong, we do it for you. And we believe that your advisers, if they advise you that you can blow Basotho about, are not really advisers at all. You are in the chair of the great Chief Moshoeshoe; we are honouring that chair, and we would not like the chair to be seen full of dust. We can come up here from time to time to wipe dust from that chair.'

They told us later that the Paramount Chief kept quiet then and looked at them steadily. At last he said, 'Among all the Chiefs in Lesotho, there is no Chief who has as hard a time in his administration as Chief Boshoane. His people are all politicians. I do not know how these people of Mats'ekheng became so spoiled! I will read and consider your letter.'

The interview was over.

But months passed and nothing more was heard about the interview with the Paramount Chief.

Then another *pitso* was called by Chief Boshoane to discuss routine administrative matters; this one was about *hlabahlabane*, the cockle burr that spoils wool and mohair. After the regular circulars had been read, it was announced that the Basutoland National Council was scheduled to sit the following month.

After this a man called Kaiser Sekoati stood up and said, 'My Chief, may we be allowed to speak?'

Sekoati was known for his views, which corresponded with those of Lefela, so the Chief tried to refuse to recognize him but the people made a hell of a noise.

'Let us speak!' they shouted. 'Let us give our views at this *pitso*! *We are free people here in Lesotho*!' The Chief was still shaking his head, but Chief Nkuebe said quietly to him, 'Let them talk!'

Sekoati was allowed to speak, and he asked the deputation that had been to see the Paramount Chief to come forward and give the people the Paramount Chief's reply to their letter. The people were told, by a spokesman of the deputation, that the Paramount Chief had promised to consider the matter and that perhaps he was still thinking it over because they had heard nothing more. Then Sekoati asked the people, 'What do you say about this, Mats'ekha?'

A man called Rabase Sekike replied, 'We had better send the deputation back to see the Paramount Chief.'

I did not think that would achieve anything, so I suggested, 'We have just been informed that the National Council will sit next month. We are represented on that Council. Why bother further? Let us hand our grievances to our representatives on the Council now.' Two men supported my suggestion, and it was adopted.

Our two representatives were Josiel Lefela and Matseketseke 'Neko. We asked them to stand up and they were formally told our grievance about the Proclamations.

'When you come to sit with the National Council,' they were told, 'speak to your fellow commoners on the Council. Place our complaint before them, and try to gain their support. Do not appeal to commoners alone, either: try to gain the ear of the Chiefs on the Council as well, and warn them that they are also in danger. As we see these matters, this will not end among headmen only; at last we might find that there are no more sub-chiefs; even Chiefs themselves might disappear as a result of these laws. So plead before the Council as strongly as you can that these two Proclamations be abolished. They are an ulcer on the body of the Basotho nation.'

The two men agreed, and *Ntate* Josiel spoke with such vigour and to such effect at the session of the National Council that when it ended he was apprehended as an agitator. It was only at the intervention of Chief Nkuebe—who was then working as a clerk to the Paramount Chief—that Josiel was released with a warning to avoid political games in the future.

But all our opposition was for nothing. The Proclamations were a fact, and they remained a fact.

*　　*　　*

Josiel Lefela had not been wrong in seeing the Proclamations as the forerunner of vast changes in Lesotho, changes that undermined the security of the lesser Chiefs and headmen. In order to secure their positions, and to make sure that they were gazetted, many of them turned to ritual murder. They wanted *liretlo* or potent medicine made from human flesh for their *manaka*. They believed that their *manaka* would have to be strengthened to protect them from the changes that were sweeping men like them from their positions.

At Mats'ekheng, then, at this time we had a series of such murders, murders that are still talked about.

I will recount to you a case concerning two men I knew who were in this insecure position. They were both descendants of Makhabane I.

Tabola and Lejaha were both lesser Chiefs at Mats'ekheng under the jurisdiction of Chief Nkutu, Tabola's father. As Chief Nkutu's first son, Tabola should have succeeded his father, but Chief Nkutu favoured Malibeng, Tabola's younger brother, as his heir and it was common knowledge that he wanted Malibeng to succeed him. Tabola was afraid that he was going to lose his rights to Malibeng. He shared his insecure position with Lejaha.

Lejaha had inherited the large area known as Liotloaneng from his grandfather, Puoane. In his position as sub-chief of Liotloaneng under Chief Nkutu he ruled a number of villages. But when Malibeng came of age, Chief Nkutu installed him in Lejaha's position, relegating Lejaha to the position of a headman over one village only, under Malibeng.

Thus the two men, Tabola and Lejaha, had a common grievance. Both had lost status and power because of the actions of a superior Chief. Both men knew that they could not appeal to higher authority or to the people because Chief Nkutu had the ear of the Principal Chief, who would make use of his new-found power to support Nkutu by gazetting Malibeng. Tabola and Lejaha had to live with the galling fact that a man younger than them, Malibeng, had dispossessed them.

They turned to ritual murder and the belief in the efficacy of *liretlo* for help.

Under Tabola there lived a man called Seleka Mosese, who was a favourite of both Tabola and Lejaha. As they both trusted him, Seleka was chosen to lure a victim to a chosen spot up in the mountains, where Tabola and Lejaha would await them with their men. The trap was set, but Seleka arrived alone, saying that the man he was bringing them was still on his way. That day the victim did not come. They returned home, telling Seleka to bring the man another day. When that day came, Seleka failed again. This time Seleka was warned that the Chiefs were getting tired of riding so far for nothing. It seemed that he despised them, they said. When Seleka arrived alone on the third occasion, the Chiefs asked him in a bantering tone how he would deal with the victim if he arrived. Going to a large tree, Seleka described to them how he would tie the man to the tree before cutting him. As he was miming the part of the victim, with his hands drawn back around the bole of the tree, the Chiefs pinioned his arms and fastened him to the tree.

'You will take your victim's place,' they told him.

In Seleka's pocket was a large sum of money the Chiefs had given him as advance payment for finding them a man to slaughter. Seleka pleaded with them to take that money and let him go, but the Chiefs said, 'We don't want money; we need *manaka*,' and they cut Seleka.

Seleka's mother had known about the plan, and was pleased that her son had been given the role of decoying a victim for his Chief. When that evening the Chiefs and their men rode past her house on their way home, she ululated stridently, running to the Chiefs' party as they crossed the stream on their horses.

'Who has been killed?' she whispered conspiratorially.

'Seleka. Your son,' they told her loudly.

At first she did not believe them, knowing that Seleka was their favourite, but Seleka did not come home. His body was found beside a stream.

Tabola and Lejaha were both hanged, together with twelve of their followers.

Cases of this type became notorious in Lesotho. The Chiefs were scared, and they seemed to follow each other in these ritual murders; they were almost like a fashion. I knew then, and I know now, that these murders were caused by the Proclamations. The Chiefs were not wicked or bad men: they were insecure men, who turned to the supernatural in an attempt to resist losing their rights.

*   *   *

The commoners of Mats'ekheng, whose feelings were so strong about the Proclamations of 1938, were right when they said, 'This will not end here.'

Between 1943 and 1945 still more changes came to our country. The British said that as we Basotho had been clamouring for independence and more control over our own affairs, they would grant us this. A good place to start, they said, would be by establishing a Basutoland National Treasury, the funds of which would come partly from a new system of law courts that were to be started.

Up to this time, the only courts we had had ourselves apart from the British hierarchy of Magistrates' courts, High Court, and so on, were the Chiefs' courts. The Chiefs could impose fines in their courts, and dispose of that income as they pleased. And in those days, our Chiefs were rich—not beggars, as they are today.

A new system of courts was introduced now, which we knew as the Basotho Treasury courts. People working in these courts were salaried officials, and fines from the courts no longer went to the Chiefs. But the Principal Chiefs still, in effect, retained the power to appoint court officials, in conjunction with the D.C.s. Previously, every gazetted Chief had had a court; now the number of these courts was cut down drastically.

The whole question of the income of the Chieftainship was reviewed, and far-reaching changes were made. For example, where previously all stray stock had gone to the Chieftainship, it now had to be sold and the money given to the central Treasury. The fines levied by the official courts were now to be paid to the Treasury as well, instead of being kept by the Chiefs. To recompense the Chiefs for losing the major portion of their income, they were to be paid regular salaries by the Government.

Suggestions for these reforms were mooted in the National Council and were approved by an overwhelming vote. The Chiefs, by so doing, signed away their rights for a mess of pottage, as the Bible says. Envisaging a steady monthly income, they thought they would gain more from the Government than they had had from their people. The voices of those few who disagreed, among them Paramount Chieftainess MaNts'ebo, were drowned.

* * *

I learned about these reforms for the first time when Chieftainess MaMakhabane returned from that session of the National Council. She sent for me and ordered me to send out circulars to convene a *pitso*. Then she told me, 'Now we are going to be paid!' She was very excited.

'What do you mean, *paid*?' I asked her.

'We Chiefs will be paid by the Government from now on, and the money collected by our administration, in fines and so on, will be sent to them, to a central treasury.'

'Are you not being paid right now?'

'No. We are not being paid.'

'Oh, you mean you don't want to be supported by your people; you want money from the Government.'

'You people don't pay us Chiefs—all you give us is the odd tickey.'

'Well, if things like this are going on, it's clear you Chiefs want to make yourselves independent of your people.'

'No, it's not that. It's of no use trying to stop this, because we've already decided upon it. It is done. There were a few who did not agree, but the rest of us simply laughed at them. The Paramount Chieftainess was reluctant to have this system introduced, but that is because she's jealous—she used to be the only Chief with a salary; now we are all going to be paid.'

I asked the Chieftainess, 'Why are you so keen on these reforms? How is it going to improve your lot? Why are you doing away with your people?'

'Money!' she replied, smiling.

'What money?' I pressed.

'You're just jealous! We will get money, cash money, from the Treasury, and we will easily support our children on it. Don't go on and on at me!'

'Chieftainess! Was there ever a day that you went to bed without having eaten? Was there ever a year when you lacked clothes? Have you ever turned to your people for money and been refused?'

'All you gave was tickeys—a mere trifle! Now I want *real* money!'

I said, 'Well, thank you! I have heard!'

When the circular arrived from the Paramount Chieftainess to be announced to the people, I approached the Chieftainess again. I asked her, 'Won't you decide differently?'

'NO!'

Chief Nkuebe arrived to help her arrange the *pitso* at which the people would be notified of all the changes their Chiefs had agreed upon, and I tried to make him see reason. I explained to him my certainty that the innovations, in the long run, would be a danger to the Chiefs of Lesotho.

'My friend Jingoes,' Chief Nkuebe said to me, 'you are right, I know that. But what can anyone do about it if all the Chiefs have voted for it? I myself can see trouble ahead for the Chieftainship, but we who saw this were beaten by the vote.'

There were more than one thousand of Mats'ekheng's people at the *pitso*; as Chieftainess MaMakhabane's clerk, I was ordered to read them the circular from the Paramount Chieftainess which set out in detail the changes that were about to take place in Lesotho. When I had finished, there was no unanimity among the crowd in their reaction. Some commoners thought that the new courts, with their more formal procedure, would rescue them from bondage to the whims of the Chief. Others recalled the words of Josiel Lefela, when he condemned change of this kind as bound to destroy the Chieftainship and the ways of our society. Some said, 'At last we will have some control over our cases in the courts because the circular says we will have to pay money to open a case; once they have taken our money, they will *have* to attend to our cases promptly and fairly. We are sick of the Chiefs' courts as they are now, because we don't pay them to hear our cases, and they mess us about!' But others said, 'These changes attack our customs. They are separating the people from their Chiefs.'

The *pitso* degenerated into a mere hubbub. The people did not see the full implications of the reforms, really, thinking only of their court cases and the beneficial effect the reforms would have on their lives. They did not look ahead.

When I saw that no powerful speaker was coming from the

people to object to the circular, I stood up and asked for permission
to speak.

'Open your eyes!' I said to the people. 'Look at this carefully.
The Chiefs do not seem to realize that our cattle, our sheep, our
grain, constitute their wealth. They do not realize that every time
they fine someone a goat, a sheep, or an ox in their courts, they are
getting wealth. They confuse wealth with cash: just because they
will get ready cash from the Government, they think they will be
richer than ever. *But they are wrong.* They are losing a revenue
from us people that cold money will never equal.

'And as for you people: you are used to sitting in the courts
and sharing the fines. If you are hungry in court from now on,
where will the Chief find a goat to slaughter for you? In winter,
where will the Chief buy grain with his cash to give to your children
when they are hungry? Haven't you heard, you people, that stray
animals and their revenue will be taken from the Chiefs? How will
they find animals, now, to make feasts for you? Do you not see
that this will bring poverty to the Basotho people and their Chiefs?'

Some shouted that I was right, but others said, 'No, he's talking
nonsense!' The Chieftainess herself was in her *lelapa*, listening to
us, and now she called out, 'Don't follow him! He's jealous because
you and I will be getting money. He does not like to see people
getting money!'

So I kept quiet. I did not tell them that their joy in the new
courts would be spoiled when they found that, because there were
fewer courts, they would have to travel further to have their cases
heard, and that, if they lost their cases, they would have to pay
costs for both parties. There were many things like that that I did
not tell them.

*　　*　　*

On the day of that *pitso*, two men from Matsieng were present,
representatives sent by Paramount Chieftainess MaNts'ebo to
gauge the reaction of the people to the circular. These men reported
my protest to the Paramount Chieftainess and the next time I was
at Matsieng in connection with a case, she sent for me to speak
before her and her advisers about these matters.

I was taken before her by Chief 'Mari Leloko Lerotholi and
Chief Khosimotse Ntaote, and was invited to speak my mind.

'My Chief,' I started, 'this is a troubled subject. Today your
rights are being taken away from you. Some people believe that you

are against these reforms because you want to be the only Chief drawing a salary, the only Chief who is paid in cash. These people are envious of your position—that is why they speak like this. There never was a child who did not envy his parents. I mention this because people have been discussing your opposition to these reforms. You receive an annual gratuity from the Government; they think that if they get monthly salaries, they will have scored over you. They are greedy for money, and have forgotten about what is good for the nation.

'My Chief, this is going to destroy some good customs of the Basotho. I foresee that the day will come that if a man comes here to Matsieng on administrative business, he will not be accommodated and given hospitality, as has always been the custom in the past. He will be like a man in a city, looking for a hotel. I am saying this because your courts are going to be controlled by the British Government, and like a British office of business, after five o'clock in the afternoon, they will be locked. If people arrive here late at night, they will not be offered the hospitality that is traditional in Lesotho. If it is winter, they will suffer from the cold. Your *lekhotla* will be closed; its officials will not feel bound to put up travellers in their homes.

'I also foresee the day when poor people will come to Matsieng saying that they are hungry and have nothing to eat. Today, before these reforms have been introduced, when a person arrives here in the evening, tired and hungry, he will find a fire burning at the *lekhotla*, and he will know that he can go and ask for shelter from the men of the *lekhotla*, and he will be welcomed. He will eat food taken to the *lekhotla* from your herds. But as from April 1946, when these reforms come into effect, where will people find such food?

'Apart from this,' I concluded, 'your cattle are being taken away from you against your will.'

The Paramount Chieftainess started and said, 'What do you mean, Jingoes? My cattle are being taken from me? By whom?'

'By the British Government,' I replied. 'Your cattle, Chieftainess, for you are the Paramount in Lesotho, are stray animals. They are your bread, and the bread of your people. . . .'

The Chieftainess nodded.

'We are cutting away our customs too fast,' I pressed on. 'I say to you, my Chief, that we Basotho are still backward; we are still far from ready to adopt Western systems. I appeal to you to approach your Government. Tell them that the time is not yet ripe. I do not

mean that I am against what the Government is introducing—I
know that we need many reforms in our country—but this is not
the time for us to change our ways so radically—not yet. Let the
British teach us first how to handle new ways; let them take some of
our people and school them overseas; when they come back, then
we will be ready to handle our own affairs. Although some people say
they will be glad to know that their cases will be dealt with quickly
by these new courts, one day they will discover that this is not so—
their cases will not be dealt with, and judgments will not be executed
as smoothly as they think they will.'

That is how I spoke that day before Paramount Chieftainess
MaNts'ebo Seeiso.

From that day I found favour with Chieftainess MaNts'ebo.
Whenever I arrived at Matsieng she expected me to report my
presence to her personally. Even after she left the regency, if I
happened to be at Matsieng, she would send for me to call on her.
Just recently, when I was at Matsieng on church business, I found
that our discussions had taken more time than I had expected, and
that I would have to leave without seeing the Chieftainess. As we
were leaving, some of the men of Matsieng asked me whether I had
called to see the Chieftainess.

'No,' I said, 'I haven't.'

'Why not?'

'Well, we were busy, and we're about to leave now. It's getting
late.'

One of them, Komiti, shouted, 'Wait!' and ran down to the
Chieftainess's place. He returned at once, and ordered the driver of
our car to wait.

'Chieftainess MaNts'ebo wants to see *Ntate* Jingoes,' he said.
'Come, Jingoes! Hurry, man!'

When I came before Chieftainess MaNts'ebo she asked me
whether I still thought of her, and what I thought these days about
the Basotho. Before I could reply, she said, 'Do you remember the
day when you talked about the reforms that were coming to
Lesotho? Well, all the things you predicted have happened. Those
who have died have been spared from seeing the things I see and
experience today. . . .'

*   *   *

If I have given the impression that the British deliberately
undermined our Chieftainship, I am wrong. They acted in good

faith. Reform was wanted and needed at that time; wanted by the people and the Chiefs alike and needed because of the conditions in some Chieftainships. I do not quarrel with that. What I do quarrel with is that the reforms came too suddenly, and altered, before we were ready for it, the customs of trust and reciprocity between Chiefs and people.

Many commoners, prior to the reforms, used to complain that the Chiefs' courts did not deal with cases satisfactorily, and their complaint was, in many cases, a justifiable one. The workers in the courts had no fixed income and were not committed to their work. Many Chiefs, too, did not take their duties seriously; they did just enough to get by so that they were not liable to reprimands or fines from the D.C.s and the Paramount Chief. Chiefs' clerks had no regular wage from their Chiefs. In my case, the Chief sometimes gave me £3 a month, other times I received £5; it depended on what we had gathered from the people during the month. The people who worked in the Chief's court were the same; what they received depended on the fines levied in the court. Consequently, they sometimes levied as high a fine as possible, to increase their own cut. It is also widely known that Chiefs' clerks took bribes to line their own pockets at the people's expense. I myself did not do so—I have never trusted bribery because it is a two-edged weapon.

In the court of a really corrupt Chief, under the old system, a court case could go something like this.

You assume your Chief is fond of beer, so you take him to the beerhouse in the morning before the court opens. You do this so that when the Chief arrives in court he is already mellow and, what is more, he remembers you as the man who paid for his beer. You pay for as much as he can drink so that when he takes his place in court he is drunk, virtually speechless, and he slumps down in his chair, mumbling, 'I am the Son of . . .' and singing his praises to himself.

When your poor opponent, let us call him Jan, who is suing you for having taken his land from him, and who cannot afford to ply the Chief with beer, starts to state his complaint against you, he barely has time to speak before the Chief tells him in a bleary voice, 'You commoner! You had better behave yourself better than this!' Jan looks at the Chief in horror, because he knows, and you know, and the court knows, that he is not the one who is at fault. But the Chief continues, pounding a plump fist on the table, 'You come to this court saying this and that against this good subject of mine. . . . I can see that in this dispute you don't know what you're talking about! If you carry on like this, my man, you will be charged. . . . There will be no mercy for your type! You are obstructing the law. . . .' And so on, in the same vein.

Then, when the Chief is ready to impose judgment in your favour against poor Jan, he stands up and says he is just going to his house for a moment. You recognize that as your cue, and get smartly to the beerhouse again, where the Chief joins you presently. Again, you produce two-and-six to buy him beer. If you want to be really sure of your case, you pass the Chief ten shillings or more, and say, 'Here is some food for you, my Chief.'

You can be sure now that the case will not go against you. The Chief then goes stumbling back into the *lekhotla*, muttering, 'Where's that little man who thinks he's so great?' Jan, the unfortunate wretch, murmurs, 'Here I am, my Chief . . . ,' and the Chief barks at him, 'Come and stand before this court!'

The Chief picks up a scrap of paper from his table and pretends to read his judgment from it. 'In this case of Thabo and Jan, who are disputing about the land at the foot of the hill of so-and-so's village, it is quite clear that Thabo is a man of law, while Jan is a person who always comes to court to argue about things he knows nothing about, only wanting other people's things. The evidence given before the court by the witnesses showed clearly that the land belongs to Thabo. As for you, Jan, this court can help you with nothing! You have wasted Thabo's time, when he could have been working for his children. You are fined a goat. Go home and keep the peace!'

Then you laugh at the poor complainant who thought he could keep his land from you, 'My friend, I told you I'd win!'

The unfortunate Jan now says, 'I appeal, Chief!' and takes his appeal before the Paramount Chief's court at Matsieng. Even there, you know your way about, and you know how expensive things can be there for a litigant whose case is delayed. You go armed with one-pound notes to smooth your way. You oil the right hinges, and Jan's appeal will be delayed for a long time until, trying to be honest, he has exhausted his provisions and his money, and goes back home, his appeal unheard. You keep his land.

I do not say that I have, myself, ever seen such a thing, but I have heard of it. Although I like the Chieftainship, these are hard things and serious.

*   *   *

From 1938 on, the changes in the administration caused tremendous confusion among headmen and Chiefs alike. For example, one of the innovations was that births and deaths were to be recorded and that all administrators were to submit a monthly report to their superiors. This sort of office work was utterly strange to lower administrative officials, and most of the men involved were unable to cope. Those who could read and write found things easier and they managed to keep abreast of events, but the Chiefs and headmen who had to rely completely on clerks to keep them informed, were lost. Many fell behind in their work, and were quite bewildered by any new instruction.

Court procedure was radically changed as well, even in the 1930s. For example, statements and answers to questions had to be recorded in writing; monthly reports had to be submitted by each court.

After the reforms of the 1940s, when headmen and Chiefs lost the right to impose fines in their courts, the situation was chaotic for some time, for many of them persisted in the old ways, and kept the fines for their own benefit. They could not realize that they no longer had official courts. They were told, repeatedly, that their courts existed only in an unofficial capacity, to make peace between their subjects. They were only mediators, without powers to enforce their decisions. This they could not grasp. What had always been tradition, had suddenly become misappropriation of property. Many headmen had to be punished in this period of confusion.

One day on my return from work, I was told that there had been a case at Tsokung's *lekhotla* before the headman, Lehlobi Rachakane. The case was between Mputi and Letsoala, who were disputing about a goat. One of Letsoala's goats had been sent with Mputi's flock to find good grazing high up in the mountains at a cattle post. When Mputi's goats returned, out of all the flock, Letsoala's goat was the only one that was missing. Mputi could not explain to Letsoala why *his* was the only one to have suffered misfortune. One of the herdboys who had taken the flock to the mountains said that Mputi had slaughtered Letsoala's goat to provide meat for his herdboys up at the cattle post.

So Letsoala charged Mputi before the Tsokung headman's court. Mputi was found guilty, and told to pay Letsoala two goats: one to replace the missing goat and one as compensation. He was also told to bring a goat to the *lekhotla* as a fine. Mputi paid the three goats that very day and the court's goat was slaughtered and eaten by the men of the *lekhotla*.

At that time I was working as an assessor in the new Treasury court, but in my capacity as an ordinary inhabitant of Tsokung, I told the people concerned that they should return the three goats at once to Mputi. I explained that their court had no right to impose fines like that, and that Letsoala should have taken the case to the Treasury court and charged Mputi there. Unfortunately for the parties concerned, the third goat was no longer there. I told them that they were breaking the law. Lehlobi pleaded with me, 'I see that I have committed an offence, and that I should be charged. But I did not do it on purpose—I did not know. . . . Please just warn me not to do it again. I'll be fined heavily if this matter ever came before the courts.'

I felt sorry for Lehlobi, but I could not, as a court official, overlook it—this kind of judicial overlap had to be sorted out. Lehlobi's wife also came to me, and pleaded with me, saying that they could not afford a fine, and that her husband had done wrong unwittingly; he had not understood the nature of the new court system. I said I could not give her an answer, but could only tell the Principal Chieftainess, and leave it in her hands.

I was not being hard. I was only carrying out the law I had fought so hard against.

The following day I met Chieftainess MaMakhabane and told her. She said Lehlobi ought to be charged before the Treasury court. Chief Dyke, the court president, said in his judgment that Lehlobi had committed an offence, but that as this was a new law, he would only caution him. If he repeated his mistake, he would feel the arm of the law. Letsoala's goat could be kept by him; the second goat he had to return to Mputi.

As Chief Dyke's assessor, I was about to bring up the question of the third goat that had been eaten by the *lekhotla*, but Lehlobi was really upset by then, so I said nothing. After they had left, Chief Dyke asked me for the whole story, and when he had heard it, he wanted to charge Lehlobi for theft, but I said, 'No, my Chief, you have already cautioned the man—don't do it.' Chief Dyke wanted to proceed further, and the other court assessor was of a like mind, but I insisted that the judgment had already been given, and pointed out that one could not have two judgments in one case. The matter rested there.

It was not only small headmen who made this mistake: several

Chiefs and sub-chiefs were guilty as well, whether knowingly or unknowingly I cannot say. The confusion lasted about three years in all, and the Principal Chieftainess had to call many *lipitso* to remind her subordinates of all their new duties. At one such *pitso* at Koma-Koma, Chief Malibeng Nkutu and headman Arone Ntsoso complained about the reforms, saying that they had accepted them foolishly and blindly.

'We have never been as poor as we are today,' they said. 'In the time before the Treasury came, money said *Baas* to all Chiefs and headmen. But nowadays, my people, we are poor. We have become beggars in our own country. How do you feel about these events and things?'

Many Chiefs and headmen at the *pitso* shouted out in agreement, but it was too late to do anything about it.

They were only starting to realize now what I had told them a long time before: that the fines they used to collect added up to much more than the salaries or gratuities they now drew. These people had not been used to dealing with cash money, and they did not fully realize the value of stock. They were tempted therefore by the prospect of cash in hand, not seeing that, in real terms, the animals were worth much more. People like myself, simply because we had more experience of working with cash, could see the difficulties ahead. The Chiefs now began to suffer from a hunger for meat. Before these reforms, we Basotho did not suffer from this meat hunger; we always got meat two or three times a week at the *lekhotla*. Now Chiefs and headmen started to know what it is like to be without meat.

Not only Chiefs and headmen had trouble in implementing the new laws: the people suffered as well because they knew nothing about the revised court procedure. For instance, in the old Chief's court, the Chief himself would, by question and answer, seek to elicit the facts of the case and break down false testimony. Anyone present at the *lekhotla* was free to question or challenge a witness whose evidence they suspected; they could bring all their own private knowledge of the case in question to bear, in order to find a just solution. In the new Treasury courts, where procedure was far more formal and inflexible, the two parties came to the courtroom as formal litigants. They had to run their whole case for themselves; they were responsible for all cross-questioning. They could not rely on the court for this, for the court only put questions to clear up vague points for itself. This was beyond the grasp of the

Ngaka and assistant

Lethuela

Mathuela

Chief Sebathali Mokhachane, Mr. Jingoes, and Chieftainess Konesoang (MaThakane Theko), sister of the late Chief Gabashane Masupha, at Thaba Bosiu in 1969. Mr. Jingoes is holding Moshoeshoe's gun

Mr. Jingoes outside the house of Chieftainess MaMathe G. Masupha, 1973

Mrs. NoMaqhesha Jingoes in her garden at MaMathe's, 1973

Mr. and Mrs. Jingoes. 'I am not ending my days leaning against the wall in the sun'

average peasant, who had no legal experience of this nature. The formality of court procedure overawed the simple man; he could find in it nothing of the informal atmosphere that characterized the men's *lekhotla*.

This sort of thing would keep happening in court. Two parties would come before the court with their witnesses. The plaintiff would simply say, 'I am claiming such and such . . .' and then he would dry up, and stand there shuffling his feet, waiting for the court to help him as his Chief used to help him. He could not go further. When his witnesses appeared, the court would ask him whether he was going to lead them with questions or whether he wanted them to give their statements unguided. He would reply, 'How do you mean, *lead* them? They are my witnesses. They know everything. They will say what they know about the case.' The witnesses were in the same boat as the litigants; without the help of skilful questions, they often missed the whole point of their evidence and either rambled on or just dried up. If either party was asked to prove his statement, he would say to the president of the court, 'You, my Chief, you are the one to talk for me, as I've brought my case before you. . . .' From the defendant, you would hear a simple denial: 'I have said, my Chief, that I have not done this thing I am charged with; I have confidence in you and your court to help me.'

At that time, then, the president and his assessors had a hard time. They not only had to hear disputes and administer justice, but they also had to take time to teach the Basotho how to speak and behave before the court. During the breaks, one would see groups of people clustered around the courtroom, asking and giving advice about how to run cases, reminding each other of what the president had said in a similar case the week before, and so on. Although they learned fast, there are still people today who fear the Local Courts—as the Treasury courts are now known—and who stammer and stutter, losing their cases because of fright and lack of know-how.

*   *   *

If headmen and petty Chiefs were insecure after the 1938 reforms, by the end of the 1940s they were desperate. There was a wave of ritual murders during those years that dismayed the authorities and made the name of Lesotho notorious. That there was a correlation between the Proclamations and reforms and the outbreak of ritual murder was clear to the people, who coined the phrase, '*Marena a ts'aba ho faoloa*'—'the Chiefs are afraid of being

8

castrated'. During those black years the saying was often on people's lips. Parents would warn their children when they were going to the fields to walk in groups and not to stay out until after dark because *marena a ts'aba ho faoloa.*

When the commoners of Lesotho began to realize that their Chiefs were finishing them off like sheep with these murders, they started to lose confidence in their Chiefs. It used to be the custom that any Chief could send word to one of his subjects, even in the middle of the night, that he wanted him to go on an errand, or that he wanted to see him urgently, and the people obeyed. From the late 1930s, however, commoners began to fear their Chiefs, and especially any summons after dark. They would simply refuse to obey such a summons, knowing that murder victims can be caught only too easily at night without anyone being the wiser. People stopped travelling after sunset, and stayed in their houses, securely locked up.

What had happened was that the Chiefs and the people had become separated by walls of mistrust.

*   *   *

Now even before the reforms of the 1930s and 1940s, the Basotho had started forming political organizations to fight for the rights of the people. The first of these, the *Lekhotla la Tsoelo-pele* or Progressive Association, started pressing as early as the 1910s that commoners be relieved of such burdens as the *letsema* custom. They laid their requests and complaints before the National Council. In respect of ploughing for the Chiefs, they were successful in the early 1920s, for the *matsema* for headmen and sub-chiefs were abolished then. Not content, they pushed their demands further, pointing out how much time a man can spend ploughing for his Chief as well as his Principal Chief on all their lands. The *matsema* for Chiefs were consequently abolished in the 1930s.

By this time a new organization had gained great popularity in Lesotho, the *Lekhotla la Bafo* or Commoners' Association, to which belonged such men as Josiel Lefela, Ramokhele Lekomola, Kelebone Rametse, and Rabase Sekike.

These two organizations succeeded finally in having the Principal Chiefs' *letsema* outlawed in the 1940s; it was replaced by a *letsema* levy to be paid by every man along with his poll-tax, the levy being one shilling per year.

It was the *Lekhotla la Bafo* in particular that I associate with those eventful years in the Lesotho administration, because this organization stirred up a lot of conflict and questioned everything the Chiefs did, in the interests of the commoners. Men such as Lefela started out with assurances that they supported the Chieftainship, and said they were only trying to warn the Chiefs of the dangers to which they were exposing themselves by supporting the reforms, but they ended up by posing quite a serious threat to the Chieftainship, so strong was their following.

You can imagine that I worked for the Chieftainship with divided loyalties at this time. The commoners obviously had grievances. While I was in the Union I had fought for the underdog, yet here I was working for the Chiefs. I could not turn my back wholly on the strong political attraction of the commoners' cause. Some of them accused me of being a sell-out to the Chiefs. Two of their leaders, Roma 'Neko and Rabase Sekike, demanded, 'How can a man of your stature keep working for the Chiefs when they pay us like they do? We have heard that you were a politician in the Union, working for the rights of the people. But it seems to us that your I.C.U. wasn't an organization at all; it did not want to help people to be free, because you work here like a slave without pay, and most of the people work for the Chiefs without pay.'

In reply I said to them, 'The I.C.U. was an organization of great strength. It taught people to respect the law until the time came for them to be free. It did not advocate taking freedom by force, prematurely. Do you expect the people to go on strike against the Chieftainship? That would be wrong. . . . The point is that we must speak softly to the Chiefs until we can win their confidence.'

I was told, at one of the annual conferences of the *Lekhotla la Bafo* at Mapoteng, that the I.C.U. and its members were not welcome among its ranks. They told me, 'We cannot invite *good boys* to our conferences. We invite only men who fight for the benefit of the Basotho or for Africans as a people, men who want to fight capitalism. Africa is a place for commoners, not capitalists. Your I.C.U. never fought capitalism.'

Despite their snub and their communistic leanings which, they gathered correctly, I did not support, I watched the way they worked with fascination. Those men were good!

They gave the Chief of Mats'ekheng a hard time on many occasions; Chief Boshoane often had to think fast to get out of the corner they had driven him into, and he often failed. They concentrated their activities on days when the Chief held a *pitso*.

First they would record the date and number of any circular that was read for public notice, so as to keep a record to which they could refer later, and then they started with their questions as soon as the *pitso* was open for discussion.

One day Chief Boshoane read a circular concerning stock; all animals, it said, had to be driven behind the mountains by a certain date every year. Oxen could only be brought to the lowlands to plough in spring, while goats and donkeys would have to remain behind the mountains all year. In addition, the number of donkeys brought into Lesotho would have to be reduced and controlled because donkeys are destructive feeders and a danger to the grasses of the lowlands.

Once this information had been read, Ramokhele opened the attack: 'May I ask some questions, my Chief?' Because Ramokhele was known as a trouble-stirrer by the Chief, he and his counsellors did not want to recognize him, but the *pitso* has a long tradition of freedom, by which people have the right to discuss what their Chief has told them, so at last Ramokhele was allowed to go ahead.

'You have read us the circular from the Paramount Chief,' he said, 'and you have read us the letter from the D.C. of Leribe and the D.C. of Berea, all talking about our stock. The Paramount Chief lives at Matsieng, and neither of the D.C.s lives here at Mats'ekheng. These people do not farm with cattle. What I, and these Basotho gathered here, would like to know, my Chief, is this: when this circular was discussed, were the Basotho people consulted and asked for their views?'

'No,' replied Chief Boshoane, 'but this law was passed by the National Council.'

'Oh. Which National Council?'

'The one that sat this year.'

'Are you telling these people that when you returned from the session of the National Council at Maseru, you knew all about this law?'

'Yes, I did.'

'Why didn't you report to us about it the day you called us here to tell us the agenda of the National Council? You said nothing that day about this law concerning our livestock.'

'I did not tell you because you have your own representatives in the National Council.'

'Who are our representatives?'

'You have Josiel Lefela, Matseketseke 'Neko, and Teboho Thokoane.'

'*What?* Were these men elected by us to represent us?' This came from Rabase Sekike, sitting near Ramokhele.

'I was just going to ask that!' exclaimed Ramokhele.

This was a telling blow, for at that time the people's representatives to the National Council were nominated by the Principal Chiefs.

'Well . . . ,' said Chief Boshoane, 'they were nominated by us, by the Chieftainship, but they are none the less there to represent you, the people.'

Ramokhele turned to the people dramatically and cried, 'Do you know, you people, that Lefela, 'Neko, and Thokoane are your representatives on the National Council?'

Some shouted 'Yes', and others shouted 'No'.

This infuriated Ramokhele, who called for a show of hands to determine how many did not know their own representatives, but the Chief intervened.

'I am sorry, Ramokhele,' he said. 'We are not here to vote today. You wanted only to know what was going on, and it is up to the people to know who their representatives are. I cannot understand you. You knew these men were your representatives; why didn't you take the whole matter up with them? Or, if you object to them, why did you allow them to represent you at this session? You could have complained to me . . . .'

'Well, if things are like that,' resumed Ramokhele, 'we ask you, my Chief, to tell the Paramount Chief and his Government from us, the Mats'ekha, that it will be impossible for us to take our stock behind the mountains on the date given, and that we cannot, above all, remove our donkeys from the lowlands. Donkeys are our transport. We use them to carry our grain from the lands to our homes, and from our homes to the mills, and from the mills to the stores to sell. We do know that donkeys are heavy grazers, but we cannot do without them.

'Again, you put us in difficulties by saying we must remove our sheep and goats from the lowlands. We are afraid, my Chief, that you have not considered our interests in making this decision. You know as well as we do that there are thieves behind the mountains, and that if we leave our stock there all year, it will disappear for certain. Would you and your Government like to see our animals stolen from us by thieves? We beg the Paramount Chief and the

Government to allow us to keep our sheep, goats, and donkeys right here with us at our homes, for we are their owners.'

Chief Boshoane agreed to place this request before the Paramount Chief. He told me later that when he did so, he was warned to beware of the organization behind Ramokhele as it would, if it could, kick the Chiefs out of the country altogether.

Although the people at Mats'ekheng were sympathetic to the aims of the *Lekhotla la Bafo*, there were many who feared to be dubbed communist, and they became wary of it. Chief Boshoane himself went out of his way not to victimize its members in any way; in fact, he gave them preferential treatment, to show them he held no grudge. He nominated Josiel Lefela for the National Council, in spite of his views, because he said it amused him to see Lefela teasing the Council by talking for a whole day, citing endless precedents from every country under the sun, scores of books lying open before him.

The whole time I was in the administration was one of change and movement. The people themselves were awakening, demanding new privileges and rights, and the Chiefs were fighting to retain what little power they had not signed away.

* * *

I remember an incident that sums up the general atmosphere of those events rather well.

A man called Mangoela from Hleoheng in Leribe wrote to the newspapers criticizing the administration of the Chief of Hleoheng. He said that while he was home on leave he went to the Chief's place and could not find him; the counsellors of the Chief were at the *lekhotla*, however, and never had he seen such ignorant people, dressed in patched clothes, placed in positions where they were responsible for hearing the grievances of the people. He was appalled to find such people in office; not one of them would have been able to help him in any way. It was quite clear, he said, that the Basotho people were still backward, and would never progress, if Hleoheng was anything to go by. It was high time that sensible people were placed in Sesotho administration courts because he knew there were some clever, educated men in Lesotho. He had been to see the Chief twice, without success. The first time he was told that the Chief was in Ficksburg. He knew, he maintained, that the Chief always returned from his visits to Ficksburg under the influence of liquor and incapable of dealing with any case placed before his court, so it was no use waiting for his return. There was no doubt, he concluded, that the Chiefs were playing with the people.

This letter appeared in the paper called *Mphatlalatsane*, and it excited the interest of Mohaila Stanley Mohale, a regular contributor to all our newspapers, who wrote under the *nom de plume* of SEPAPATLELE MOSHEMANE OA HO LI BONA—The-vagabond-boy-who-sees-things—or SEPAPA for short.

In his reply to Mangoela's outburst, SEPAPA wrote: 'May I draw Mr. Mangoela's attention to the fact that those *ignorant* people he mentions are the people who built Lesotho, for the founders of our nation were the same kind of men as those he saw at the *lekhotla* of Hleoheng.

'My friend, those people you despised as the counsellors of the Chief had grandfathers who were even more *ignorant* than they, yet they were the advisers of the great Chief Moshoeshoe. Your forefather, Mangoela, was a famous man, and his exploits are widely known, but he did not know how to read or write. It is also a known fact that this, your ancestor, did not help when Moshoeshoe was asking for missionaries to come and educate the Basotho. I say this because at that time the Bataung were not in Lesotho, and your ancestors are Bataung. Our forefathers were the ones who battled to bring missionaries into Lesotho. What you are today, or what your sons are today, has only been made possible by the struggles of these *ignorant* people you talk of so disparagingly.

'You may be highly educated, but you did not send yourself to school; the man who paid for your education was *ignorant*. Those counsellors of the Chief for whom you have so little time are not as *ignorant* as your forefather was. I think you have been too quick to jump to conclusions; I think you saw them wearing blankets and assumed they were fools. The Chief would hardly have left half-wits to deal with the administration of his people. It is because he knows he was brought up by them, that he trusts them. They were the ones who advised his father to educate him.'

Mangoela's reply did not impress me. He said that SEPAPA was really a *sepapatlele*, a vagabond, poking his nose into other people's affairs. 'Perhaps the people of Hleoheng have a right to comment, but SEPAPA, who does not live there, no!' There was much more, along those lines.

Then I joined the battle. Among other things, I wrote, 'If the Chief of Hleoheng was absent the day Mangoela wanted to see him, it was Mangoela's duty to speak to the man left by the Chief to act on his behalf, because it is a known fact that Chiefs often have to leave their villages on administrative or private business. Mangoela is not ashamed to tell the world how foolish he is. He is an inhabitant of Hleoheng, so who does he expect will come in from the outside to fix matters there for him? He is free to see the Chief's staff if he wants reform, and not go shouting his mouth off to people who have nothing to do with Hleoheng's administration. He criticized the men he saw wearing patched clothes, assuming stupidly that that made them *ignorant*. I must tell him that those men have better brains than his, and I have grounds for saying this. If you go to the appeal court of Tsikoane, the ward into which the village of Hleoheng falls, you will find that very few appeals come from Hleoheng's court, whereas the other courts in the ward have many appeals going to Tsikoane's. The men who work in Hleoheng's court, then, are obviously settling cases to the satisfaction of the other people in the village besides Mangoela.

'My word to you, my boy, is when next you go home, make an appointment and see your Chief; tell him you are not satisfied with his counsellors. I am sure he will tell you that he wants no other counsellors, because he has chosen them for their brains, and not for their clothes.'

The editor cut short our debate at this point. It was a well-known dispute in Lesotho, and from that time, Mangoela spent three years without putting his face at Hleoheng, being afraid of the Chief and his counsellors, who had all followed the correspondence with keen interest. Mangoela's views showed the attitude of many people in Lesotho at that time. Many commoners had started to hate the Chiefs and all they stood for. Educated Basotho resented the arrogance and privileged life of the Chiefs, and started to think of the Chieftainship as outdated and redundant. The simple people had been scared by the ritual murders. The old ways of our Chieftainship were finished forever, and I regretted the fact.

*   *   *

When I think about the old ways of our country, and how the Chiefs' power was progressively strangled, I think of what happened to Chief Hlajoane in the dying years of his life, and how that warrior was finally broken in a South African prison.

It happened that once when Chief Hlajoane was at Matsieng for a case, he eloped with someone's wife, and the Paramount Chief

summoned Chief Hlajoane to appear before his court because of
this. Hlajoane, being Hlajoane, refused to go. The Paramount
Chief sent Chief Palamang to Chief Peete to ask for Hlajoane to be
handed over to him. At that time Chief Peete was very sick, and
Chief Mitchell was nursing his father. Chief Boshoane was not at
home. So that left Chief Nkuebe, then about twenty years old, to
carry out the Paramount Chief's orders. It was the first time that
Nkuebe had been given such a difficult task to perform.

Chief Nkuebe announced at once that he would ride to fetch
Chief Hlajoane the following day, and ordered his men to accompany him. Nkuebe's horse, a gleaming brown gelding, was stabled
at Tsokung, and his men came for the horse before sunrise. Headman Lehlobi Rachakane and I rode with them to join Chief Nkuebe.

We rode slowly past the Mukunutlung store, and from there
past Ralekeke's to Nchochoaneng, opposite which we reined in our
horses. About a mile ahead of us lay Chief Hlajoane's village, Chere's.
Chief Palamang ordered us to dismount, and then he stood and
looked at the village for a long time.

By this time we were all as cold as ice, knowing Hlajoane, whose
praise name is Mokoara, which means Determined Fighter.

> Hlajoane of Seshophe,
> Great-grandson of Makhabane,
> The knight of Peete and Seshophe,
> The stick of iron of Mitchell,
> Of Boshoane and Nkuebe;
> The child who is like his parents,
> He is like Mokhachane and Makhabane;
> The brother of MaThabeng,
> The rod of iron of Mitchell.
> Hlajoane was given the name Mokoara
> During the war of the Boers and the British.

Then Chief Palamang said to Chief Nkuebe, 'Son of the Chief,
I have been given an order by the Paramount Chief. He said I must
come before you, for today you are Chief Peete, so that you will
hand Hlajoane over to me. I was ordered to take him from your
hands alive; I must go and hand him to the Paramount Chief alive.
I am telling you that Chief Hlajoane must not be injured—not a
hair of his head must be touched. Now I want Hlajoane.'

Chief Nkuebe looked us over and then he ordered headman
Lehlobi, *Ntate* Jannie Ramotso, and me to fetch Chief Hlajoane.
'Tell him I want him here. Tell him he must not waste time.'

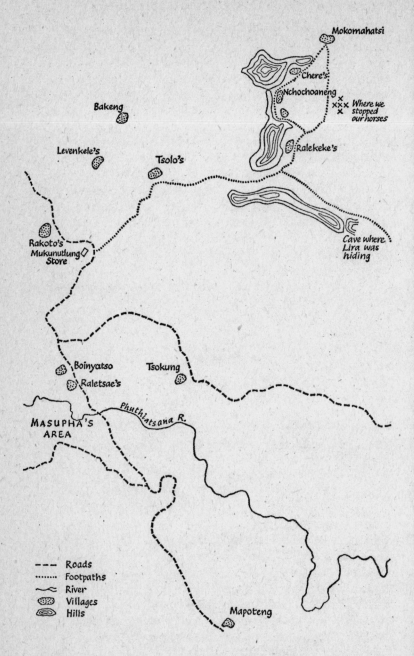

6. Where Nkuebe tried to capture Hlajoane

Khele! The three of us mounted under the eyes of the rest, and stepped out towards Chief Hlajoane's village, taking with us Mafu-roane, Lehlobi's brother. Although both Lehlobi and Jannie were headmen, with men from their villages in our group, no one else followed us. Perhaps they were thinking how dangerous it is to cross Chief Hlajoane.

We rode forward at a very slow walk along the footpath, each of us trying to let the others get ahead of him; each of us wanted to be last. As we went along in silence, I thought of Chief Hlajoane in battle:

> Hlajoane is Mokoara, the one who takes without asking.
> He refused to part with his father's land
> When it was decided to end
> The Government of England,
> The Government of Moshoeshoe.
> MaThabeng's whirligig beetle,
> The one who escaped in the midst of arrows;
> He escaped the Boer generals Cronjé and De Wet,
> When they said they would kill him.

When we were about thirty yards from Chief Hlajoane's *lekhotla*, we saw him walking towards a small hill. We raced there, but he was gone. We returned to the *lekhotla* and asked the men where their Chief was, and they told us he had only just gone into his *lelapa*. Very politely, we asked them to go and tell him we wanted to see him at his *lekhotla*, and someone went off with our message. While he was gone, we looked around and slowly started to relax: none of his men was armed, and there were no weapons in sight. We knew Chief Hlajoane's men would have their weapons hidden nearby, but we stood a better chance because no one was actually holding a weapon. When the messenger returned, he said the Chief was not in and could not be found.

At that moment a ragged beggar passed us wearing the most ancient hat I have ever seen, and clutching a grain bag around his stooped shoulders with one hand. The other hand was closed around a stick, upon which he leaned hard. He was walking painfully, slowly, his head thrown back to see where he was going. I hardly had time to notice him before our party spokesman said we had better go and search the Chief's houses.

'What *is* all this?' demanded one of Chief Hlajoane's men. Another snapped, 'We told you the Chief is not here. Were you sent to come and search his house?' Among these men was one called Sekobi, a man who had been with the Chief during his raid on Thota-Moli when I was an infant; he was a man known for his utter bravery and lack of patience—he never wasted time before hurling himself into battle, and he would not hesitate to shoot anyone who tried to obstruct him.

Perhaps it was the look on his face that decided us. Anyway, we turned our horses with as much dignity as we could, and rode slowly back to report our failure. The cold feeling had left my shoulder-blades: I knew we would be out of range before the men at the *lekhotla* had fetched their guns.

We reported to Chief Nkuebe, who in turn went to relate our detailed statement to Chief Palamang. 'I don't want excuses!' said that Chief. 'I want Hlajoane!' Chief Nkuebe spoke to us very harshly, ordering us to search Chief Hlajoane's homestead at once.

So we four rode once more down to the village, where the men of the *lekhotla* refused to allow us into the Chief's houses. Chief Nkuebe was a fine youngster. When he heard this, without a word, he swung into the saddle and turned his horse towards Chere's village. Most of the men fell in behind him and we rode down again. When the men of the village saw our horses coming, they left the *lekhotla* and went out to meet us. Nkuebe rode straight up to Sekobi and asked, '*Ntate* Sekobi, where is my uncle?'

'He is not here, my Chief,' replied Sekobi. 'He *was* here, but he left us and went into his *lelapa*. When we went there to tell him he was wanted, he was gone.'

Suddenly we thought of the beggar we had seen earlier, so we told Chief Nkuebe about him, saying we suspected he might have been Chief Hlajoane in disguise.

'Where is he now?' cried Nkuebe.

We pointed out the way the beggar had taken, but there was no sign of him when we started to search. Then we noticed that there were no women or children in the village at all. It was all still and deserted, except for the men near the *lekhotla*.

Men were despatched at once to Mokomahatsi, Chief Seshophe's village, for the beggar had gone in that direction. They returned to say that there was no sign of Hlajoane, but that Chief Seshophe had promised to hand him over if he appeared. 'But,' Hlajoane's father added a challenge, 'I am surprised to see that Chief Peete has entered my area without my consent.'

Lepekola, Hlajoane's younger brother, started gathering his men to fight us, but nothing came of it because his advisers stopped him. Men were sent to Levenkele's, Bakeng, and Tsolo's, but Chief Hlajoane had slipped away.

While all this bustle was going on, someone noticed that there were children and women hiding in a cave off to our rear, and that there were horses with them which someone recognized as belonging to Lira, Hlajoane's son. Chief Nkuebe ordered us to go and seize the horses; if Lira was in the cave, he wanted him taken as well. Just as our horses started the steep descent to the cave itself, Lira appeared with a companion, burst past us, and galloped off towards Boinyatso. We shouted to him to stop, but he galloped the faster, and so we spurred our horses after him. We saw him disappear into a *lelapa* at Boinyatso and we surrounded it at once, but when we got inside, only his companion, an old man called Malikonopo, was inside. We seized him and demanded Lira. The old man looked up across the Phuthiatsana River, and there we saw Lira, already some distance into Chief Masupha's area, where we could not follow him. While we were taking Malikonopo back to Chief Nkuebe, some of our men who had been following us in our chase met up with us, and at once they started shouting at Malikonopo, and being very rough with the old man. Jannie and Lehlobi stopped them.

'It's funny', I said to those men, 'that when the Chief ordered us to chase Lira, you did not join us; you hung back until we had captured Malikonopo ourselves. Now you shout at him rudely as if you had captured him yourselves. You talk too much, you rough men. Leave him alone!'

A man called Khetla had been with Lira in the cave, and he now joined our group as we rode to Chief Nkuebe. 'Hey you! Son of Ngolozani!' he yelled. There were four or five of us Ngolozani's there that day, so no one replied. 'I mean YOU!' shouted Khetla, 'You, son of Makhuba!' I turned to him and waited for him to speak.

'Why do you show these men of Nkuebe's which direction Lira took?' he demanded, shaking with anger. 'You used to pretend that you were Lira's friend. Have you become his enemy?' He raised his stick. 'I'll knock you down!' he screamed. As he brought his stick down, I blocked his blow with my own stick.

'Stop fighting!' Chief Nkuebe shouted. 'Who's that fighting over there?'

'It's Khetla, Chief,' someone said.

'Bring him here!'

'They cannot take me!' shouted Khetla. 'These cowards of yours cannot take me! *I am Khetla*! I can crush their heads with my stick!'

I am sorry to say I found that day that some of my family were cowards. I realize that if Lira or his father had tried to fight, my people would have fled. Those relatives of mine, although they heard this Khetla insulting me and saw him trying to hit me, they made no move against him.

'You're born cowards, eh?' Chief Nkuebe said to them. 'A man insults your young brother in your presence, and you do nothing. . . .'

By this time it was sunset. Chief Nkuebe feared that Chief Hlajoane might ambush us in the dark, so he ordered us to meet at the same place the next morning to continue our search.

I rode home, my head full of the words of Chief Hlajoane's praises, thinking of how he had outwitted us all.

> Tell the Lion of the Litlhakola, Mitchell,
> To present Mokoara with a man's stick. . . .
> You refused with the land, Mokoara,
> With the land of your father,
> When Cronjé and De Wet wanted to take it. . . .
> The Lion handed him the rod
> Of iron, the stick of men. . . .
> The war song, the song sung only by men,
> Was raised to the sky. . . .

In the morning, we fanned out to cast a wider net for Chief Hlajoane, but we failed. Chief Palamang ordered Chief Mitchell, when he found Chief Hlajoane, to take him to Matsieng, because he still had to face the charges against him.

Three weeks later, Chief Ntina came across Chief Hlajoane sleeping in a valley near Chief Nkuebe's village. He was still on the run. Chief Ntina fell upon him, screaming, 'Ha! I've got you now! *Help*! People, *HELP*! I've got him!' Hlajoane staggered to his feet, still half asleep, but Ntina held him fast.

Chief Hlajoane's praises now end with:

> You, Ntina, son of Lehomo,
> We will meet one day.
> You will remember the day
> You fell upon me.

Chief Hlajoane was taken before the Paramount Chief and

sentenced to four years' hard labour. Moreover, the Paramount Chief said that a Lesotho prison would not treat him as the Chief wanted him to be treated, and so he had him sent to a gaol in Boksburg called Blue Sky.

Khetla was right: I was a good friend of Lira's, and when Chief Hlajoane later told Lira about his years in Blue Sky, his son said he used to weep. He said that when he was eventually released from Blue Sky, he felt he had to be dreaming—he had lost hope altogether of ever living, in that place, to see the outside world again.

Chief Hlajoane, the reckless warrior, the Iron Rod, the Gun of Mitchell, changed completely because of Blue Sky.

If you had ever seen Blue Sky you would understand why Chief Hlajoane changed; you would have seen, in that place, things like a cart full of stones being pulled by men; those poor wretches being whipped with what the Boers call a *duiwelspyp*—an ox whip, doubled over. People there cringed. What a pitiful sight!

Chief Hlajoane used to say to Lira, 'My son, I never thought I would see you again. I lost hope . . . .'

NOTES

1. *Thaba Nchu* is the South African version of *Thaba Nts'o*, meaning 'black mountain'.
2. 'The two proclamations, together with an explanatory memorandum, were published in English in a blue jacket, and in Sesuto in a red, *khubedu*, and these and the subsequent Native Administration reforms came to be referred to locally as the *khubedu*' (G. I. Jones, op. cit., pp. 42-3).

CHAPTER EIGHT

Without law, people are animals

ANY boy growing up in Lesotho in my time absorbed knowledge about the laws of his country without conscious effort because, from an early age, he joined the men at the village *lekhotla*. There he would hear disputes being settled, points of law argued and customs discussed. There anyone, even a boy, could put questions to the disputing parties and their witnesses, and a boy was never too young to add whatever knowledge he had about the case before the *lekhotla*.

The first case I remember ever going to was at Potjo's village, Thota-Moli, during the first year I attended school.

Someone's fowl disappeared one evening. He reported to the headman, who ordered the whole village to be searched. My cousin, Tlalinyane, had built his homestead right near my father's, so that when the searchers went to his place, I could hear everything clearly. As the searchers entered the *lelapa*, I heard Tlalinyane's wife, NoMkichimi, asking, 'What do you want now, at this late hour?'

'We are looking for a missing fowl.'

'So why do you come to my place?' That was Tlalinyane's voice.

'We have been going into every house in the village. No person is excluded from our search.'

They must have gone to the hearth where NoMkichimi had her cooking-pots out, for we heard Tlalinyane say, 'Get out of here! You said you were looking for a missing fowl, but now you're scratching around on our hearth!'

Just then we saw Mthengi Sotshangani, the one who started that village with my father, enter Tlalinyane's place. We heard him say, 'Let them search your place, Tlalinyane.'

The dressed fowl and its feathers were found near the hearth, covered with a basket.

The following morning Tlalinyane had to go before the *lekhotla*. Of the adults of our family, only my uncle Maphuphuta attended the case. We children were eaten up with curiosity, though, because it was the first time we knew of a thief being tried before our *lekhotla*. Our feelings flew between horror and awe; we were sure Tlalinyane would be beaten, but we had no experience of a theft case, so we imagined the most frightful things.

The court itself consisted of Potjo, the headman, Phahlane (who had been acting headman for Potjo before he had the courage to move to the village), Mthengi, Sekhamo, and Mohapi, headman of the village nearest to Thota-Moli. Most of the village men were there, and of course so were we boys.

When the case started, Tlalinyane was told he was being charged with stealing a fowl. I wondered what he could possibly say to avert the dreadful judgment hanging over him. This is what he said:

'I confess that I did steal that fowl. I could not do otherwise: I had a strong appetite for meat. I had been drinking for a solid two weeks, and I had no meat to eat during that time. I tried to get some, even a tiny piece, but I got none. I went to Sehlajaneng to ask if someone there could let me have a fowl, but they said they did not have any fowls. I plead with the court for mercy.'

The court found him guilty and ordered him to pay three fowls in all: two to the owner of the stolen fowl, and one to the court as a fine. He was given seven days to find the fowls.

We wondered where Tlalinyane would find three fowls—had he not told the court that there were none to be had? Then we heard that he had managed to buy three fowls from the Mukunutlung store. On the seventh day, we were at court again to see what would happen.

Tlalinyane placed his three fowls before the court. The owner of the stolen fowl took his two, while the third was slaughtered right there. We were sent out to gather firewood, and when they had a good fire going, the fowl was cooked and its meat shared out. Both Tlalinyane and the man whose fowl he had stolen ate of its meat. We boys were given small bits. While we ate, people were scolding

Tlalinyane jokingly: 'Don't come and steal our fowls hoping that you will eat meat at the *lekhotla* every day!' A drumstick and some white meat were put aside for the headman, and that was where the trouble started.

Potjo reached out for the meat, but Mthengi pushed his hand aside roughly, saying that he had built that village, and had fought for it—he should get the headman's portion. Potjo flew into a rage saying that he was headman, and would eat the meat. They started shouting at each other, until they leapt up, ready to fight, but Phahlane stepped between them.

'You're doing a bad thing in the presence of the children,' he reprimanded them. 'Don't you see that they will think you greedy?'

Then the two men subsided.

We learned later that they both went to see Chief Mitchell soon after that, to discover who was the headman of Thota-Moli. The Chief—remember, his wife was related to Potjo—said that Potjo was the one who had applied to him for a village to rule, and was therefore the true headman. Mthengi, said the Chief, had only been sent to Thota-Moli to guard the *moli* grass growing there, and was thus a caretaker of the grass, and that was all, even if he *had* built the village.

That was when Mthengi and my father moved back to their fathers' villages at Tsokung, because they did not want to live under that coward, Potjo.

*   *   *

In those days women did not accuse each other at the men's *lekhotla* when they had a dispute; they had a hearing before the headman's or Chief's wife, in a special women's court.

It was a great shame for a woman to appear in the men's *lekhotla*, so women either came to blows when they fought, or had to ask more senior women to settle their disputes.

I remember a case that happened in the women's court of Sotshangani's village at Tsokung, involving two of Sotshangani's daughters-in-law.

NoMzimkulu, it seemed, used to go about talking badly of people, insulting them and accusing them of lying and other bad things. One of the people she talked about most was her sister-in-law, NoMthendeki; she called her a whore and a witch, and insulted her at every opportunity. When NoMthendeki realized that, by herself, she could not stop NoMzimkulu from insulting her, she turned to Qenase, the senior daughter-in-law of Sotshangani, for help.

Genealogy 6: NoMthendeki and NoMzimkulu

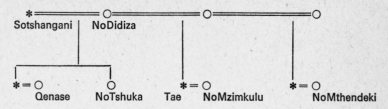

Qenase talked to NoMzimkulu, trying to get her to stop insulting people, and to stop talking badly of their sister-in-law, NoMthendeki, but NoMzimkulu paid no attention whatever.

At last NoMthendeki could stand it no longer, and appealed to NoDidiza, Sotshangani's first wife, to hold a court where she could charge NoMzimkulu for insulting her. NoDidiza agreed, and called together all the women of the villages ruled by her husband, about five villages in all.

When they had gathered, NoMthendeki stated her case before them, saying, 'It was not my intention to come before the court in this way, but I had no choice. When I first heard the things NoMzimkulu is saying about me, I went to her myself, asking her why she said such things. She ignored me. Then I went to *Ausi*[1] Qenase to ask her to bring us together and sort out this matter, but again NoMzimkulu paid no attention. None of this had any effect on her. Even yesterday, although she knew she would be coming before your court, she insulted me again. She called me a witch and a whore. Now before all of you and our mother-in-law, mother NoDidiza, I would like to ask *Ausi* NoMzimkulu: why does she call me a witch? When did she find me witching? With whom has she ever found me whoring? My witnesses are here. The first is *Ausi* Qenase and second *Ausi* NoTshuka. I can prove that I have been insulted and these two sisters of mine will corroborate what I say. If NoMzimkulu can prove I am a witch or a whore, I will withdraw my case against her, and apologize.'

The old lady, NoDidiza, said that the case was too heavy for her, and should be heard by men; women alone could not make a decision in such a serious matter. After she had reported the case to her husband, Sotshangani, he called together the men of his villages to help his *lekhotla* hear the case. When the men had gathered and heard the details, someone said it was wrong that NoDidiza had forwarded the case to their court without having come to any decision herself about the issue. Once she had reached some decision in her own court, they would be prepared to hear the case.

So once more a day was fixed for the women's court to sit. NoDidiza picked a sort of committee consisting of responsible women, headmen's wives and so on, to help her, five of them in all.

When NoMzimkulu went before them, she broke down at once, saying that she had indeed called her sister-in-law those bad names without any provocation, and that she was sorry, and would never do it again.

The court said it was a bit late to be sorry: she had had all the time in the world, and repeated opportunity, to ask for forgiveness. It seemed, they said, that she was afraid of being sent back before the men's *lekhotla*. She could have saved everyone a lot of trouble, both men and women, if she had confessed and asked for forgiveness sooner. She was clearly guilty, and was fined one goat. The court added that had she been fined by the men's court, she would have been punished severely. If she repeated her offence, she would be fined a cow.

Within two weeks of this decision, Tae, the husband of NoMzimkulu, went to NoDidiza and handed her the goat that his wife had been fined. Then he laid a chicken before the old lady, saying, 'I am very thankful, Mother. I was so frightened, when my wife was before your court. Please see to it that you and your court teach my wife better manners.'

'What is the fowl for, my son?' the old lady asked him.

'I am just giving it, Mother, to accompany the goat. Had this case gone back to the men's *lekhotla*, I should have had to pay a cow or even a couple of cows for what my wife said. Insult is a serious thing, and my wife has made a habit of it. The fine would have been heavy because this is not the first time my wife has insulted NoMthendeki, who treats her kindly. NoMthendeki did not fight my wife, as she might have done, or take her before the court at once; first she tried to settle their quarrel peacefully. It is entirely my wife's fault that their dispute went before a court.

'This fowl is a gift to the court for its mercy towards me. I am not trying to bribe the court. Please see to it, Mother, that you stop my wife from insulting people. May your court live long!'

The goat and the fowl were slaughtered and cooked, and people passing by were given meat to eat and gravy to drink. Even boys were given a share. I am sorry to say that men are greedy creatures; whenever an animal was slaughtered in their *lekhotla*, you never saw women coming to ask for a share in the meat, but when the women's court slaughtered something, the men always sent someone along to collect some meat for them.

The customs concerning women in courts started changing with legislation from about the 1920s, and today women are as free as men to appear in court. Yet even today, there are women who always send men to represent them in court, because they were brought up in the custom that it is unseemly for a woman to be seen in court. There are no women's courts of this kind left in Lesotho, and today even minor quarrels between women go before the courts as cases. There are still some women left, though, who go before the court trembling at their own temerity.

*   *   *

When I was a boy, two things fascinated me: the first was teaching; the second was being a court president. Had I been able to go further with my education, I would most certainly have trained to be a lawyer, for that was my greatest dream. When children play games, they always pretend to be the people they would like to be when they grow up. Some of us had clay oxen with which we ploughed imaginary lands; others pretended they were working on the mines; others had their own courts of law. I always played court games when I was small, especially games in which I had to defend myself or other people against charges.

Ever since my youth, I have kept a notebook in which I record events and interesting cases. When I returned from France, Dane Rachakane and I used to attend court cases as often as possible, and keep a written record of each case, simply for interest. Unfortunately this experience did not help me much the first time I was charged before a court in the 1920s.

Dane and I had been in charge of a group of herdboys who had let their cattle graze the *leboella* of Makhobalo's village, and we were charged in the Makhobalo *lekhotla* for this. Perhaps the men there knew of our interest in the law, and how we always attended cases and took notes, for they called in three men from Nthoba's village and two from Chief Peete's court staff to help them try us, all of them men who were known in the district for their knowledge of the law and their expertise in taking cases. Dane and I pleaded not guilty before that court, but those five men soon broke down our hopeless defence and we were fined. Because he was the son of a headman, Dane was fined two goats or two bags of grain, while I was fined one goat. The court said that I should have been fined two goats as well, being just as guilty as Dane, but that I might get swollen-headed, as a commoner, if I were fined the same amount as a headman's son.

Like most men of my age, when I was in my twenties, I had a reasonable knowledge of the law and of procedure in a Chief's court. I had been charged in the odd case, and I myself had charged other people. My success in court was no better than average and I had had no need to brush up on my knowledge of the law or to seek to improve my ability as an orator.

My years with the I.C.U. changed all that.

First as Secretary of a branch of that organization, and then as District Secretary, I discovered that I could best help my fellow Bantu by knowing thoroughly the laws to which we were subject. I had to consult and engage legal counsel on many occasions. I watched those lawyers in court, doing my best to learn their style and copy their ways before the court; through them, I started to learn the law.

Among those lawyers with whom I associated, it is especially Mr. Edmund Ellenberger and Mr. Wolfardt whom I remember with gratitude and pride, for they taught me patiently. In Mr. Ellenberger's office I spent many hours reading up on law and discussing cases. These men helped me prepare myself in case I should one day have to speak for myself in court, or defend a fellow without their help. They told me that even if I had little chance of success, it was better to have a go at it rather than simply to give up without trying. Through them, and through the circumstances of working for the I.C.U., my real interest in law was born.

During my years as a clerk in the Principal Chief's administration, I did all I could to foster and increase the knowledge I had gained through the I.C.U. I kept abreast of the latest laws and changes in court procedure, and tried by every means to become skilful in cases.

When the Treasury courts were opened on 1 April 1946, I was not among those appointed by Chieftainess MaMakhabane to serve in the new courts. I must confess that I was a little disappointed. I was on leave at that time from my duties as a clerk in her administration. The following day I received a letter at home from the Chieftainess saying that she wanted me to take the position of assessor in the Koma-Koma Treasury court. She explained that the man she had nominated for the post, Koenyama Cheba, had turned down her offer because he had pressing responsibilities as a farmer and stock-owner, and so she wanted me to take his place. She asked me not to think badly of her because she had not nominated me initially; she had wanted to keep me in reserve, she said, in case a vacancy came up.

This last was nonsense, of course. Chieftainess MaMakhabane and myself were on bad terms just then because Makhabane had returned from school to claim his rights as Principal Chief, and his mother, who did not want to give up the regency, held me responsible. Although I accepted the post, I did not do so with an easy mind, knowing that Chieftainess MaMakhabane had appointed me only through force of circumstance, and not because she wanted to. I started my new profession on 3 April 1946 as assessor under the presidency of Chief Dyke; the second assessor was Mapeshoane Posholi. An assessor's duties were simply to advise the president of the court, question the parties and their witnesses when necessary, act as prosecutor, and participate in the judgment. This was not unlike being an adviser in the old Chief's court.

Early on, each assessor was given a case to preside over by himself, in order to test his knowledge of the law. Ironically, I was given the case concerning Makhabane's elopement damages. Makhabane had eloped with Nkhala, from Pitseng, and her people brought a case against Chieftainess MaMakhabane for failing to pay the required number of cattle as compensation for the elopement.

Before the case, Chieftainess MaMakhabane told the people from Pitseng, 'I am sorry to be brought before this Jingoes, who thinks himself Makhabane's father. I have been disputing with Jingoes because he did not consult me when he advised my son to go and elope with your daughter. *He* is the one you should have charged, instead of me, for I had nothing to do with it.' She totally refused to appear before the court if I were to preside over the case, and pleaded for a postponement until she had consulted some people to help her prepare her defence. Whatever happened, she was quite determined not to pay those cattle for the girl she did not want as her daughter-in-law.

Chief Nkuebe could not bear to see Chieftainess MaMakhabane in this predicament, so he summoned the people of Mats'ekheng to a *pitso* where he laid the matter before them. He asked the people,

'Would you like the bridewealth of Chief Makhabane's wife to be discussed in public and squabbled over in a public court?' The people replied that they definitely would not like such a thing to happen.

'Then give me the cattle,' he said.

And they did. In a matter of days the people of Pitseng had their cattle—even though Chieftainess MaMakhabane tried to delay things by having the cattle seized, as I have related—and the case before our court was dropped, to everyone's satisfaction and relief.

*   *   *

To be a court president is not an easy task. The reader who does not know Lesotho must remember that a court president is not separated from other men. In Western countries, judges are paid huge salaries and are powerful men, living apart from common men and not associating with the people who appear before their courts. For us, it is different. You cannot tell the court president from any other Mosotho; he lives in a hut which is in a village, which is under a Chief, who is under a Principal Chief, just like other men. He has to try his relatives, friends, and enemies, and he also has to try the Chiefs, their friends, and enemies. In many ways he is like mealies between two grinding stones. I know a president of a court whose nerves are so bad that he takes a nip of brandy before every important decision he has to give.

It is particularly difficult to give objective judgments where Chiefs are involved. Your friend in court might *hope* that you will favour him; the Chief regards you as his subject, and *expects* you to favour him.

This happened to me in the hearing of a dispute between two headmen under a Chief whom I shall call Chief Khotso. The first headman, Thabo, claimed that the other, Mari, was trying to encroach on his area. Thabo's area had been allocated to his grandfather originally by Chief Lesaoana so that he could act as a bulwark against incursions by Chief Molapo. Before my court—for I was a president by this time—Thabo's witnesses gave clear and convincing evidence of this. I had no doubt that Thabo was in the right. Besides, Mari's witnesses, even though one of them was a Chieftainess, gave contradictory and confused evidence. It was clear to me that Mari was trying to enlarge his area at the expense of Thabo.

The court went to inspect the area under dispute. When we

returned, there was a message that Chief Khotso wanted to see me. He said to me, 'I think that as you have now seen the place and as you have heard the evidence, you have found to whom the portion in dispute belongs.'

'Yes,' I said.

'But,' he continued, 'as my subject, you know that the president of the court should follow the decision of the Chiefs, *because they are the Chiefs*. As president of the court you are something like a Chief now. No Chief should fight another Chief.

'In this case I suggest that you award the portion of disputed land to Mari, who is a loyal person, and who complies with all my orders. Thabo is rebellious; he has no time for the Chieftainship, and just states baldly that he was allocated his area by Chief Lesaoana. Although his witnesses are strong, and are telling the truth, Mari's witnesses include a Chieftainess, and it will not do to call her word in doubt. Give the decision in favour of Mari.'

'My Chief,' was my reply, 'I am afraid of the dead Chief Lesaoana. The evidence of the Chieftainess you talk about is weak. There is no doubt that Chief Lesaoana gave the whole area to Thabo's family. If I turn against Lesaoana's decision, what am I going to be? I am afraid of the ancestors of the Chiefs. I understand your reasons, my Chief, but we cannot do it—it would be unjust.

'By calling me here to discuss my decision, you yourself have tacitly admitted that Mari has no case. Let me tell you straight: you yourself should be here as Thabo's witness, because you *know* that your own grandfather allocated that area to him. I too, even as a private individual and not as a court president, *know* that this is so: in my father's time, our cattle used to graze at a cattle-post in that area, and they were herded there by Thabo's family.'

He said, 'H'mm . . . I thought I had a chance of talking you round. Can't you help me out, Jingoes? Mari is a good headman.'

'No, Chief. I'm afraid to act otherwise. I cannot put myself out of line with the law.'

You can see that I had to talk seriously here: if a court president allows himself to be swayed like a branch, he becomes nothing, and, through his actions, the law becomes nothing. And if I believe in anything, I believe in the law. The law is there . . . .

*   *   *

I did not remain in Mats'ekheng long as an assessor. In 1949 a circular from the Paramount Chieftainess cut down the number of assessors in each court from two to one. When this happened, Chief Makhabane was Principal Chief, and I have already told you that we were not getting on. Consequently, of the two assessors in our court, I was the one to be dismissed. When I asked the Chief why he had dismissed me, he replied only, 'Because I choose . . . .' He also did not tell me that there were vacancies in each of the nine districts of Lesotho for relieving court presidents, but I came to hear about this and made application. Despite Chief Makhabane's opposition, in brief, I was appointed as a relieving court president.

While I was a court president, I found many relatives I did not know I had, and I was offered many bribes.

One day a man called Makiki came before my court claiming compensation for his dog, which had been killed by a man called Monakoli. That was all I knew about the case when it first came before me, but as the case developed, some very interesting facts emerged.

It appears that Monakoli's wife was sick. One night she heard noises on the roof of their house, and she started sweating inexplicably, even though it was winter. Monakoli went outside and found that an extraordinary thing had happened. He had, like most sensible people, placed what we call *lithakhisa* or wooden pegs treated with *litlhare* in the roof of his house to ward off witchcraft. When he went out that night, he found his *lithakhisa* lying on the ground; they had been pulled out of his thatch. He looked up in horror and saw a dog which he recognized as belonging to Makiki on the roof of his house. The dog ran away, straight back to Makiki's place.

Monakoli went to Makiki the following day and told him about his dog. 'I don't want to see your dog near my place again,' he warned Makiki. 'Are you witching me with this dog of yours? You take care!' Monakoli then went to the headman of the village, and told him what had happened and how he had warned Makiki. The headman summoned Makiki and told him to keep his dog home in future.

Matters might have ended there had Monakoli not found the dog on the roof of his house for the second time. It was evident to him that the dog was witching his place, because his wife did not seem to be recovering from her illness. This time he killed the dog.

He went to the headman again, and showed him how his *lithakhisa* had been pulled out and thrown on the ground. Makiki was taken before the headman's court, where he behaved insolently, not as a man should when he is about to be charged for witchcraft by his headman. So unpleasant was he before the *lekhotla* that some of the men present wanted to beat him for despising their court. They said to him, 'You are a witch. You admit that this dog is yours. It must be a *thokolosi*[2] that you send out at night to witch people for you. What other reason would a dog have for climbing on top of someone's roof?'

Makiki protested, 'I am not a witch. My dog does not witch.' But he failed to explain what his dog could have been doing on top of Monakoli's house if it were not witching.

The headman's *lekhotla* found Makiki guilty, and the headman said, 'This court has no power to fine you, Makiki. My court is only there to try to make peace. It is up to you now, Monakoli, to make your own decision. If you want peace with Makiki, you can drop the matter, but if you want to charge him, you can take him before the Treasury court.'

Monakoli did want to charge Makiki. For one thing, he had to force Makiki somehow to undo the mischief that his dog had caused, so that his wife would recover, and while Makiki denied that he was a witch, this was impossible to do. But before Monakoli had time to register his case with the Treasury court, Makiki jumped in and sued him in that court for compensation for the death of his dog. It was Makiki's case, then, that came before me first.

After the first day of the case Makiki realized that things were not going well for him. In fact, all the evidence was against him. When the court had adjourned for the evening, he came to me.

'Do you know me?' he asked.

'I know you as a plaintiff in my court,' I replied.

'But don't you know me as a person?' he persisted.

'No, I don't know you.'

'I am the son-in-law of Mohao.'

'Which Mohao?'

'Mohao of Tshabalala, the one who married the daughter of Mokhajoang.'

'Well, I know that Mohao, but I do not know you.'

'Yes. . . . Well . . . I am his son-in-law, . . .'

So he had married into my clan, and was a distant relation by marriage. I waited for what I knew would come.

'Won't you have pity on me, and make this man pay for my dog?'

I kept silent.

'Don't say I'm a witch! Let's talk, man!'

'No.'

'Don't you want food for your children?'

'You have a case before my court. I do not want to be seen with you.'

'But I am your son-in-law. . . .'

'Even so. . . .'

'Don't you want to buy food for your children? You have to work here for your children. Won't you say, in your judgment, that my dog was killed for no reason, and that I must get compensation for it?'

I had no choice. I stood up and walked out, leaving Makiki with my wife. He asked her to beg me to accept his money so that I would favour him in the case. If I did not, it would mean disgrace for him. He did not want to be exposed as a witch among the people of his village. If he lost this case, he said, he would take an appeal to the Central court where he knew he would win, because he would be able to buy that court.

'Please,' he begged my wife, 'tell *Ntate* not to make a bad judgment for me. Let that man pay for my dog. It's a valuable dog.'

'What kind of a dog do you have', my wife asked him, 'that climbs people's houses?'

'My dog was a big dog,' he replied. 'If I win my case I will ask heavy compensation for it.'

My wife told him that she was afraid to talk to me about bribery because she knew how I hated it.

Then Makiki fetched his wife to plead for him, and she told my wife many things. 'You must tell your husband', she said, 'that court presidents here are paid by the people who want to win their cases, and they are also paid by the Government. He must act like that too. People will pay him. He'll be rich in a month, with cattle and horses.'

'But what if the Government finds out?' my wife asked.

'Who will tell the Government?' Makiki's wife scoffed. '*Hao*! Take the money!'

Well, my wife was lucky, and did not take the money.

Needless to say, Makiki was not awarded compensation for his dog by my court.

Shortly after this, Monakoli lodged his case with my court against Makiki. The charge was witchcraft. Monakoli's witnesses were men of the village and the headman.

Makiki admitted that his dog had been seen on top of Monakoli's hut, and that he had been warned not to let it climb on the hut again. His only defence was that someone else might have put the dog on the hut to frame him. He was asked by the court whether he was prepared to take Monakoli's wife to the doctor, and pay for her to be cured, for he knew she was very sick, and he replied, 'No. Why should I?'

'Do you agree that your dog was on top of Monakoli's hut?' I asked him.

'Yes.'

'What was it doing up there?'

'I do not know.'

'There are many dogs in our villages. Do they go up on top of people's houses and pull out their *lithakhisa*?'

'No, I've never heard of that before. It seems that only my dog did that.'

My judgment was as follows:

'Your dog, Makiki, was found on top of Monakoli's hut, and you admit that you saw it there. You also admit that you have never seen another dog on anyone's hut. So this is a marvellous affair, eh? You have admitted that you often hear people talking about witchcraft, but that you yourself have never seen any evidence of it. You said that someone else might have caused your dog to behave so strangely.

'You agreed with the court that if your dog had killed a man's sheep, you would be responsible to pay for the damage. This is the same thing. This court orders you to take Monakoli's wife to the doctor and to pay whatever his fees are. Failing that, Monakoli can do with you what he sees fit. Go home and keep the peace.'

Makiki took the woman to hospital and he also called in his own *ngaka* to cure her. She recovered.

It was a pity that the body of the dog had been thrown away. I wanted to cut some of its flesh to make *litlhare* for myself. It was clearly no ordinary dog, but a *thokolosi* that only turned into a dog in the eyes of the people. Who ever heard of a dog that left the ground?

*   *   *

A court president is like a Chief in many ways. He is exposed to witchcraft and the use of *litlhare*. He must be on his guard because we Basotho believe firmly that a court case can be influenced, and its outcome controlled, by the use of *litlhare*.

I was fortunate as a court president in that, being a *ngaka* myself, I know about *litlhare*. Consequently, I was not as scared as some court officials I have known when they found that *litlhare* was being used in their courtrooms to influence their decisions. I was also not afraid that my relative, Makiki, would try to witch me—it is certain that he was a witch—for having given a judgment against him. I have faith in my own *lenaka*. I never caught anyone at Mats'ekheng using *litlhare* in my court, because people there are clever at such things, and would not be caught out easily. But in other areas people blatantly tried it.

Let me tell you about some thieves who did this. I must explain, first, a little about thieves in Lesotho. The Basotho have been stealing cattle from South Africa for many years. In the early days these cattle thieves were regarded as heroes, and were often Chiefs leading raids against the Boers. This idea is still strong in Lesotho. So many cattle are still stolen from the Republic that the South African police have had to come into Lesotho in an attempt to control the problem. The thieves are generally brave and arrogant men, and the common people very often help them and regard them with admiration.

They do not only steal from South Africa, but in Lesotho itself they make of stealing a challenge. They send a letter to a village saying that they are going to raid on a certain night. As they put it, 'We are coming to fetch the calves of our cattle, and the lambs of our sheep, and the kids of our goats.' You must know that they mean this. It is their way of testing the bravery of the villagers against their own skill as stock-thieves. But more than that, they are testing their *litlhare* as well. These men usually have powerful *lingaka* working for them. The village they raid often does not even see them when they come.

There used to be a powerful gang operating in the area where I live now, when I first moved here as court president. They wrote to the village of Morolong, saying that they were coming. The men of that village prepared themselves and spent every night around their kraal, keeping watch to guard their stock. When the thieves arrived one night and found the men there, they used their *litlhare* and the men guarding the cattle fell asleep, except for one. The one who managed to stay awake had obtained a very special *lenaka* from a *ngaka*, but although he was awake, he was helpless to act. He watched the thieves opening the cattle kraal and driving the animals out. He came to his senses only when the thieves were well on their way, driving the cattle ahead of them. He tried to awaken his companions, but they were sleeping so heavily that he had to hit them over the head to get them up, and then they set off after their cattle.

The thieves abandoned the cattle at Sebalabala, the place where Chief Masupha I used to stop to count his booty after his cattle raids into the Free State. The thieves were content to let the people of Morolong's have their cattle back; they had proved they could steal them, no matter what Morolong's men tried to do to stop them.

Within a month, they returned. They wrote again to say that they were coming. This time the villagers had gone to their own *lingaka*. They were well fortified, and they did not fall asleep. But the thieves meant business. When they found the village well guarded, they set fire to the thatch of a house to create a diversion. Some village men ran to extinguish the flames while others remained to guard the kraal. Seeing that they had not yet cleared a passage to the kraal, the thieves set fire to yet another house, and after that another, until utter confusion reigned in the village, and all the men were running around to fight the fire, fearing for the whole village as there was a wind blowing.

Then the thieves opened the kraal and drove out the cattle with a rush. They did not get away this time; the village men ran them down at Phoofolo's village, quite near by.

Their case came before my court.

I knew the thieves, and I knew that they were past masters at using *litlhare*, so I was on my guard when they appeared before me. I need not have bothered to look for a surreptitious use of *litlhare* as it happened; when they came to use their medicine, they were quite open and defiant. One by one, they dropped things on the floor of the court, things like whistles, a pip that resembled an apricot, and bits of roots and sticks. As he threw down his *litlhare*, each man spoke to it: 'We are in trouble. Please help us.' They said this aloud, right in court.

My clerk and prosecutor started trembling. 'What shall we do?' they whispered to me, and I saw their teeth clamped so as not to chatter. It was clear that I had to act quickly.

I got up and walked to the thieves. Picking up the *litlhare* from the floor, I said, 'I am not a boy, you people.'

I did not have *litlhare* to counter theirs, but I was trying to bluff them into believing that theirs was powerless against mine. I wanted to make them shake. I picked it all up, and told them right in their faces that they were making a habit of their *litlhare* and their thieving, and I advised them to make an end of it.

Once I had done this, the members of my court perked up. 'Hey!' cried one of them. 'This Jingoes is a strange one; he simply stands up and takes the thieves' *litlhare*! I can see that one of them has started trembling already. . . .'

I sentenced them all to £10 or two months' hard labour in gaol. They all paid their fines.

That same day as I left the court, I walked past a *lethuela*,[3] and she fainted. When she recovered, she said my shadow was too heavy for her.

After this people came to realize that I was a *ngaka* myself, and did not waste their time with trying to use *litlhare* in my courts. It is a useful thing for a court president to have a heavy shadow.

*   *   *

I am old now, and I have not worked in law courts regularly for some years, but I am still absorbed by the law. I still try to keep up with the latest gazettes and acts and I spend hours every week in the courts in this village. I think, in some ways, it is my interest in the law that has kept me alive, because every case I follow compels my complete attention.

I have come to be known in the district where I live as a specialist in law. People come to me for advice on how to proceed with their cases, and I act as a kind of lawyer for them by outlining the strategy they should adopt in their cases. Even though I no longer work for the Chiefs or the courts, I am often called upon to help preside over difficult cases in the village, and Chiefs still travel to consult me. Because of my long association with the Makhabane Chieftainship, I am known as the 'Briefcase' of Mats'ekheng, and I am one of the few old people left who can remember the boundaries, the succession, and the affairs of that Chieftainship. Even where I live today, I am known as the 'Door to the Chief', because I have the ear of the Chief, and because I know so well all the paths one can take to reach a Chief.

So I am not ending my days leaning against the wall in the sun. My life is fuller than ever.

NOTES

1. *Ausi*, from the Afrikaans *ousus*, means 'elder sister', also 'aunt, girl, miss'.
2. A *thokolosi* is a witch's familiar.
3. A *lethuela* is a type of diviner and healer who has been cured of a form of nervous or hysterical affliction known as *motheketheke*.

EPILOGUE

THE winters are long in Lesotho, and desperately cold. Darkness comes early.

One afternoon I was walking past the place where the buses stop in our village when I saw an old woman getting off a bus with her luggage, looking bewildered. Something about her was familiar, and I walked closer in the dusk. A chilling drizzle was descending on the village. I saw that the old lady being jostled by the other passengers was a Chieftainess I used to know when she was young and able. Now she was senile and lost.

I greeted her, and asked her what she was doing in our village, and where she was bound. She said she was travelling to see her daughter, who was married and living in a near-by village.

I knew that the old lady's mind was playing tricks on her: that daughter of hers had died some years before.

'Come, Chieftainess,' I said, picking up her suitcase and blanket roll, and I led her to the place of the Chief.

Chieftainess MaMathe welcomed the old Chieftainess, and saw that she was given food and a warm place to spend the night.

Chieftainess MaMathe and I have known each other for a long time, and as we walked down the steps of her house together she turned to me and said, in a strange tone, 'You've always helped us Chiefs, eh, Jingoes. Why?'

'I don't know, *Morena*. I really don't know. I haven't got much out of it. . . .'

As she turned to go in she laughed and said, 'I don't know either, but you will serve the Chieftainship until the day you die.'

APPENDIX

THIS appendix is not in any way intended to be an anthropological commentary on Mr. Jingoes's autobiography. It is provided with the primary purpose of supplying the reader who is unfamiliar with Lesotho with a general context in which to place Mr. Jingoes's narrative. It has the secondary purpose of providing the interested reader with a few central references from which he can pursue his own researches.

Terminology and Orthography

An inhabitant of Lesotho is known as a Mosotho, of which the plural form is Basotho. Sesotho is the language they speak. The Basotho also use the word Sesotho to qualify things specifically of their culture; for example, they would speak of Sesotho custom. In colonial times the country was known as Basutoland, and its people as Basuto.

Some notes are necessary to assist the reader with the pronunciation of Sesotho words used in the book. Generally speaking, the consonants are pronounced much like English ones; the vowels approximate to those of Italian. There is no letter *d* in Sesotho, but an *l* before an *i* or a *u* is pronounced like the English *d*. Thus *moli* is pronounced *modi*. The vowels *o* and *e* before other vowels are pronounced *w* and *y* respectively: *molutsoane* is thus pronounced *modutswane*, *Lesaoana* is *Lesawana*, and so on. The 1959 South African orthography uses the letters *d*, *w*, and *y* in the above instances. We have, however, preferred to retain the traditional Sesotho orthography, largely because the South African is not used in Lesotho. Further, where a double consonant occurs, each one is pronounced. Thus both terminal *l*'s of *leboella* are sounded and the name *Anna*, to take another example, is spoken as *An-na*. The letters *kh* are pronounced gutterally in much the same way as the *ch* in *loch*. *Q* is the only common click sound in Sesotho, and is produced by pressing the tongue against the roof of the mouth and then drawing it sharply away. Where *h* appears after another consonant, it usually indicates that the consonant preceding it is aspirated. Thus *th* is not pronounced as it is in English, but simply as an aspirated *t*.

Women's names are commonly spelled in various ways, including 'M'amakhabane, 'Mamakhabane, Ma-Makhabane, and 'Ma-Makhabane. The way we have elected to spell them, i.e. MaMakhabane, is not uncommon, although the first example given is perhaps traditionally the correct one. We have adopted this device for two reasons: the initial apostrophe has been dropped because it is so unfamiliar to an English reader, while the root of the name (in this case, the child's name) has been capitalized to avoid the reader's confusing mother and son. Some men's names also begin with *Ma-* as, for example, Masupha, but the reader should have no difficulty in discerning whether the name belongs to a man or a woman if he bears in mind our explanation.

References

DOKE, C. M., *and* S. M. MOFOKENG
1957   *Textbook of Southern Sotho grammar*, Longmans, Green, London and Cape Town.
MABILLE, A., *and* H. DIETERLEN
1961   *Southern Sotho–English dictionary*, reclassified, revised, and enlarged by R. A. Paroz, new edition using the 1959 Republic of South Africa orthography, Morija Sesuto Book Depot, Morija.

The Country

Lesotho is a small, beautiful, ruggedly mountainous country entirely enclosed within the Republic of South Africa. Of its total area of 11,716 square miles, the eastern half or 58 per cent is comprised of mountains ranging from 8,000 to over 11,000 feet. Here, on what is primarily grazing land, the population density averages 39 per square mile. Dropping down westward are the foothills, more densely populated and fertile. Bounded on the east by the foothills and on the west by the Caledon River and the plains of the Orange Free State, sprawls the lowland region. Inhabited by 38 per cent of Lesotho's population of about one million people, while comprising just over 17 per cent of the country's total area, the population density here ranges to over 200 per square mile. The Basotho divide their country into two distinct parts: the mountainous regions and the lowlands. There is a feeling in the country that it is the lowlands that have been affected most by change; 'behind the mountains', people say, true Basotho still live and provide a repository for tribal values. But the mountains, too, are changing as the lowlands become progressively more overcrowded. Once primarily grazing grounds, a shortage of land is forcing people to attempt to colonize the steep slopes of the Maluti range.

Koeneng and Mapoteng, where Mr. Jingoes's narrative is largely set, lie in an area where the lowlands start to shade into the foothills of the Maluti. Here villages are set high above densely cultivated valleys. Over the scene towers the changing face of the mountains. The country-side is stark and intimidating. The mountainsides are harsh and rocky with no forests to soften their outline. There are few trees, except for the poplars that have been introduced to stop the ravages of erosion, one of Lesotho's gravest problems. Many changes have taken place since Mr. Jingoes's youth; population pressure has placed increasing demands on the land. The dongas Mr. Jingoes mentions are now ravines, scarring the countryside with livid wounds. Many of the marshes where herdboys used to drive their cattle to drink have dried up or been ploughed under in the quest for more arable land. The reedbeds that fringed the rivers of his youth have largely been turned up, victims to Lesotho's desperate struggle for subsistence. Although Hlajoane's path to the *moli* pasture still exists, it now runs through straggling cultivated fields.

This small country has a healthy, vigorous climate. Winters are cold, summers are not unbearably hot. The rainfall would be adequate (29·26 inches in the lowlands) if it were favourably distributed, but Lesotho is subject to crippling droughts, destructive hailstorms in summer, and torrential storms which often provide a surfeit of water at the wrong times. With little provision made for channelling or storing excess water, agriculture is often a tragically hit-and-miss affair.

According to the 1966 Lesotho *Population Census Report*, 87·4 per cent of the *de facto* population is 'largely dependent on agriculture' (vol. I, p. 95). In theory, all men are entitled to three fields to cultivate, as well as a garden site, but with present pressure on the land, not all land holdings are viable and the land has become overworked. Under the system of land allocation, permanent rights to land are unobtainable, and there is little incentive to effect improvements consequently. The three fields ideally allocated to a man are also often widely scattered geographically, a factor critical in inhibiting efficient land utilization. Leistner describes succinctly further impediments to agricultural progress:

> What basically impedes the development of a dynamic agricultural economy is the interaction between an archaic form of land tenure, a social system biased against rapid change, mounting population pressure, and the physical features of the land. From the interaction of these four factors has evolved a pattern of eroding soils, declining output per unit of land, malnutrition, and labour migration, with all the attendant social and moral evils (1966, 6–7).

Lesotho does not grow enough to meet her needs, and must import cereals to balance her deficits. The country is better suited to the keeping of stock than to agriculture, but a variety of factors have resulted in poor returns in this field as well. The decline of pasturage, as a result of population pressures and inadequate grazing control, is not the least of these. The future of the pastoral way of life has been summed up by Leistner as follows:

> ... it is clear that the future of the livestock industry is inextricably bound up with the effectiveness of soil stabilization and reclamation measures.

Unless these efforts are successful, the country seems destined gradually to become a mountainous wasteland uninhabitable by man and beast (ibid., 9).

In the village where Mr. Jingoes lives today, the changes that have occurred since the events he describes are graphically present. In this village it is impossible to buy fresh milk, for example. What little milk the children get is obtained mainly from missions in powdered form. Fewer people now have spans of oxen to plough their fields and there is little grazing available. Older people in the village regret the passing of the pastoral way of life and say that young boys grow up today knowing nothing about cattle, and that their lives are the poorer for it. Few men still play the *lesiba* and know the tunes associated with driving cattle.

When Mr. Jingoes was a young man there was minimal opportunity for employment in Lesotho outside traditional subsistence activities. He, like many of his compatriots, was forced to turn to the South African labour market to earn money. Since that time, industrial development has been extremely slow in Lesotho; by 1966 only 1,880 people were employed in this sector of the economy. Job opportunities within the country are still severely limited, and many Basotho are not able to exist only as farmers and herders. Surrounded as they are by South Africa, they pour from the country to supplement their income by working on the South African mines, in South African industry, and on South African farms.

Even before Mr. Jingoes was born, migrant labour was an accepted and integral part of the Sesotho way of life. Williams says that as early as 1892 there were 30,000 Basotho working in South Africa (1971 a, 149). This trend, present so early in the history of Lesotho, is far more marked today than it was when Mr. Jingoes went to the mines. Estimates vary on the number of men who are away from Lesotho at any given time, but Williams states that as many as 15 per cent of the total population fall into this category, 'comprising the most productive elements of the society' (ibid., 149–50). Spence estimates that 'at least 43 per cent of the adult male population of Lesotho is away at work on the mines, industries and farms of South Africa' (1968, 64), while Leistner's estimate of absentee adult males is as high as 62 per cent (1967).[1]

The migrant labour system has become notorious throughout Africa for the social dislocation it causes. In Lesotho family life is disrupted by it, and wives and children often do not see the head of the household for months, or even years, at a stretch. In addition to these long separations women must, in the absence of their husbands, take agricultural decisions and supervise the farming of their fields. In effect the country is deprived of her most effective citizens at a time when they are at peak productivity. Labour migrancy also perpetuates Lesotho's economic dependence on South Africa, a position that irks many Basotho.

So ingrained has the habit of migrant labour become, that at coming-out ceremonies to mark the end of initiation, young initiates are rigged out with gifts of gum-boots, mirrors, and other articles characteristic of life on the mines. At these ceremonies, when the young men chant the praise-songs that they have composed for themselves during their seclusion, one often finds that their chants deal with their forthcoming adventures in travelling by train to the place of gold. The numbers of men one meets in a village in Lesotho who have suffered mutilation on the mines or who have contracted phthisis underground bear testimony to the hardships of the mines. Some years are dated by reference to catastrophic mine disasters, and the presence of the mines even in remote villages is never far away.

The United Nations Economic and Social Council states

If South Africa imposed restrictions on migrant labour from Lesotho, it is hard to see how Lesotho could cope economically with the loss of income which would follow or contain the social and cultural crises which would follow the return of thousands of Basotho.[2]

References

COATES, AUSTIN
1966 *Basutoland*, H.M.S.O., London.
HALPERN, JACK
1965 *South Africa's hostages; Basutoland, Bechuanaland and Swaziland*, Penguin, Harmondsworth.
LEISTNER, G. M. E.
1966 *Lesotho: economic structure and growth*, Africa Institute of South Africa, Communication no. 5, Pretoria.
1967 'Lesotho needs aid and gifted leadership', Johannesburg *Star*, 27 January.
MOROJELE, C. M. H.
1963 *1960 Agricultural census reports* (six parts), Agricultural Department, Maseru.
SHEDDICK, VERNON
1954 *Land tenure in Basutoland*, Colonial Research Studies no. 13, H.M.S.O., London.
SMIT, P.
1967 *Lesotho: a geographical study*, Africa Institute of South Africa, Communication no. 6, Pretoria.
SPENCE, J. E.
1968 *Lesotho; the politics of dependence*, Oxford University Press for the Institute of Race Relations, London.
WALLMAN, SANDRA
1969 *Take out hunger: two case studies of rural development in Basutoland*, London School of Economics Monographs on Social Anthropology no. 39, Athlone Press, London.

10

WARD, MICHAEL
1967   'Economic independence for Lesotho?', *Journal of Modern African Studies*, 5, 355–68.
WILLIAMS, JOHN C.
1971 a 'Lesotho: economic implications of migrant labour', *South African Journal of Economics*, 39, 149–78.
1971 b *Lesotho: three manpower problems: education, health, population growth*, Africa Institute of South Africa, Communication no. 16, Pretoria.
1972   *Lesotho: land tenure and economic development*, Africa Institute of South Africa, Communication no. 19, Pretoria.

History

One of the most striking features of the Basotho is their sense of identity, their belief in themselves as a people and a nation. This feeling has been forged by their long struggle to preserve from many competitors their mountain fastness with its rich arable lands along the Caledon River. Central to their idea of nationhood is their reverence for Moshoeshoe who united a number of disparate and heterogeneous clans and tribes and welded them into the Basotho nation.

When, in the early nineteenth century, Chaka, famous Zulu empire-builder, started to expand his territorial power, his *impis* drove the shattered remnants of tribes to take refuge across the Drakensberg range. These refugees from the power of Chaka fell upon the peoples in their path who, in turn, fell back upon others in their fight for survival. Starting in the early 1800s, this time of horror is known as the *Lifaqane*, the Wars of Calamity. As people struggled for life, fleeing always from the threat of raid, there was little time to plant or herd, and the devastated countryside soon gave up what little food it had. It was at this grim time that cannibalism became known in Lesotho. Even today reminders of the troubled times remain. The caves of the cannibals are now used as byres, and folk-tales contain many references to these dreaded figures. It was during the *Lifaqane* that Mr. Jingoes's grandfather became separated from his family who fell victim to one of the roving bands.

It was also during this period that Moshoeshoe, a relatively minor chieftain of one of the Sesotho clans, began to gather about him the people who were to become the Basotho nation. In the early 1820s he was at Butha Buthe in northern Lesotho, and right in the path of the fleeing bands from Natal. His small group had suffered the shock of defeat at the hands of marauders and, seeking a more secure position, Moshoeshoe struck southwards on a desperate journey across the inhospitable terrain of the foothills to find the mountain that his scouts had assured him would give them safety. On this journey Moshoeshoe's grandfather, Peete, was captured and devoured by cannibals.

When his men later captured cannibals, Moshoeshoe would refuse to put them to death, saying that they were living sepulchres and should therefore be protected, given grain and cattle, and encouraged to turn from cannibalism.

Moshoeshoe established a secure fortress on his eyrie at Thaba Bosiu. Less vulnerable to enemies, he could start the career of diplomacy that was to mark him off as one of the most astute leaders ever to have ruled in Southern Africa.

> When his position was threatened by a tribe who were among Chaka's enemies, Moshesh[3] sent gifts to Chaka. At times he sent gifts to both. The shifts and turns of Moshesh's diplomacy during these years have an Elizabethan astuteness about them, reposing—as Elizabeth's did—in the reality of the possession of an island; and though the Zulu armies wrought havoc in many parts of the region, Moshesh remained unmolested, his people and his cattle increasing. Here he would befriend a man known to have wronged him; there he would capture a chief who had attacked him, and instead of putting him to death would send him back to his own people with a gift of cattle. It was a policy running contrary to all that had gone before, keeping fighting to the minimum, and avoiding making permanent enemies. To traditionalist African chiefs it looked like weakness, yet it bred a continuingly gathering strength. Before he had been on Thaba Bosiu six years Moshesh was the most considerable chief among his people (Coates, 1966, 23).

By the early 1830s Moshoeshoe had about him the beginnings of a new nation. As a man of perception, when Moshoeshoe heard reports of white missionaries in the interior, he recognized that these were men who could play a decisive role in the future of his people, and he welcomed three members of the Paris Evangelical Missionary Society, Casalis, Arbousset, and Gosselin, laying the foundation for the long and continued co-operation between the Basotho and Christian missions, a process that has been crucial in the evolution of Lesotho.

Moshoeshoe was acutely aware of the threat posed to his mountain chiefdom by the Boers, who, having trekked from the Cape Colony, were looking for new territory. The fertile lands of the Caledon were to become the scene of ever-increasing tension between Boers and Basotho. As more Boers settled in the area, relations between the two emergent nations worsened, the Basotho striking at the Boers, cutting out cattle and horses from the farmers whom they saw as encroaching on their territory. As the tempo of contact increased, Moshoeshoe came to feel that security against the Boers lay in protection from the British. In 1843, by the Napier Treaty, Moshoeshoe became an ally of the Cape Government and the boundaries of his territory were roughly delineated. This treaty did nothing to alleviate antagonism between Boers and Basotho, and the British found it necessary, in order to contain the strife, to declare their sovereignty over the territory north of the Orange River. Moshoeshoe still remained an independent leader, and the pattern of raids and disturbances continued. In 1852, to stop the Basotho raiding, Lieutenant-General Cathcart mounted an inconclusive offensive against Moshoeshoe, after which Moshoeshoe successfully sued for peace. He had demonstrated superior military and diplomatic skills in this encounter. At this time Moshoeshoe was at the peak of his power; the Boers had not yet deprived him of land to any great extent, and he had secured for himself British friendship and protection.

With the abandonment by Britain of the Orange River sovereignty two years later, Moshoeshoe was left to face the independent Boer republic of the Orange Free State on his own. The strife for territorial domination between the two emerging powers came to its climax during the following fourteen years. In 1858 the Orange Free State declared war on Moshoeshoe. Their expedition against the well-armed and mounted Basotho ended in defeat at Thaba Bosiu and they sued for peace. The peace could not be lasting, however, as the real cause of difference, the question of land, was unresolved. Moshoeshoe, too, was growing old, and did not have many more years to rule. The second Free State War (1865–8) brought the Basotho to the brink of defeat. The country was only saved because Britain at long last heeded Moshoeshoe's repeated requests for protection, and declared the country British territory in 1868. The terms of the peace were such that the Basotho lost a large portion of their best grazing and arable land to the Boers. The effects of this loss were to be seen with force in later years as population pressures mounted, and even now the Basotho still covet the lands that they regard as having been unrightfully taken from them.

Two years later Moshoeshoe died, to be succeeded by his son Letsie. Moshoeshoe's achievements were truly remarkable, and he is still venerated in Lesotho as the father of his people.

In 1871 Lesotho was annexed to the Cape Colony. Not only had the Basotho not been consulted about this move, but they were not allowed representation in the Cape Parliament. In 1880 the Cape presumed to attempt to disarm the Basotho—a short-sighted move when it is considered that the Basotho had only preserved their territorial integrity by dint of the very arms the Cape was attempting to confiscate. The Gun War (1880–81) that resulted, although some chiefs supported the Cape, proved to be an expensive and fruitless drain on the manpower and resources of the Colony. The Basotho retained their arms, and the Cape appealed to Britain to take over the territory. As a consequence, Lesotho was disannexed from the Cape Colony in 1883 and the British Government took over the administration of the country the following year, an administration that continued until 1966 when Lesotho was granted independence.

The events of these early years seem to have left a legacy of profound mistrust among the Basotho regarding South Africa and her intentions.

The Basotho continually feared that they would be incorporated into South Africa. With the rise of an apartheid-dominated ideology in that country, the differences between the two states have been thrown into sharp relief. Lesotho finds herself in the anomalous position of being an independent African state within the boundaries of a country where black men are treated as 'second-class citizens'. Since her economic viability depends to such a large extent on maintaining good relations with her encircling neighbour she must, of necessity, find the means to co-exist with the extreme right-wing policies of Mr. Vorster's government. The government that has brought Lesotho from Independence to the present, under Chief Leabua Jonathan's Basutoland National Party, has often been accused of pandering to South Africa, but any government in Lesotho would have to come to terms with this problem.

References

BECKER, P.
1969   *Hill of destiny*, Longman, London.

CASALIS, REVD. E.
1965   *The Basutos*, G. Struik, Cape Town. First published in 1861, James Nisbet, London.
1971   *My life in Basutoland*, G. Struik, Cape Town. First published in 1889.

ELLENBERGER, D. F.
1912   *History of the Basuto, ancient and modern*, Caxton, London. Written in English by J. C. MacGregor.

GERMOND, ROBERT C.
1967   *Chronicles of Basutoland*, Morija Sesuto Book Depot, Morija.

HADLEY, PETER (ed.)
1972   *Doctor to Basuto, Boer and Briton 1877–1906; memoirs of Dr. Henry Taylor*, David Philip, Cape Town.

LAGDEN, SIR GODFREY
1909   *The Basutos; the mountaineers and their country* (in two volumes), Hutchinson, London.

TYLDEN, G.
1950   *The rise of the Basuto*, Juta, Cape Town and Johannesburg.

WILLIAMS, J. GRENFELL
1950   *Moshesh, the man on the mountain*, Oxford University Press, London.

The Chieftainship

At the apex of the traditional tribal structure in Lesotho is the Paramount Chief (or King, as he is now called), who is the supreme tribal authority and in whose care the land of the nation is vested. Directly below and responsible to him are twenty-two principal and ward chiefs, each controlling a territory or ward. Below each of these chiefs, in turn, is a hierarchy of chiefs, sub-chiefs, and headmen, each having jurisdiction over an area.

The traditional political hierarchy has largely been created by a process whereby close relatives and descendants of Moshoeshoe were placed in positions of authority over portions of the country. This process is best summarized by Ashton:

> As soon as Moshesh was in a position to do so, he divided the area under his control into districts, over each of which he placed someone whom he could trust. At first he placed his principal warriors and later, as the people became more amenable to his rule, he placed his sons. In a few cases, the tribal chiefs were left directly under him, either because their loyalty was unquestioned or because they were too strong to be tampered with. This system was continued by his successors, each of whom rearranged some of the districts, and made fresh appointments as the claims of his sons and followers and political expediency dictated, with the difference that the major appointments were confined to sons. Consequently, to give them a caretaking commensurate with their status, districts were amalgamated and the old authorities degraded. Power has thus gradually been concentrated in the hands of the Paramount Chief and his near kinsmen . . . (1938, 296).

Hamnett comments that it is in this 'placing' system, as it has come to be known, that 'the Moshoeshoe dynasty has found one of its most potent political weapons in its march to supremacy' (1965, 244). Of the present holdings of the twenty-two principal and ward chiefs, he says that

> The senior cardinal lineage, that of Letsie I, . . . enjoys the pre-eminence of holding twelve principal chiefdoms, . . . the second (Molapo) holds three, two of them very large, the third (Masupha) holds 'Mamathe's, again a major ward, and only the fourth (Majara) is poorly endowed (ibid., 245).

Thus of the twenty-two principalities, seventeen are in the hands of descendants of Moshoeshoe's four senior sons.[4] Of the remaining five, one is under the jurisdiction of the present Chief Makhabane, great-great-grandson of Lesaoana, Moshoeshoe's nephew. In the district of Berea, in which Makhabane's ward is situated today, there are three principal chiefs, Masupha, Makhabane, and Majara, with 21,000, 12,583, and 3,833 taxpayers respectively in 1969. These three principal chiefs are all descended from men who were granted their wards because of their genealogical propinquity to Moshoeshoe.

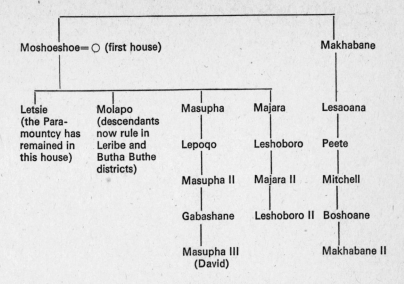

In a principal chief's ward, the process described above reproduced itself. Principal chiefs placed close relatives over sections of their own area, and administered their wards through this hierarchy of chiefs, sub-chiefs, and headmen, all ultimately responsible to them.

A chief's tasks were multifarious, among the most important of them being the allocation of land to loyal subjects and the dispensing of justice at the men's *lekhotla*. The chief was entitled to services, but his subjects could call upon his extensive resources in times of hardship. The title of Mr. Jingoes's book is a translation of the Sesotho maxim, *morena ke morena ka batho*. These words refer tellingly to the fact that in traditional times chiefs seem to have ruled always in consultation with their people. A balanced reciprocity existed then between chiefs and their subjects.

Mr. Jingoes's account of the chieftainship focuses on the period of reforms of the 1930s and 1940s, a time during which the nature of chieftainship in Lesotho was irrevocably altered. He spells out how relations between ruler and subject became progressively more formalized, and how the balance between them became distorted under the impact of reforming legislation. His discussion centres around the fact that chiefs became salaried officials, rather than servants of their people, and that the chiefs' courts were transformed into formal bodies, which many tribesmen found unfamiliar and intimidating. The reforms and the effects they had on Sesotho life are analysed in all their complexity by Lord Hailey and by Jones (1951).

Mr. Jingoes leaves the history of the chieftainship in the early 1950s. Since that time, many further changes have affected the position of chiefs in Lesotho. The greatest of these has been the rise of modern political parties and the emergence of leaders who have often been extremely critical of the place and role of chiefs. Lesotho gained constitutional government and independence from Britain in 1966. Since then there has been further legislation that has served progressively to circumscribe the power and authority of chiefs. In Lesotho today people often say that the chief is no more than a clerk for the government and, in fact, he has come in many ways to resemble a bureaucrat. The reciprocity between chiefs and people that Mr. Jingoes dwells on so nostalgically can no longer be discerned in the form that he knew it and, although the chieftainship is still respected and still plays an essential part in contemporary Lesotho, the chief can no longer, by any stretch of the imagination, be regarded as 'father to his people'.

References

ASHTON, E. H.

1938   'Political organization of the Southern Sotho', *Bantu Studies*, *12*, 287–320.

1947   'Democracy and indirect rule', *Africa*, *17*, 235–51.

HAILEY, LORD

1953   *Native administration in the British African territories, Part V, the High Commission Territories: Basutoland, the Bechuanaland Protectorate and Swaziland*, H.M.S.O., London.

JONES, G. I.

1951   *Basutoland medicine murder; a report on the recent outbreak of 'diretlo' murders in Basutoland*, H.M.S.O., Cmd no. 8209, London.

1966   'Chiefly succession in Basutoland', *in* Jack Goody (ed.), *Succession to high office*, Cambridge University Press, Cambridge papers in social anthropology, no. 4, Cambridge.

HAMNETT, IAN

1965   'Koena chieftainship seniority in Basutoland', *Africa*, *35*, 241–51.

KHAKETLA, B. M.

1971   *Lesotho 1970; an African coup under the microscope*, C. Hurst, London.

STEVENS, RICHARD P.

1967   *Lesotho, Botswana and Swaziland; the former High Commission Territories in Southern Africa*, Pall Mall Press, London.

VAN WYK, A. J.

1967   *Lesotho: a political study*, Africa Institute of South Africa, Communication no. 7, Pretoria.

WEISFELDER, RICHARD F.

1969   *Defining national purpose in Lesotho*, Ohio University Center for International Studies, Papers in International Studies, Africa series no. 3, Athens, Ohio.

Liretlo or 'ritual murder'

Of the term 'ritual murder', Jones says

> This term 'ritual', which implies the taking of a human life for religious
> purposes or in accordance with a religious or magic rite, is not a particu-
> larly happy one for there is no such element of human sacrifice in these
> Basutoland murders. They are not committed from any religious motives
> but for the purely material objective of cutting from the body of the victim
> strips of flesh or portions of particular organs, called by the general term
> *diretlo* . . . and used in the making of certain magical compounds usually
> called 'protective medicines' (1951, 12).

The origins of *liretlo* murders are uncertain, but Jones gives two
explanations based on the information he gathered during his research.
The first common view is that *liretlo* murders were a relatively new
phenomenon, whose impetus came from Natal, where witch-doctors are
believed, by the Basotho, to be very powerful innovators of new concepts. The flesh used originally in *manaka* was taken from large animals
such as bulls or buck, for which human flesh was later substituted. The
second view, also commonly held, was that, far from being a new thing,
liretlo murders are a variation of an ancient custom; human flesh had
always been used to make powerful *manaka*, but the flesh was taken from
the bodies of enemies killed in war. When, after the turn of the century,
Lesotho became more settled, battle-felled enemies became more rare,
and this formidable ingredient of a *lenaka* had to be sought from other
sources. 'The truth', Jones comments, 'appears to lie between these two
extremes' (ibid., 14). There is no doubt that parts taken from slain
enemies were used by the Basotho during the nineteenth century to
compound medicines, such parts being called *litlo*, and there is ample
documentation for both Boers and British finding their dead mutilated.
But *liretlo*, Jones goes on to say,

> . . . is a new term an extension of the word used for slices of flesh cut
> from the body of an animal killed for eating, and *diretlo* is obtained not
> from the bodies of strangers or enemies, but from a definite person who is
> thought to possess specific attributes considered essential for the
> particular medicine being made. Such a person is usually a member of the
> same community and is frequently a relative of some of the killers. He is
> killed specifically for this *diretlo* which has to be cut from his body while
> he is still alive (ibid., 14).

Jones gives a detailed summary of the case for the Crown in High
Court Criminal Case 14/48, the trial of Chieftainess MaMakhabane and
fifteen others. His summary is given here in full.

> On a Saturday evening in January, 1948, Mochesela Khoto sat in a hut
> drinking beer with Dane Rachakana and a number of other people who
> had come to a wedding feast in Moloi's village. While the party was pro-

ceeding the Chieftainess of his ward arrived with a number of her men, others were summoned from the party and when they came were told: 'I want you to kill Mochesela for me, because I want to make a medicine horn (*lenaka*) which I will use in the placing of my son. Anyone of you who disobeys this order will be killed.' One of them was then sent to let Dane know that all was ready and when he saw him Dane got up and said to Mochesela 'Cousin, let us go outside for a while.' Mochesela followed him to where sixteen men were waiting for them with the Chieftainess and two of her women attendants. She greeted Dane, reminded him that he had already had her orders, and told the men to seize Mochesela. As one of them caught hold of him, Mochesela cried out: 'My father Pholo, are you going to kill me?' and when he did not reply, continued: 'Let me free and I will give you my black ox.' 'I am not your father and I want you, not your ox' replied Pholo. He started to shout, but they gagged him and marched him off away from the village, while Dane threw stones to drive off some boys who had been attracted by his shouting. When they reached a satisfactory spot they removed their blankets stripped deceased of his clothes and held him naked on the ground. An oil lamp was produced and by its light they proceeded to cut small circular pieces of skin from his body with a knife. Pholo cut a piece from the calf of his left leg, another man a piece from his groin, a third from beneath his right breast, a fourth from the biceps of his right arm. The pieces as they were cut were laid on a white cloth in front of Mosala the native doctor who was going to make the medicine, and one of the men held a billy-can to collect the blood from these and later wounds. Then Dane took the knife and with it removed the entire face of Mochesela. He cut right down to the bone, beginning at the forehead and ending at the throat and he finished by taking out the throat, the tongue and the eyes. Mochesela died while his throat was cut. The Chieftainess who had stood by watching is then reported to have said: 'I thank you, my children, for having killed this man for me. I know the Police will come here to investigate this matter and no-one must tell them about it. If they do, I will kill them in the same way as I have killed Mochesela. Take the body now to the house of Steve, where it will remain until Tuesday, when those of you who live near will take it to a place where people will see it.' After this she left for her home with her two attendants followed by the doctor and another man carrying the billy-can and the pieces of flesh. The rest carried Mochesela's body to Steve's hut where it remained wrapped in his blanket and placed in a wool pack until Tuesday night. Then it was carried to some low cliffs near the village and after some of the clothing had been placed on the grass and on a tree nearby, it was thrown over and then dragged a little further downhill, to be found there the following morning (ibid., 11–12).

Jones elsewhere comments on the motive for the murder as follows:

. . . the chieftainess said she wanted medicine for the placing of her son Makhabane, but a study of the correspondence relating to the placing of this young man shows that his mother was intriguing to achieve the exact opposite, to prevent his being placed as Chief of the Peete Ward, as this would mean that she lost her position as its Regent . . . (ibid., 17).

Jones's report on *liretlo* is so thorough that little else need be said but to refer the reader to it directly. Perhaps one might point out, however, that he sees the reforms of the 1930s and 1940s as a direct cause of the sharp rise in incidence of the murders during the latter decade, culminating in no fewer than twenty murders in 1948. He gives the total of suspected *liretlo* murders before 1938 as twenty-three; those between 1938 and 1949 as seventy. The greatest number of murders—twenty—took place in Berea District (ibid., 104).

Liretlo is still a controversial and contentious subject in Lesotho. Many Basotho do not accept that Jones was correct in the conclusions he drew in his report. Concerning the role of senior chiefs in *liretlo* murders, Khaketla writes as follows:

> Some of our most senior Chiefs like Bereng Griffith and Gabashane Masopha[5] were found guilty of these murders and hanged. But to this day, there are still grave doubts whether they had, in fact, been responsible for the murders. Many people believe they were the victims of a vicious, premeditated frame-up. . . . One of the most outspoken in this connection was Josiel Lefela. He regarded the murders as a 'mere trick' of the white people who wanted to destroy the Chieftainship. . . . Unlike other people who disbelieved the gruesome stories of the murders but were afraid to talk openly, Mokhehle[6] was as bold as a lion. He spoke openly and vehemently against the murders which he regarded as a 'trick intended to discredit the Chiefs and pave the way for the eventual incorporation of Lesotho into the Union of South Africa' (1971, 49–50).

Unfortunately, Khaketla adduces no evidence in support of these extreme viewpoints. But there is little doubt that some Basotho believed —and still believe today—that the hanging of some of their most prominent chiefs represented a miscarriage of justice of the gravest sort.

Further relevant reading

Social structure of the Basotho

ASHTON, E. H.
1946   *Social structure of the Southern Sotho ward*, University of Cape Town communications from the School of African Studies, no. 15, Cape Town.
1952   *The Basuto*, Oxford University Press for the International African Institute, London.

SHEDDICK, VERNON
1953   *The Southern Sotho*, Oxford University Press for the International African Institute, London.

Sesotho law

DUNCAN, PATRICK
1960   *Sotho laws and customs*, Oxford University Press, Cape Town.

PALMER, VERNON V., *and* SEBASTIAN M. POULTER
1972   *The legal system of Lesotho*, Michie, Charlottesville, Virginia.
POULTER, SEBASTIAN
1972   'The place of the Laws of Lerotholi in the legal system of Lesotho',
       African Affairs, *71*, 144–62.

Labour movements in South Africa
KADALIE, CLEMENTS
1970   *My life and the ICU: the autobiography of a black trade unionist in
       South Africa*, Frank Cass, London.
WALSHE, PETER
1970   *The rise of African Nationalism in South Africa: the African National
       Congress 1912–1952*, C. Hurst, London. (This work has an outstanding
       bibliography.)

NOTES

1. Cited by Williams, 1971 a, 165.
2. Report of the Basutoland Educational Planning Mission, Appendix; cited
   by Williams, 1971 a, 170.
3. Moshesh is an alternative spelling of Moshoeshoe.
4. For a detailed break-down of how Moshoeshoe's line dominates the tradi
   tional political structure of Lesotho, see Jones, 1951, diagram IV, facing p. 78.
5. Masopha is an alternative spelling of Masupha.
6. Leader of the opposition Basutoland Congress Party.